Leading On Purpose

LEADING ON PURPOSE

The Black Woman's Guide to Shattering the Glass Ceiling

Dr. Julianna Hynes

Leading On Purpose: The Black Woman's Guide to Shattering the Glass Ceiling
Copyright © 2020 Dr. Julianna Hynes, PhD

Edited by: Guia Nocon and Paulette Nunlee
Photography by: Rachel Radcliffe
Cover and book design by: Tywebbin Creations, LLC

Contents

Acknowledgments

Too many people to count supported me in bringing this project to fruition. I want to thank each one of you, whether you offered feedback on the content or book title, or you expressed interest and encouragement along the way. You are the wind beneath my wings.

I want to particularly say thank you to my husband, Bakari Akil, and my children, Chester, Assata, Julian, Jakari, and Joi. You all give me the love I need to thrive. Thank you, Dr. Abby Jandro, for walking through this journey with me from start to finish. You are a fantastic coach and friend. Dr. Vanessa George, if it weren't for you and your encouragement, I might not have seen this project through to fruition. Thank you. To my late sister in Christ, Mrs. Chandra Felicia Wallace, you always boosted my spirits and helped me to believe I could fly. I'll forever miss you and will be ever grateful that the Lord brought you into my life. I'll see you again in Paradise.

Introduction

A Brief History

The history of black working women begins in the United States at the point of slavery. For some, if not most, the work ethic of working long hours, sometimes multiple jobs for little pay, in conjunction with nurturing and ensuring the family's survival and well-being, exists to this day.

From the time of slavery to the present, black women have worked outside the home to provide for their families, often being the sole breadwinners. Simultaneously, work has represented an opportunity for black women to integrate into society by attaining status, recognition, affiliation, and other psychological and sociological advantages which are often needed to counter the effects of overt and covert racism.

The shift from slavery to post-slavery did not show much of a conversion in work opportunities for black women. We transitioned from working in the fields to working as domestic servants in the homes of white employers. Although slavery had ended, most black women were still psychologically enslaved as they labored and made very meager wages. It was not until World War II that black women's economic status showed signs of progress. Although the majority of black women still worked in domestic service, a small minority started working in non-domestic industries such as manufacturing. In the 1960s, when the Civil Rights Movement forced the federal government to look at racial discrimination in employment, black women finally had access to more traditional (white) female occupations, especially clerical work, that had for so long been denied them.

Title VII of the Civil Rights Act of 1964 made discrimination in hiring on the basis of "race, color, religion, sex, or national origin" illegal. Studies conducted after the law went into effect revealed that black women should have advanced professionally, with less difficulty, in roles once only occupied by white women than they would have pursuing white men's jobs and pay levels. However, in spite of the forecast, black women's opportunities did not increase and instead, they began to pursue traditional male professions, such as medicine and law.

Although black women had high motivation, they had low aspirations and expectations of succeeding because of discrimination and lack of opportunities when it came to planning their careers. Women who were successful and advanced in their careers most often did so because of equal opportunity legislation. Most were young and well-educated. Many came from families, either nuclear or extended, that supported their efforts in school and in the job market, whether through financial aid or enthusiastic encouragement. Their place of residence and access to jobs also affected the young women's opportunities.

Throughout history, black women have always had to overcome sexism and racism in the American workforce in order to not only advance but to simply maintain employment. From the 19th century to present day, we have had to literally and figuratively fight because of being a double minority. As blacks, we've been subjected to prejudice and racism. We were stereotyped as manual laborers, incapable of possessing enough intelligence to perform any other type of work. As women, we were restricted to positions presumed to be "women's work."

In spite of these historical challenges, however, black women have exemplified a strong work ethic throughout history. We have overcome obstacles with a great deal of strength, dignity, and determination. In spite of barriers, our foremothers inherently passed down their strategies to their daughters, granddaughters, great-granddaughters, nieces, goddaughters, and mentees. And in the pages of this book, I am passing down what I have learned in my own career, as well as from others, to you.

About Leading on Purpose

Leading on Purpose is a career management and leadership development tool for black women in their early- and mid-careers. Whether you're in a support role, first-time supervisor or manager, or looking to advance beyond middle management, you can have the mindset of a leader starting today. This book will encourage and inspire you to be the best in your current role while also helping you prepare for your next opportunity. Not only is it a book written about my journey from being an administrative assistant to becoming the CEO of my own firm, it also draws together others' voices and stories of accomplishments. Additionally, it contains the results of research I've conducted over the years with a little inspiration from my book, *Living on Purpose: Keys to Discovering Your God-Given Destiny.*

Becoming successful in whatever field you choose is not the result of "luck" or "being in the right place at the right time." With the help of God, it is the direct result of focused and deliberate hard work while leaving room for the unexpected and enjoying the process every step of the way. Through this book, I want to encourage you to aspire to achieve your professional dreams.

Growing up, I had strong black female role models in my mother, some of her friends, my aunts, my sister, and my older cousins–all strong, hard-working, and independent women. However, few of them spoke to me in much detail about their experiences of being young, black, and female in the primarily white-male environment of corporate America. I learned many of those lessons either by observation or through my own experiences. Teaching my adolescent daughter these lessons is a gift I am trying to give her and other young women who are put on my path.

Even though I'm just now putting pen to paper (or really, fingers to keyboard), I've been writing this book all my life. I have stockpiled information through my early personal and professional experiences, through conversations I've had with mentors, through recent research and coaching, and through the reflections I've made being a professional black woman in white corporate America. Truth be told, many of our experiences are not limited to being black women. I've had numerous conversations with women who are not black about the challenges of simply being female, let alone a woman of any color, creed, or orientation, in the workplace.

Throughout this book, you'll see I've shared studies and statistics on the low representation of black women in senior executive positions, boardrooms, and other leadership roles of our largest corporations. But you really don't need the data to tell you what is going on in today's organizations. If you're working, you're living it. The stories and strategies you will read are not new. They're the collective lived experiences of many black women.

How do you know if this book is for you? This book is written for the woman who:

- is interested in being more effective in her current role while also developing the skills that will get her to the next level (whatever the next level is for her) yet doesn't yet know what to do or where to start.

- already wants to be a leader without the fancy corporate title or degrees.

- doesn't know how to go beyond where she is at the moment. She aspires to take on a role with more responsibility, but she doesn't know where or how to start or what's missing. She doesn't think she has models or examples to draw from.

- is content in her current position, but wants to make a bigger impact in her role.

This book is also for mentors and managers of professional black women who want to learn more about their unique perspective and how to better support them. Within these pages, I offer the mentoring insights I've received over the years from men and women of differing backgrounds who were interested in not only seeing me advance and achieve my goals, but also supporting me in the process.

I am so excited I am free enough from my mental and emotional limits to share this information with you, as over time and in turn, you will share your lessons with others. The beauty of learning is that there is always something to learn; we never truly stop as long as we stay open to it.

You'll read about the insights, pearls of wisdom, experiences, and strategies I've gained as well as what I've learned from the women (and men) I've talked to. I'll also share common competencies I have found as an executive and leadership coach that professionals, regardless of gender or level, need in order to be successful. There isn't just one way to achieve success (or one way to achieve a goal, vision, or strategy, for that matter), and success means different things to different people. So, I invite you to think critically about the information I am sharing. Some of it will fit your situation, some of it won't. Use what works and pass it on.

My prayer is that you will be inspired to take action and move forward in your career. Rather than wishing for something better, you will be motivated to do something better. As my pastor often says, "I don't want you to just talk about it, I want you to be about it!"

If you're serious about focusing on you and your career, start right now, shift out of autopilot, and set your mind to being intentional. If you are a woman of purpose, then join me as you learn to lead on PURPOSE!

Outline

Leading on Purpose is outlined into three sections: The Why, The What, and The How.

1. The Why provides support for the importance of having black women as leaders in their organizations.

2. The What outlines key concepts such as leadership, career success, and the critical strategies and qualities of a leader.

3. The How takes you through a strategic planning exercise that will help you to take all of what you've gleaned from the book and place in one document.

At the end of some chapters, I offer questions as *FOOD FOR THOUGHT* and you will also have an opportunity to *TAKE ACTION!* As important as it is to be thoughtful about your answers, it's even more important to be intentional about your resulting actions. Capture your insights within the pages of this book and then transfer them to the strategic planning document you'll find in the last chapter.

If you determine that you are going to do something deliberate each time you get an idea or identify an opportunity, I guarantee you by the end of this book, you'll be much closer to your goals. It's up to you.

Are you ready to lead on purpose? Let's go!

FOOD FOR THOUGHT

- In thinking about your career development, why do you want to advance?

- What could interfere with you successfully creating the space and time to focus on you and your career right now?

- What can you put in place to minimize, if not eliminate, the challenges or obstacles you identified above?

TAKE ACTION!

Based on the obstacles you identified in #2 above, decide which actions you need to take to minimize them. Identify who, what, when, where, why, how, and how much you'll need (you might not have a strategy for each of these).

If you can enact the strategies today, do so; if not right now, add them to your to do list or schedule them and give yourself a deadline.

Find an accountability partner who will support you as you go through this process.

My accountability partner(s):

What other actions can you take? When will you take them?

THE WHY

1. My Story

Many great books start with a compelling story to draw the reader into the subject matter. I debated which of my stories I wanted to start with: Should I start with my divorce when I was twenty-three after only one year of marriage while carrying my first child, or entering corporate America as a young, black female, recently divorced, single mother? Perhaps the opening story I tell should be about when I got my master's degree while dealing with sexism and racism at work. Or about when, a few years later, I remarried, blended two families with my husband, worked full-time, and pursued my doctoral degree. I could also start my story at the point when, while in my doctoral program, I became depressed after my mother passed away and struggled to make it through the day, let alone any academic program. And no sooner than I recovered from the depression, I found out I was pregnant, right before I was supposed to take my comprehensive exams. My goal to complete my degree was delayed eighteen months due to these different circumstances. So where should I start?

Like many, I've been through marriages, separations, and a divorce; I've had the challenges of blending a family and raising children, some with special needs; I've dealt with loved ones who were chemically-dependent; I've suffered through major losses, illnesses, and learned to manage my own mental health issues while supporting others in managing theirs. I am in the process of overcoming the trauma of the sexual abuse I suffered in childhood and the resulting baggage I brought with me into adulthood. With all that said, the best place to start is with my first book, *Living on Purpose: Keys to Discovering Your God-Given Destiny*.

In the Beginning

Living on Purpose chronicled my life from an undergraduate student in my early twenties to the time I received my doctorate degree some twenty years later. I shared the ups and downs of my personal and professional lives that brought me to a place of feeling broken and in need of direction. I unpacked lessons of going from being on autopilot to living a life of intention and purpose, which meant becoming clear and deliberate about my choices and actions. Contemporary popular and academic literature calls this idea of being deliberate and purposeful, mindfulness: the practice of being fully present and more aware in the current moment rather than dwelling on the past or projecting yourself too far into the future.

In addition to being intentional about living your life in the present moment, Living on Purpose also includes being intentional about pursuing your goals, the day-to-day decisions you make, and the actions you take to reach those goals. It's being aware of whether your decisions are moving you closer to or further from where you want to be, and then making the appropriate, conscious adjustments needed as you assess your progress.

As One Chapter Ends...

My journey of living purposefully began the day my first marriage ended. Up until then, I was a dependent, immature twenty-three-year-old girl who went from relying on my parents' and other family's financial and emotional support to depending on my new husband whom I'd married at twenty-two. I hadn't learned the difficult yet liberating experience of being independent, and because of that, I had a lot of hard lessons ahead to learn. The marriage only lasted a year because we both made choices that did not serve the relationship—such as the extramarital affair my husband chose to have. Devastated, depressed, and pregnant, I moved back home with my parents (still with a dependent and unconscious mindset) and started the process of trying to rebuild my life, not really knowing how.

Soon after my son was born and I could fit into a suit, I started applying for positions and going on interviews. Although I had an undergraduate degree in psychology, my technical skills were office administration. Therefore, I applied to positions that fit my skill set.

It took me about five months to land a job at a terminal operator in Oakland as an administrative assistant. My starting salary, while modest, was more than I had ever made before and was enough for me to support myself and my infant son. We were able to move out of my parents' home and into our own space. Although not what I envisioned, I was getting my life back on track and thankful to be working and providing as a single mother.

Initially, I enjoyed my job. I was learning a good deal and meeting great people, but about a year in, I became dissatisfied with my role. I realized my mostly male colleagues—often the same age and with equal or less education and work experience—were making more money. Because of many factors—I was a woman, I was black, I was young, I was in a support role, I was immature—I wasn't treated as the professional I thought myself to be. Because of the lack of financial and professional recognition I thought I deserved, I began petitioning my employer for higher-level, higher-paying positions.

Although my manager was open to the conversation, he discouraged me from applying to any other positions. The company I worked for was a twenty-four-hour operation, and as a single mother, I had to have set hours. To be close to work, I moved away from my immediate support system which meant I relied on a daycare provider who closed at 6 p.m. every day. As a result, I couldn't work additional hours like my other co-workers. In hindsight, I can see how my own limitations kept me from advancing. I was still very young and professionally immature and had gotten in my own way. I had not developed the emotional wisdom (now known as Emotional Intelligence or EQ) required of an individual in a management or leadership role. I pursued a promotion because of the sense of financial security it provided. While there is nothing wrong with that, it wasn't the only thing I should have been paying attention to. I hadn't developed the proper business acumen required in the industry, and quite honestly, I lacked an interest in learning the industry at all.

Unaware of it at the time, my lack of knowledge, effort, and interest prevented my promotion to a higher paying, more responsible position. Not to mention, because I was a single mother, I was not able to work the extra hours required for better management and supervisory roles. While my parenting responsibilities didn't allow for a lot of flexibility, I also did not consider an alternative solution (how to be a single mom and have a role with more responsibility). Having the desire to grow and develop professionally, I had not figured out how to do it. And with the exception of one amazing family member, I didn't have anyone to guide me. I was still driven. So, I did the easiest thing I knew how to do: go back to school for another degree.

A girlfriend had recently graduated with her master's in psychology from a program that catered to working adults. When I saw her graduate, I was inspired to do the same.

Thankfully, my son's father kept him two nights a week. At first, I hated that my son was gone, but soon realized his time away would allow me to go to school and study. I started seeing the possibilities and benefits of my circumstances rather than the challenges vying for my attention. After about a year on my job, I applied and was accepted into a master's program. My son had just turned one and I was twenty-five.

In some ways, my decision to go back to school was to gain more of an advantage at work, and, in many ways, to bolster my confidence. If I wasn't confident in anything else, I was confident in knowing I could learn. None of my coworkers had graduate degrees—including many of the senior leaders. So I thought earning an advanced degree would help level the playing field.

New Beginning

Getting my graduate degree was the first in a series of many good career decisions I made after my divorce. Being a working student and mother taught me self-discipline, problem solving, and how to think critically in various situations. I also developed a stronger work ethic. Because I had more to balance and much more at stake, there was no time for the procrastination or goofing off that I did when I was younger and still dependent on my parents' support. Additionally, I learned to be more of a strategic thinker. I had to think many more steps ahead than I had to when it was just me. I also began to take more pride and interest in my work and the success of the company. Something I hadn't done before. And although I still had time constraints, I started managing my time and work better and volunteered for various projects of interest at work. At school, as I interacted with other working professionals, I started to develop my business acumen and became increasingly able to engage in discussions with leaders, both within and outside of my organization.

I was introduced to a process of visioning and goal setting that became the catalyst for my career and leadership development. Although I wasn't a leader by title, it was in the administrative support role that I learned much more about myself and being a professional, about working in a corporate environment, and about what it means to be young, black, and female in a primarily older-white-male-dominated organization. I also learned achieving career success, especially for women, isn't solely about being smart and competent. It's also about the strategies you employ to help achieve your goals—especially in the face of adversity. Further, I learned that I could begin developing leadership competencies such as developing and implementing a vision, influencing and working with others to achieve results, and collaborating with a diversity of people throughout the organization, right where I was. And while I had aspirations of developing beyond an administrative role, I could start my development in my current role. But these lessons didn't come without their challenges.

Countless times after expressing interest in pursuing other opportunities within the company, I was told I was either underqualified or wouldn't be considered for the job because of my schedule constraints. My job was threatened more than once because I couldn't stay beyond an eight-hour workday. I experienced sexual harassment by a number of the men I worked with (mind you, we were working on the waterfront)—including a manager. It wasn't easy; but I persevered.

Although I initially returned to school to become a therapist, a natural and rational progression for someone with an undergraduate degree in psychology, because of what I experienced at work, I developed an interest in helping people in the workforce, particularly those in leadership positions. After all, work is where we spend so much of our time. Why shouldn't it be a place everyone enjoys, or at the very least, doesn't hate? So I made another critical career decision midway through my master's program, I decided to combine my passion for helping people succeed with my growing interest for leadership development and transitioned into the organizational psychology program (I call it a business degree focused on people). As a result, I decided to build a career around helping leaders to be their best.

Starting the Climb

As a young woman in my first corporate role, I knew very little about career development. My first few years were tough. I didn't know how to dress properly for the culture which impacted how people viewed and treated me. I took advantage of sick time, not demonstrating I'd been raised by parents with a strong work ethic, and I allowed my personal life to interfere with my professional one. These choices, along with my mediocre work product, also impacted how others regarded me. Truth be told, I wasn't really a good fit for my job. I wasn't passionate in any way about being an assistant. It was only by the grace of God that I made it through those early years and stayed employed. Even though I had a mentor encouraging and supporting me, it would be a while before I took work seriously, listened to sometimes very difficult feedback, and started paying attention to how my behavior affected my opportunities to advance. But I eventually got it—after bumping my head a few times—and began to carry myself as a leader.

In the simplest yet broadest of terms, I define a leader as someone who others want and are able to follow, they who have a clear vision, and are able to bring others along for the journey. A leader is a leader not because of a title but because of their ability to realize success for themselves and others. As I learned the various qualities of leadership in school, interacted more confidently with others across the organization, and had informative conversations with men and women I admired, my development showed in my work and my efforts began to pay off. About a year into my graduate program, a manager in another department approached me and asked if I would be interested in becoming a customer service supervisor—an operational and front-line management role in which I had no experience. It offered more responsibility, more visibility, and more money. I happily accepted the offer.

I thrived as a supervisor and enjoyed the additional responsibility of leading others and managing the work of the department. More engaged in my work, I began taking my job even more seriously. I started to attend various management workshops and volunteered for special projects as they became available. My manager and peers took notice, and that changed my relationship within the organization and others I worked with and for.

A year later, I was asked to join a committee to oversee the management training program that was under my responsibility. Made up of many senior leaders in the organization, I was the only non-executive and woman on the team. The group's mission was threefold: 1) to ensure the participants of the program were receiving the proper training and mentoring, 2) to verify whether they were completing the program in a timely manner, and 3) to ensure that new, qualified trainees were recruited into the program. Being on that committee was an opportunity for me to show what I had learned in school as well as demonstrate my abilities as the program manager. Taking the baton, I ran with it, being fully involved and immersed in the role while still supervising my department. Once again, the management team took notice and invited me to manage the entire program. I gladly accepted.

Yet another year later, I was completing my master's degree in organizational consulting and was approached by the human resources vice president about becoming a regional human resources business partner. The role did not yet exist, nor did I have previous experience working in human resources. They were creating the position for me; I would be responsible for working with leaders in the Northern California region. Although the vice president and I discussed making it a manager role, I was told to wait; I would receive the title after I started the job. This should have been a red flag. So eager and ambitious, I didn't take issue. But just four years going after joining this company as an administrative assistant, uncertain of my career direction or even interests, I was beginning my career as a leadership development professional, and had a position created that fit my knowledge and skill set. God is truly amazing!

Soon after stepping into my new role, my manager and I began discussing how I could shape the position into a manager role. We created a year-long action plan, and I got busy working towards my goal. I volunteered for projects and made every effort to be a visible and available resource to the leadership team, working hard to better understand the industry and the HR profession. My son was older, and I was able to work whatever hours were needed to get the job done. In spite of my hard work and efforts, however, I found myself once more banging my head up against the proverbial glass ceiling. The more I pushed to take on more responsibility, the more my manager—in spite of our agreement—pushed back and said, "Not yet." My newfound career had quickly come to a standstill; I didn't quite know what the stall was about or what to do about it.

A year passed without any news from the vice president about the manager role. Although I received an excellent performance review, I discovered the possibility of becoming a manager within that organization was further away than I thought. One Friday afternoon while once again discussing my career goals with my manager during my second-year performance review, I was informed I was going to have a new boss the following Monday. Her title? Human Resources Manager—the very role I was trying to attain. I was not notified the position had been created or interviews were taking place. I was disappointed, hurt, and very confused.

I had given my all, only to be told my all wasn't good enough. I decided to make the best of the situation and do my best to work with and support my new manager, teaching her everything I could about the company and the nuances of the role so she could be successful. It wasn't easy training someone who was in the position I worked my butt off to get. To top it off, it seemed the vice president told my new manager about my wanting the title as she bluntly noted in one conversation that she knew I was interested in her job.

I stuck it out for another year and learned a lot about talent management, organizational politics, and myself. When it was obvious advancement was even less of a possibility than when I first started, I decided it was time to move on. My confidence and self-esteem were so eroded from that experience it was difficult to even believe another company would want me. It felt like I was getting out of a bad relationship. And I was. It was too unhealthy to stay, but the future was so uncertain.

About a year after I left, I learned the human resources manager never really fit into the culture and was terminated. Of course, all the "what ifs" came flooding in: what if I had stayed and stuck it out, what if I had been more aggressive in going after what I wanted, what if I wasn't black, and on and on. In the long run, I'm glad I left. It was time for me to apply my talents somewhere else.

As I started looking for new opportunities, I noted what I enjoyed most about my previous position and looked for roles that would fit. At first, I questioned whether I should even apply to the positions as I only had a year's worth of HR experience but I thought, *Why not? I have nothing to lose by just applying.*

Better Days

Not long into my search, I found a position in leadership development at a fast food restaurant chain. Although I had never worked in training and development before, I decided to apply to the entry-level position the company had posted. The worst that could happen is I'd get a "no." To my pleasant surprise, I didn't get a no. They offered me the job! And not only that, but because of my master's degree, they brought me in at a mid-level position and salary rather than in the entry level position I had sought. Some of the confidence that had eroded because of my prior experience started to return.

For two and a half years at the fast food company, I honed my technical and leadership skills until I once again felt I had come to a standstill. While I enjoyed the company, my coworkers, and my manager, I was becoming bored with the work. There was more for me to do professionally. So I made another conscious (and bold) career decision, I decided to pursue my doctorate.

By this point in my story, I was remarried with a blended family; our four kids ranged in age from one to fourteen. My son from my previous marriage was ten. I found it hard to juggle work, home, and school. With my husband's support, I made another critical career decision and decided to leave the company I enjoyed working for and start my own business. It was a long-time goal of mine and the timing was right to pursue it. Being independent allowed not only the flexibility I needed as a wife, mother, and student but also the freedom to create the programs and opportunities that were my passion and would help others. These series of decisions have led to a very fulfilling career as a leadership coach, facilitator, and author.

When people often ask me now how I succeeded, I always say first and foremost, I wouldn't have been able to do it without my faith in God and much prayer. He enabled me to develop the confidence and provided the assurance I could do what I set my mind to, and He provided me the support of friends, family, colleagues, sponsors, and mentors (more about the support system later) who helped me along the way.

I tell this story for many reasons. First, throughout my career progression, many women and men have shared their stories of success and failure with me. Their stories inspired me to find my path and purpose. I'm hoping my story will inspire you to do the same. I tell it from the perspective of someone who has achieved some goals while still in pursuit of others. My second reason for sharing my story with you is that based on conversations I've had and research I've conducted, I've learned my story is not much different than many others as you will read in subsequent chapters. Although my story, as everyone else's, continues to unfold, I have learned a few lessons along the way that now I'm sharing with you.

My path, from vision to plan to goal accomplishment, wasn't a straight or easy shot. There were peaks and valleys, detours, road bumps, and dead ends. There were a few loops in there too; moments when I had to backtrack, retrace my steps, regroup, and try again. Like I mentioned earlier, while pursing my goals, life happened. To get through one challenge after another took tenacity, optimism, determination, focus, a clear intention of where I was heading, and for me—a lot of prayer, sleepless nights, and countless conversations with those who wouldn't let me quit. I had to be deliberate. I consciously made choices knowing if I said yes to one priority, I was saying no to another. I couldn't be with my kids, work, and go to school, all at the same time. There were evenings when I wanted to be home, but I had to go to class or to an event. And there were days I'd planned to go to work, but one of the kids was sick, so I stayed home.

I have found a woman's career progression often looks less like a linear progression and more like a maze. I can personally attest to that. But through the encouragement and support of others, as well as my own drive and tenacity, I can say I'm living my vision and truly living my life on purpose. Now, it's your turn!

FOOD FOR THOUGHT

Now that I've shared my story, what experiences (the highs and the lows) have created the person you are today?

What themes do you notice about these experiences?

What elements of your story could you share with others that would encourage and inspire them? If you don't know, simply share your story with someone your trust (whether they've already heard it or not), and ask them to share what they heard that was encouraging and inspiring.

TAKE ACTION!

Create a timeline of your journey, highlighting themes and noting trends that you notice.

Step 1. List out the highs and lows of your life and career to date. For example, you might identify being elected Student Body President in ninth grade as a high and losing your first pet when you were five as a low. Don't worry about the order of events yet. Just list the highs and lows however they come to you.

I've provided space for you to capture your thoughts. If this isn't enough, you don't want to write in your book, or the book format you have is electronic, use a designated notebook to capture your thoughts for each exercise (there's more!).

Understanding ourselves is the first step in creating lasting change in our lives. Creating a timeline of the experiences (both positive and negative) that have impacted who you are today enables you to more clearly see why you're passionate about certain things, how particular situations trigger you, and what circumstances brought out the best and worst in you.

Step 2. Craft the timeline. To do this get a piece of paper, turn it horizontally, and draw a straight line across in the middle of the paper. The space above the line will be where you note the high points and the space below the line you'll note the low points.

Step 3. Arrange the events you identified in step one along the timeline you crafted in Step 2.

Step 4. Write your answers to the following questions:

1. What was it about the high points that made them high?

2. What was it about the low points that made them low?

3. How did these experiences shape you as an individual, professional, and leader and what lessons did you learn?

4. Who were the key players in your life at the time?

- Who influenced you and how?

- Who were your mentors?

- Who else supported you?

- Who inspired you?

5. What decisions (whether you considered them "good" or "bad," conscious or unconscious) did you make that impact who you are today?

Write a summary of your leadership journey and how that journey influences you today.

2. Why Lead on Purpose

I attended an executive leadership training for a healthcare company recently, and I had the opportunity to hear senior executives proudly tell stories of the company's culture and its diverse labor force. Hearing this made me wonder how much of that labor force and the communities they serve were represented in the room of executives. So I looked around. In a room of about 50 people, there were many women, which was expected as currently, about 75% of those in healthcare are female[1], however, I saw few other visible "minorities" in the room. Besides me, no one else, either male or female, was black, and as far as I could tell, there were only two other people of color: one Asian woman and two Latino men. The senior executive panel was made up of eight men and two women. All Caucasian. Although this company's workforce, as a whole, might have been culturally diverse, the executives in the room visibly were not.

This scene, unfortunately, is not uncommon. It is replicated across organizations, industries, cities, and states throughout the United States. While there is more to diversity than how someone looks, our first impressions are often always based on what we see and/ or hear. And visibly not seeing those who look like you can have a great impact on your career aspirations and confidence in what opportunities are available to you. Additionally, there are certain nuances to being black, being a woman, and being a black woman. Our own individual experiences, as well as our collective cultural heritage, add value to a senior team and its conversations, ideas, problem-solving, and decision-making.

Racial disparities are not only prevalent in our workplaces but in our society as a whole. For example, according to the United States Census Bureau, the United States is made up of 13% blacks, of which 52% (a total of about 7% of all Americans) are black and female[2];

further, 61% of all blacks are in the labor force[3] with black men making up 11% and black women making up 8%of the entire workforce. We would reasonably expect to see an equal distribution of these numbers throughout an organization. For example, 8% of roles in any company, statistically, should be occupied by black women across all industries, professions, and levels of an organization; however, this just isn't the case. The numbers drop significantly as we look higher in the hierarchy. Top leadership teams rarely reflect the demographics of our nation. The societal impact of sexism, racism, and other-isms that occur because of implicit and explicit bias make it difficult, particularly for black women, to advance their careers and, thus, increase the numbers of those in higher level positions.

While black women make up a small percentage of the workforce, the numbers are higher in lower paying occupations. For example, while 28% of black women work in service occupations, 12% work in management, business, and financial operations positions—of which 42% of all women occupy. Our percentages are high as sole-income earners (53.3%), yet we have a higher representation (28.6%) of those who earn income below the poverty level[4].

Given that there's a large percentage of black women in lower-income jobs and an even larger percentage that head households or are the primary breadwinners, it's imperative that more black women secure opportunities to earn higher wages. Obviously, this is a systemic problem and not the scope of this book. However, for those who find themselves within these statistics, this information will assist in developing their professional skills and careers which will increase their earning potential.

Logically, the concentration of certain groups in certain regions of the country does not allow for an even distribution of groups. For example, you're generally going to find more racial diversity in urban areas than some suburbs and many rural regions. Additionally, the availability of education and resources to these same groups, namely black women, along with the sheer interest or disinterest in certain fields or industries, impact the number of us going into certain professions.

For example, the STEM (Science, Technology, Engineering, and Math) professions are trying to figure out how to interest and recruit more women and particularly women of color into their companies.

And many other industries are grappling with the same challenge. Some young girls, like my fifteen-year-old daughter, are more interested in English than science; more arts and fashion than algebra. They just don't have the interest or passion for more technical topics or professions. Taking sheer interest (or lack of) into the equation creates a clearer picture of why there might be a dearth of women in certain fields.

As you'll read in the next chapter, poverty, unemployment, social norms, and a broad spectrum of violence committed against women also contribute to having a smaller pool of black women in certain professions or at higher levels of an organization. For example, the significant rate at which black men and fathers are being incarcerated and murdered often leave mostly black women and mothers as the sole breadwinners of the family. This, in turn, lessens the number of professional women even more as they focus their energies on finding more readily-accessible work to support their families. While some of us are able to pursue our dreams and care for our families, others have to sacrifice their dreams in order to provide for theirs.

Finally, we also have to account for an individual's own lack of motivation and drive, self-worth, and confidence in pursuing or achieving her goals, as well as her fear of failure as well as success. Fear of success occurs when a woman sabotages her own career out of concern of no longer fitting in with her social group once she succeeds. These challenges have kept some women from pursuing more difficult, heavier responsibility, decision-making roles—a reality that is rarely written about or discussed.

I share the above considerations because often it is assumed that systemic racism and sexism are the only reasons black women aren't more visible in positions of power. Which, in turn, leaves a shortage of role models, mentors, and sponsors for those up-and-coming. While racism and sexism do play a major role in the lack of representation, each of us also has a responsibility for our careers. We can't always blame our lack of advancement on others, even if they contribute to the issue. It's important to remain focused on what we can do to change our situations rather than focusing on the obstacles—unless we have control over removing them. In understanding the obstacle yet putting our energy into the strategies that will help us get over or around them, we will not only achieve our goals, but make an easier ascent and be models for others to follow.

While not all women, let alone black women, and those in the workplace in general, want to be executives, the lessons in this book from those in executive roles can be applied at all levels throughout the organization.

FOOD FOR THOUGHT

1. Even if it's not a high-level position, what more do you want out of your career that you don't currently have? Besides money, is it recognition, reputation, fulfillment, enjoyment, the opportunity to help others?

2. What gets in the way of you having what you want? How can you overcome that barrier?

3. If you were to intentionally go after what you want, even if that meant first minimizing or eliminating a barrier, what kind of impact could having what you want to make in your life and the lives of others?

TAKE ACTION!

After answering the above questions, identify one intentional step you can take in making this desire a reality.

How soon will you start or complete this step by?

After you take that step, identify the next and follow through on taking it, and the next, and so on. List your next three steps here:

What other actions are you motivated to take?

Notes

1. https://www.bls.gov/cps/cpsaat11.htm
2. http://Blackdemographics.com/Black-women-statistics/
3. https://www.bls.gov/opub/reports/womens-databook/archive/women-in-the-labor-force-a-databook-2014.pdf
4. https://www.bls.gov/opub/reports/womens-databook/archive/women-in-the-labor-force-a-databook-2014.pdf

3. Valleys

Have you ever gone through something and felt you were the only person in the world who's ever suffered from it? Me too! I felt I was in a valley when I went through the divorce, when I experienced racism and sexism at work, and when I had my first bout of anxiety and depression. We all undergo life struggles that I call valleys, but because we tend to not talk about them with many, if anyone, we feel isolated and alone. But then when we open up and share our stories, we discover that others have survived like experiences and felt just as we had. That's how the #metoo movement came about. In 2006, after having a conversation with a young survivor of sexual abuse, at a loss for words, Tarana Burke, the originator of the #metoo movement, simply replied, "You're not alone. This happened to me too.[1]"

We're only liberated from our seeming isolation in the valley by speaking up, thereby, allowing us to connect our experiences to others, receiving and offering support in the process.

Another valley experience that I think is common, but not often talked about, is being the "first" and/or the "only;" the only black, the only woman, the only black woman, the only young black woman, the only black woman who is a single mother...the list can go on to include religious beliefs, sexual orientation, disability, birthplace, nationality, and ethnicity, to name the more common. The more identities you claim, the fewer of others like you you see, and the rarer, and sometimes more isolated, you feel.

In addition to work challenges where I felt I was the only one who ever experienced a situation, like you, I've often had to simultaneously juggle personal situations over the course of my career and adult life. I've struggled financially, physically, and emotionally; my current marriage has had its ups and downs; and

I've had to manage feelings of inadequacy sometimes during moments when I was projecting confidence.

There's nothing new under the sun. If someone else has successfully climbed out of a valley, so can you. And if we all would just share a little more about who we are and what we've been through, it has a way of liberating us from the bondage of shame, guilt, anger, and loneliness that we tend to bottle up. And our liberation enables others to free themselves as well. Sharing our stories fosters trust, builds relationships, strengthens bonds, and creates a sisterhood. You're not alone in any valley you've experienced—especially in the workplace. For every challenge you've encountered, there's another black woman who has encountered it too. Let's review some of the more common.

Black women experience four primary threats that can jeopardize their career advancement. They are:

1. societal barriers such as poverty[2], racism, and sexism[3]

2. organizational challenges because of the glass ceiling or cultural differences[4]

3. personal issues that arise due to conflicting responsibilities or a lack of personal and emotional support[5]

4. not having a success mindset

Poverty

The biggest challenge black women have had to overcome on the road to career success has been the economic and psychological barrier of poverty, as it can completely undercut work and career development[6]. Many academic studies have looked at the effects of poverty and socioeconomic status on motivation and achievement. The general finding from those studies was that women who were of a lower socioeconomic status weren't as ambitious and determined and possessed less of a desire to achieve[7]. Although this is a generalization that has been disproven time and time again by those who have achieved tremendous career success, this finding provides one explanation for the lack of black women in high-status positions. About 29% of black women are below the poverty line (compared to roughly 11% of Caucasian women[8]). Breaking through this barrier requires focus and determination.

Sexism

One study I read examined a diverse group of 325 women who represented several career fields[9]. Twenty-five percent of them were in senior-management positions, and the remaining 75% occupied middle- or upper-middle-management roles. Eighty-three percent of those studied reported experiencing specific issues related to sexism that affected their careers. I define sexism as any bias against women on the basis of gender. This bias can include attitudes, actions, or decisions and is not necessarily limited to men.

The researcher's first finding, which shouldn't be a surprise for anyone, was that the women's gender influenced their earnings. Sixty-eight percent of the participants in the study remarked that sexism affected their current and future salaries.

The second finding was that just because the women held positions in middle-, upper-middle-, or even senior management, their current role was not a guarantee for advancement to a more senior level. Sixty-seven percent of the participants reported being female negatively influenced their opportunities for promotion.

The third finding the researcher discovered was that one's talent was not a guarantee for development opportunities. Sixty percent of the participants believed that being a woman limited their prospects for professional development.

The final finding was that nondiscrimination policies in the participants' workplaces did not prevent discrimination against them, even though they were part of a "protected class." Also, the policies did not help participants advance; they needed additional support from managers to be successful.

A researcher of another study found that prejudiced performance norms reinforced an organizational culture of gender bias and sexual harassment practices. These norms were considered to be the greatest barriers to the women's advancement as those in positions of power—generally men—set the norms. The findings fly in the face of common career development assumptions that talent and visibility afford career opportunities. As will be discussed in another chapter, in addition to being good at what you do and positioning yourself, having someone in a position of influence, what's known as a sponsor, is also critical.

The Glass Ceiling

In 1991, the Glass Ceiling Commission released a study that examined the challenges women and people of color faced while aspiring to positions in management. They found that an institutional barrier existed that prevented diverse talent from advancing in their organizations simply because of their gender or race[10]. This institutional barrier is commonly known as the glass ceiling. Whereas the glass ceiling was at one time the more commonly used term, black women have also referred to it as the concrete ceiling or wall[11]. Although the experience of racism and sexism is not unique to black women, certain challenges can be distinctive for difference races[12].

For example, all women might experience sexism to some extent, however, black women and other women of color experience sexism and racism, and each racial group can experience these barriers in different ways.

At the core of this issue is unconscious (and at times, conscious) bias. Simply put, unconscious bias is a prejudice or preference one applies to a group of individuals outside of one's awareness. For example, a man might hire more men than women because of the assumptions he makes about the quality of a man's performance over a woman. We all have biases. They're how our minds make sense of the world; we group like objects together. Our biases can become harmful when we overgeneralize our experiences and assumptions.

Oftentimes, the racial and sexual elements are downplayed in the work environment[13], but there is sufficient evidence to support that the combination of these two constructs creates the concrete wall. These two biases which have been termed racialized sexism[14], are so often combined that it can be difficult for black women to discern when to ascribe another's behavior to racism, sexism, both, or something else.

This often-invisible barrier called the glass ceiling manifests as lack of opportunities to gain significant management or operational experiences, exclusion from formal and informal networks, stereotyping, preconceptions of women's roles and abilities, and failure of senior leadership to assume accountability and commitment to the advancement of talented black women[15]. Additionally, being unable to secure highly visible assignments, being under constant scrutiny, having one's authority and credibility continuously challenged, experiencing double outsider status as a person of color and woman, and feeling a lack of fit in the workplace[16] also contribute to the organizational barrier that black women reported experiencing while trying to achieve their career goals. Because of this, black women have not easily gained access to the needed organizational knowledge. This, in turn, has affected our ability to develop the required skills to compete and advance in the workplace. On top of that, even when the skills and knowledge are attained, because of other's biases, a black woman's behavior is often perceived as something other than intended. For example, a black woman asserting herself has often been seen as anger or hostility.

Cultural Differences

There are two considerable barriers to achievement at the interpersonal level for black women. First is perceptions of cultural differences and ethnocentrism, and second is what is called minority group density[17].

Cultural differences in how groups manage conflict and how they communicate are examples of interpersonal barriers; two types of groups can generally perceive and behave differently if put in similar situations which can cause misunderstandings between people of different cultures.

Ethnocentrism is the propensity to evaluate other cultures' behaviors and customs based on the standards and norms of one's own culture. Ethnocentrism coupled with perceptions of differences between groups are typically what create unconscious bias. And unconscious bias is often what influences many hiring, professional development, and succession-planning decisions as those in the decision-making roles make certain implicit assumptions about a particular individual or group. Hiring and promoting people who someone more naturally identifies with not only contributes to a lack of diversity in the organization but also to what is considered minority group density.

Minority group density is the proportion of a particular group (e.g. whites, men, baby boomers, etc.) in a department, team, or organization. It affects how black women, other woman, and people of color are treated within a group and the organization as a whole[18]. Perceptions of cultural differences, ethnocentrism, and minority group density all affect how individuals within an organization interact with one another, the attitudes they display[19], and the career development opportunities available.

Interpersonal

One challenge that is not unique to black women but is a common challenge for all as it relates to career and professional development, is interpersonal differences. While there can be a cultural or gender component such as in how men communicate compared to women or the way blacks express themselves over whites, I did not find any research to suggest that interpersonal issues were more of a unique challenge to one gender or race than another and therefore, I will not address that here. However, in later chapters we will discuss interpersonal strategies to ensure your success.

Personal

Researchers have found that a woman's family and personal responsibilities are a barrier for some[20]. black women have found it increasingly difficult to balance family and career as it has become even more prevalent over time for us to be the spiritual, emotional, and financial heads of our families. One author noted that "combining marriage, family, and career may be more damaging to career goals than discrimination"[21].

Moreover, lack of support from family and friends, going so far as trying to prevent a woman from achieving her career goals, is another barrier black women have experienced[22]. When women do not feel emotional support or appreciation from loved ones, career goals often suffer[23].

Fourteen percent of the women in one study reported that friends, family members, and colleagues tried to block their goal achievements. For instance, one respondent contended that some of her coworkers would not refer to her as Doctor but would refer to her as Miss, demonstrating their disrespect for her educational attainment. Another respondent complained that peers and even mentors "unsuccessfully tried to stymie several of us from completing the doctoral degree." Another respondent experienced problems with other black women who refused to support her[24].

All the above barriers—societal, organizational, interpersonal, and individual—are external to the professional black woman. The final barrier, that of your mindset and beliefs about yourself and others, is internal and, arguably, one of the more difficult barriers to overcome.

Studies of a concept called the achievement motive came out of the assumption that striving toward success was the norm for most people[25]. However, because many female participants in the study did not demonstrate that they were motivated to succeed, the idea that women might have a fear of success as a way of explaining gender differences was introduced.

Americans tend to assume that success is a universal aspiration, and they have a difficult time conceiving that someone would have a true fear of it[26]. They can understand a fear of failure perhaps, but not a fear of success. After all, why would someone be afraid to realize a dream? However, when negative social consequences are the expected result, some women make efforts to sabotage their own achievement[27] in order to avoid such consequences; consequences such as rejection or alienation from others and, for more non-traditional careers (those in which men primarily occupy), includes the pressure to deny one's femininity in order to compete for or maintain professional positions[28].

Fear of success is a learned characteristic that is more easily aroused in women than in men, and it has long been considered a potential inhibitor of achievement behavior[29]. Low self-esteem, self-sabotage, concern with others' evaluations of performance, and the competitive implications that follow, all characterize a fear of success.

One author studied fear of success and achievement-related motives in black college women and found a difference among the women in different socioeconomic classes (middle class versus working class)[30]. She found that middle-class women did not display as much of a fear of success as working-class women. This finding was evidenced in the middle-class women's competitive behavior with male counterparts both before and after receiving feedback on a given task. The result was associated with the women's middle-class upbringing in which standards of excellence were more so taught and social assertiveness was highly encouraged. Additionally, it was found that fear of success not only affected current, but also, future goals, and planning for both formal education, and career development.

In another study, fear of success influenced future goals by redirecting women to more neutral, achievable, traditional careers such as social service. When career success was associated with aggressiveness (for instance, when one competes in more traditional male-dominated occupations), and aggressiveness was associated with more conventional male behavior, for some black women, the fear of success seemed to be aroused[31]. One author also found that working-class women were socialized to be more feminine and were conflicted in displaying more aggressive behavior because it placed them outside of traditional female roles. Therefore, fear of success appeared to be a bigger obstacle for working-class black women than it was for the middle-class women due to the socialization each received as children.

The fear-of-success barrier somewhat brings this discussion full circle, as the above referenced study found that college women in lower socioeconomic groups—those closer to the poverty line, a societal barrier—were more likely to display a fear of success by redirecting their career goals towards more female-friendly professions, such as psychology or marketing. While our attitudes and mindsets have changed over the years, many still struggle with fear of success and other limiting beliefs that sabotage our careers.

In addition to fear of success, many of us are plagued with fear of failure; we lack the confidence in thinking we can succeed. Therefore, we often unconsciously sabotage our actions either behaviorally or in our decision making, before we even give ourselves a chance to achieve. For example, I dreamed about being a doctor when I was in high school and even took pre-med classes in college. But I didn't have the confidence or support that I needed at the time and, therefore, gave up the idea of becoming a physician after I earned my undergraduate degree. My grades were mediocre, I didn't have the drive, and I was distracted by other desires like wanting to be married and have children. Had I a different mindset and the support of others, the outcome might have been different. But at the time, I didn't see it as a possibility. I didn't want to fail trying.

Henry Ford of Ford Motor Company has been quoted as saying, "whether you think you can or think you can't, you're right." Because I didn't think I could get accepted into medical school, I didn't even try. My mindset is so much different now. Ourselves, alone, ultimately determine whether we succeed or fail. While there are external forces beyond our control that can get in the way, the biggest force that keeps most people stuck, is their own mindset. If you change how you think and approach a challenge, you can change the probability of overcoming it, and ultimately, realizing a desired outcome.

FOOD FOR THOUGHT

1. What barriers in your career have you encountered?

2. How have the barriers impacted your ability to develop new skills or make the career progression as you'd like?

3. What strategies did you use to minimize or eliminate the barriers?

4. We'll talk about strategies in a few chapters, but what strategies come to mind that you can implement now to overcome some of the controllable obstacles you've encountered? Don't forget to include how you're thinking about the obstacles.

TAKE ACTION!

With the list of barriers above, use a colored pen or highlighter and identify those barriers you felt were insurmountable. List them here:

Use a different colored pen or highlighter to identify those barriers you were able to overcome. List them here:

For those obstacles you felt were insurmountable, in hindsight, what did you have control over in each situation that you could have done differently?

This exercise will help you to distinguish between challenges that are controllable and those that are not. For those that are not, you have the opportunity to adopt a different mindset that will get you through the challenge until it's resolved. If the challenges are controllable, your opportunity is to identify the strategies you successfully used before and apply them the next time you're in a similar situation.

What other actions are you motivated to take?

Notes

1. Biography.com, 2019, https://www.biography.com/.amp/activist/tarana-burke.

2. Fleming, J. (1978). Fear of success, achievement-related motives, and behavior in black college women. Journal of Personality, 46(4), 694–716. Retrieved June 29, 2006, from http://0-web.ebscohost.com.library.alliant.edu/ehost/pdf?vid=125&hid=107&sid=e24542d0-5d2b-4ac4-99ab-771d665137bc%40sessionmgr102.

3. Bell, E. L. J. E., & Nkomo, S. M. (2001). Our separate ways: black and white women and the struggle for professional identity. Boston: Harvard Business School Press.

4. Bell, E. L. J. E., Nkomo, S., & Hammond, J. (1994). Glass ceiling commission: Barriers to workplace advancement experienced by African-Americans. Retrieved November 22, 2006, from http://digitalcommons.ilr.cornell.edu/key_workplace/118/.

5. Catalyst (2004). Advancing African American women in the workplace: What managers need to know. Retrieved January 20, 2006, from http://www.catalyst.org/bookstore/freematerials.shtml#woc.

6. Fleming, J. (1978). Fear of success, achievement-related motives, and behavior in black college women. Journal of Personality, 46(4), 694–716. Retrieved June 29, 2006, from http://0-web.ebscohost.com.library.alliant.edu/ehost/pdf?vid=125&hid=107&sid=e24542d0-5d2b-4ac4-99ab-771d665137bc%40sessionmgr102.

7. Turner, C. (1983, February). Psychosocial barriers to black women's career development. Paper presented at the Stone Center for Developmental Services and Studies, Wellesley College, MA.

8. Fleming, J. (1978). Fear of success, achievement-related motives, and behavior in black college women. Journal of Personality, 46(4), 694–716. Retrieved June 29, 2006, from http://0-web.ebscohost.com.library.alliant.edu/ehost/pdf?vid=125&hid=107&sid=e24542d0-5d2b-4ac4-99ab-771d665137bc%40sessionmgr102.

9. Swiss, D. J. (1996). Women breaking through: Overcoming the final 10 obstacles at work. Princeton, NJ: Peterson's Pacesetter Books.

10. Wrigley, B. J. (2002). Glass ceiling? What glass ceiling? A qualitative study of how women view the glass ceiling in public relations and communications management. Journal of Public Relations Research, 14(1), 27–55. Retrieved November 24, 2006, from http://0-web.ebscohost.com.library.alliant.edu/ehost/pdf?vid=37&hid=109&sid=8af1260c-0629-4cdc-a853-96061bb389c8%40sessionmgr109.

11. Bell, E. L. J. E., & Nkomo, S. M. (2001). Our separate ways: black and white women and the struggle for professional identity. Boston: Harvard Business School Press.

12. Bell, E. L. J. E., & Nkomo, S. M. (2001). Our separate ways: black and white women and the struggle for professional identity. Boston: Harvard Business School Press.

13. Gallagher, C. (2000). Going to the top. New York: Penguin.

14. Bell, E. L. J. E., & Nkomo, S. M. (2001). Our separate ways: black and white women and the struggle for professional identity. Boston: Harvard Business School Press.

15. Bell, E. L. J. E., & Nkomo, S. M. (2001). Our separate ways: black and white women and the struggle for professional identity. Boston: Harvard Business School Press.

16. Bell, E. L. J. E., & Nkomo, S. M. (2001). Our separate ways: black and white women and the struggle for professional identity. Boston: Harvard Business School Press.

17. Bell, E. L. J. E., & Nkomo, S. M. (2001). Our separate ways: black and white women and the struggle for professional identity. Boston: Harvard Business School Press.

18. Bell, E. L. J. E., Nkomo, S., & Hammond, J. (1994). Glass ceiling commission: Barriers to workplace advancement experienced by African-Americans. Retrieved November 22, 2006, from http://digitalcommons.ilr.cornell.edu/key_workplace/118/.

19. Bell, E. L. J. E., Nkomo, S., & Hammond, J. (1994). Glass ceiling commission: Barriers to workplace advancement experienced by African-Americans. Retrieved November 22, 2006, from http://digitalcommons.ilr.cornell.edu/key_workplace/118/, p. 40.

20. Bell, E. L. J. E., Nkomo, S., & Hammond, J. (1994). Glass ceiling commission: Barriers to workplace advancement experienced by African-Americans. Retrieved November 22, 2006, from http://digitalcommons.ilr.cornell.edu/key_workplace/118/.

21. Catalyst (2004). Advancing African American women in the workplace: What managers need to know. Retrieved January 20, 2006, from http://www.catalyst.org/bookstore/freematerials.shtml#woc

22. as cited in Nichols, J. C., & Tanksey, C. B. (2004). Revelations of African American women with terminal degrees: Overcoming obstacles to success. The Negro Educational Review, 55(4), 175–185. Retrieved June 16, 2006, from http://0-web.ebscohost.com.library.alliant.edu/ehost/pdf?vid=13&hid=109&sid=8af1260c-0629-4cdc-a853-96061bb389c8%40sessionmgr109, p. 180.

23. Nichols, J. C., & Tanksey, C. B. (2004). Revelations of African American women with terminal degrees: Overcoming obstacles to success. The Negro Educational Review, 55(4), 175–185. Retrieved June 16, 2006, from

24. Nichols, J. C., & Tanksey, C. B. (2004). Revelations of African American women with terminal degrees: Overcoming obstacles to success. The Negro Educational Review, 55(4), 175–185. Retrieved June 16, 2006, from http://0-web.ebscohost.com.library.alliant.edu/ehost/pdf?vid=13&hid=109&sid=8af1260c-0629-4cdc-a853-96061bb389c8%40sessionmgr109, p.178.

25. Canavan-Gumpert, D., Garner, K., & Gumpert, P. (1978). The success-fearing personality. Lexington, Massachusetts: Lexington Books.

26. Turner, C. (1983, February). Psychosocial barriers to black women's career development. Paper presented at the Stone Center for Developmental Services and Studies, Wellesley College, MA.

27. Canavan-Gumpert, D., Garner, K., & Gumpert, P. (1978). The success-fearing personality. Lexington, Massachusetts: Lexington Books.

28. Tresemer, D. (1977). Fear of success. New York: Plenum Press.

29. Fleming, J., & Horner, M. S. (1992). The motive to avoid success. In C. P. Smith (Ed.), Motivation and personality: Handbook of thematic content

analysis (pp. 179–189). New York: Cambridge University Press.

30. Fleming, J., & Horner, M. S. (1992). The motive to avoid success. In C. P. Smith (Ed.), Motivation and personality: Handbook of thematic content analysis (pp. 179–189). New York: Cambridge University Press.

31. Canavan, D. (1989). Fear of Success. In R. C. Curtis (Ed.), Self-defeating behaviors: Experimental research, clinical impressions, and practical implications (pp. 159–188). New York: Plenum Press.

THE WHAT

4. What Is Leadership?

There are certain components of leadership that are essential at every level of an organization. Being a leader is not about a title, although plenty of people make it out to be. Leadership is a way of being. It is also about how you carry yourself, the mindset you have, your character, and how you choose to treat others in order to get results.

To lead means you're willing to go before others and take responsibility if you take them in the wrong direction. There are those who are considered leaders because of their position and title. While it doesn't always happen this way, I have found the leaders who are most effective are those who lead first through action and, as a result, are appointed to a position.

How leaders lead really depends. It depends on the environment they're in, be it work, school, church, the community, etc. It also depends where, geographically, they are, the generation they were born in, and the role models they have. How a leader leads also depends on their gender, ethnicity, and upbringing. Leadership can also be situational. In some moments, you might have to step up to lead more than in others.

Leadership is a highly-written and talked about topic. You can pick up ten different books or ask ten different people what a leader is and you'll get ten different answers. Because there are enough books on leadership to fill countless libraries and bookstores, I'm not going to focus how others have defined leadership. I'm going to help you define what leadership is to you.

The key to defining leadership for yourself is to think about what it means to lead. In a notebook or journal, write what qualities, traits, beliefs, and behaviors you think make a good leader. Then, list the qualities, traits, beliefs, and behaviors you think make a poor leader.

If you have a hard time coming up with qualities that make a leader, think about those you've worked with. What has been your experience? What constitutes a good or bad example and why? What about a person's behaviors led you to consider your experience a good or bad one?

Next, take a look at the list you came up with and see if you can group any of the traits together or whether a theme emerges. Then, in a few sentences write your definition of a good leader. What observable traits do they possess? How many of these traits do you have? Which would you like to develop?

I define a leader as someone who is strategic, has a clear vision of the desired outcome, clearly communicates that vision, and brings others along to see the vision realized. A strong leader doesn't work in a vacuum; she's open to others' ideas and holds herself, her team, and her colleagues accountable. A strong leader also knows how to problem solve, and, even if she doesn't know the answer, she knows how to leverage her relationships with others to find answers and make decisions. Finally, she knows and is inspired by her purpose, and in turn, she's able to inspire others.

Remember, leadership is based on action, not title. While all managers might not be good leaders, all good leaders can be managers, supervisors, administrative assistants, specialists, coordinators, etc. You can be a leader at any level of the organization, no matter what role you're in. Don't wait until you get to a certain place in your career to develop your leadership behaviors and skills. I've worked with many senior-level women who hire me to help them develop behaviors they wish they'd learned early in their careers. While people are often promoted for their technical and not their leadership skills, imagine demonstrating both skills early on. How much more successful and satisfied could you be in your career?

FOOD FOR THOUGHT

If you think about the leaders you've worked with over the course of your life, what behaviors, characteristics, and competencies made them what you'd consider to be an effective leader?

TAKE ACTION!

Write what qualities, traits, beliefs, and behaviors you think make a good leader (and while you're at it, list the qualities, traits, beliefs, and behaviors you think make a poor leader).

Which of these traits do you already demonstrate?

Next, list the traits you have an opportunity to develop.

As you read through this book, keep a running list of strengths and development opportunities you identify. Decide which traits you'd like to develop first, second, third, and so on and why. List them here:

What other actions are you motivated to take?

5. What Is Career Success?

In the United States, striving for success is an almost universal way of life. As a culture, we discuss success and failure constantly. We tend to look up to, emulate, and put on pedestals those we consider "successful." And we don't admire or pay much attention to those who haven't lived up to our society's idea of achievement. There are two broad ways of looking at success: internally and externally.

Internal success is about how you feel about your accomplishments. Are you more satisfied or dissatisfied with the things you've done to date? Do you feel you're successful? Why or why not? Perhaps you feel proud of what you've achieved, like earning a degree or achieving a desired position. Or maybe you feel a sense of fulfillment in the work you perform, regardless of your title or pay grade. If you have a sense of satisfaction in your career or are striving for it, you're more so driven by internal success.

External success, on the other hand, typically includes the more visible attainments such as income, title, and status, and material possessions like homes, cars, and clothes.

While most people celebrate and highlight external success, it's equally, if not more, important to genuinely work towards being internally successful. You can have all the cars, homes, and vacations you want, but those who have external success and lack internal success can ultimately become very unhappy.

If you want to achieve both internal and external career successes, being intentional and crafting a strategic career plan helps you get there in a more focused and accelerated way. It involves identifying what you want from your career, assessing your strengths and weaknesses in relation to these goals, and deciding what steps need to be taken, within a certain time frame, to realize your goals in the light of your strengths and weaknesses. It comprises a series of individual decisions that ought to be made as rationally and systematically as possible if the plan is going to be successfully implemented. We'll talk more about a strategic career plan a little later. But for now, start thinking about:

FOOD FOR THOUGHT

1. How do you define success?

2. How close or far are you in matching your definition to your reality?

3. What's missing?

If you were successful, according to your definition, what would be different?

If you never earned another dollar, but you were doing work that made you feel fulfilled and like you were making a significant impact and the contribution you wanted, how successful would you feel? Why?

TAKE ACTION!

Re-write your definition of success.

List which components of your above definition of success you "have to have," like a particular salary or job level, in order to feel successful?

Now, list which components of your definition would be "nice to have" (but are not necessary, like a new car every year)?

What actions are you motivated to take after reading this chapter?

6. What Is Power?

Many women I coach struggle with an inability to persuade or influence others the way they'd like to. For some, it's because of their body language and how they communicate; some don't present their thoughts and ideas in a compelling way; others' have developed reputations in the workplace or their industry that first need to be repaired.

We all possess some form of power and, therefore, the ability to influence. Without having an awareness of the type of power you have or can have, you won't be able to successfully collaborate, lead, or work with colleagues, higher level managers, or your direct reports.

In 1959, John French and Bertram Raven conducted a social psychology study on power. From that study, five types of power were identified, and later, Raven added a sixth. In this discussion, power is the capacity to influence a person or group of people. Power can be used to inflict hurt and pain; it also can be used to uplift and support. While power usually has more of a negative connotation, it doesn't have to. Let's look briefly at each form of power that is used in the workplace.

Coercive Power is the type of power exercised to control another person or people. Coercive power is leveraged through bullying, threatening, and intimidating a person or group to do what you want them to do. While this type of power might be effective in getting people to act, it's the least effective in creating motivation, engagement, and loyalty in others, given that you will only influence their behavior when you're being a witch (or choose another first letter if you like). While coercive power is a means to an end, it carries a lot of consequences, such as fear, disrespect, rebellion, and outright defiance.

I am currently working with a leader who has two direct reports. One of the challenges she's facing is that one report is bullying and intimidating the other, even though they are peers. You don't have to have a title to exert this type of power, but it'll only get you so far. While, in the short-term, you might get others to do what you want, in the long-term, it can result in a lot of damage to your relationships and professional reputation.

Legitimate power is the power someone has because of their position, title, or role. Chief executive officers, vice presidents, executive directors, directors, managers, and supervisors all wield varying degrees of legitimate power over others and use it to influence and persuade. This type of power is often associated with a command and control environment where one person has been given the formal right to make demands and expect others to be obedient and carry them out. Legitimate power often goes hand in hand with coercive power.

While I've been subject to all six types of power, the first organization I worked in used a combination of coercive and legitimate power to force employees to act. While some individuals thrive in this type of setting, I found it to be oppressive and limiting for my personality and career aspirations. It wasn't until I recognized how damaging this type of power was to my psyche, health, and even relationships that I decided to move on. Recognizing the types of environments you thrive in or don't is key to your engagement, satisfaction, and success.

Reward power is the ability to influence with rewards in return for another's obedience or compliance. It's based on the idea that, "If you do X for me, I will give you Y in return." Reward power can be useful at first, but the effect of the reward can diminish the more often the reward is used. Over time, the reward becomes less desirable. If you are trying to use this form of power to influence peers and direct reports, you might find this strategy initially effective; however, you'll have to continually stay mindful of what works and what doesn't with each person you work with in order to keep them motivated. If you are interested in influencing up in your organization, reward power can also be useful. However, the strategy will not be effective long-term or with multiple individuals. You'd have to continue to come up with different forms of rewards to offer to those higher in the hierarchy. Often, these are the scandals we often hear about and see in the media.

If you are in a hierarchical situation, the above three forms of power could be useful; however, if you're looking to build or maintain relationship as well as influence, consider the next three forms of power.

Those whose personalities or presence are charismatic, alluring, or captivating, use **referent power** to influence. Because of the experiences and successes they have had in their careers, and others' admiration of them, these individuals are able to gain followers. Social media influencers use this type of power.

A person who has **informational power** has control over information that others need, and without it, are unable to do their jobs. One can use informational power to influence by offering what they know in exchange for something else. It's similar to reward power, but more specific to giving out inaccessible information. You might be chosen to lead or collaborate on a team, for example, because of your educational background that others don't have. In turn, that allows you to be influential not just in your particular area, but overall. Others see you as smart and knowledgeable, even when you might not feel that way yourself.

Expert power can be used by anyone who has knowledge, information, skill, or expertise in an area that others find valuable. Those with expert power can have a great deal of influence over others because of the respect and trust they've earned in their careers. To make a difference in your organization and the world at large, developing a subject-matter expertise in an area you are passionate about provides you a platform to influence others to choose a certain course of action.

Expert power has been found to be the most effective form of power in organizations. You don't have to have a title or position to be a subject matter expert. You also don't have to have a degree (although formal education could boost your influence even more). If you feel like you have not developed an expertise in any one area, this is your opportunity to explore and decide what topic you want to be more knowledgeable about.

Regardless of what form of power you use, another key element of influence is understanding and keeping in mind the other person's WIIFM (What's In It For Me?). When you approach a situation considering the other's perspective, desires, expectations, and needs, you are positioning yourself to be a great influence because you can approach them in a manner that arouses their interest. If you approach a discussion solely focused on you and what you want, you're more than likely going to get even less of what you were expecting. Building relationships based on trust, understanding power, and another's perspective is a great cocktail for success.

FOOD FOR THOUGHT

1. To apply the concept of power and influence on yourself and your career, think of how you've experienced power:

    a. Who has had it and how did they use it effectively?

    b. How did they use it ineffectively?

    c. What qualities or characteristics of leadership can you glean from each example?

3. When have you had power, how have you used it effectively and ineffectively?

4. How do you think your race, gender, social class, or any other

identity, impacts the power you have or want to have? How can you use it to influence and impact others positively?

TAKE ACTION!

What specific actions can you take as a result of reading this chapter?

7. The Foundation of Goal Achievement

Understanding your leadership style, clearly understanding what success means to you, and understanding the kind of power you possess is the beginning of leading on purpose. Now I want to give you some fundamental strategies to getting where you want to be. We will discuss setting goals specifically in the final chapter, however, let's examine the underlying processes that support goal-achievement.

Passion

Passion is the first essential key to achieving any goal. Passion is an intense and sometimes uncontrollable emotion—whether positive or negative—about a person, idea, challenge, or issue. Think about passion as a flame that burns within you. It can bring about great joy and fulfillment and it can also bring about great change in you, others, and the world. You know when you're passionate about the work you do when you're so focused on it that time just seems to fly. Some refer to it as "flow." We can be passionate about our careers, our families, a sports team, a social issue, or anything else where we have an intense emotional response.

Our passion easily comes through when we talk about anything related to it. Our faces light up, our energy changes, we get more animated, and our voices might even go up an octave (or two), and the volume can increase. Some of us are passionate about a social issue that angers us, such as poverty, homelessness, or human trafficking. If we can find a way to channel that energy into positive action, we can bring about massive transformation.

Following your career passion means you're willing to pursue it in spite of lack of money, time, education, or anything else. For example, I have a friend and colleague who has a degree in biochemistry, however she was passionate about the theater and acting. So, in her spare time, she supported her local theater and eventually turned that side gig into her main gig.

Do you know what you're passionate about professionally? Some leaders I work with have strong feelings about a particular subject matter, like accounting or engineering. Others have a passion for social issues, such as the environment. Still others, although well-established in their careers, are not yet engaged in their passion and are trying to figure out what really brings them joy and a sense of fulfillment. You can have more than one career-passion. You can be passionate about helping people with chronic pain as a pharmacist, physician, or physical therapist, for example, and be just as passionate about helping others with weight loss. The more able you are to combine your passions, the more fulfilled you will be at work.

I am passionate about supporting women in leadership. While I enjoy working with all my clients, I have a different energy level talking to and engaging with professional women. Whether an individual contributor or a senior executive, I feel I could spend all day helping a female client strategize on how to achieve their goals. It's just in my DNA. I feel really blessed to be able to work in an area I'm passionate about.

Our passion leads us to our purpose—that greater reason why we are here on Earth at this point in time and place. There is a reason I was born in 1969 as a black female to working-class parents in the San Francisco Bay Area. There's a reason I grew up in a culturally-diverse suburb with a variety of friends from different backgrounds. There's a reason I experienced the things I did as a young woman and professional even though some were confusing and painful. They became my cause, if you will—my desire to enact change. This is my reason for doing what I do. It's my "why".

If you take the time to think and reflect on the themes of your life, over time, if you don't already know what it is, your purpose will materialize. There's a need that only your passion, gifts, talents, skillset, personality, interests, and background can fulfill. You are the answer to that need. This is your purpose. Plug anyone else into the equation, and it won't be the same. If you align your passion with your purpose, you can create a powerful vehicle to transform your life and the lives of many others.

I became passionate about coaching women leaders because of my own early career experiences. I wanted to see organizations be more inclusive of women and people of color, and I work tirelessly to see organizations make that change. I invest a lot of mental and emotional energy and sometimes end the day with nothing left to give. But I love every minute of it. I encourage you to find a career that will engage your gifts and talents and that you're excited to go back to day after day. If your current role doesn't excite you, find out what does.

Our career goals, ideally, would be born out of our passion. Almost 90% of employees, according to one study[1], do not feel passionate about their work and, therefore, are not engaged; they are unable to contribute to their full capability. If you want to be more involved and excited about going to work every day, identify what would get you out of bed every morning, motivated to get to work. Think about the ideas or activities which you'd enjoy engaging in most. How can you bring more of that experience into your day to day?

I worked with an executive once who was interested in the arts, but was working in academia. We discussed the possibility of her finding a job in a more artistic environment. Because of her family and financial obligations, however, she was unable to change professions at the stage of her career that she was in (although some do). So instead, she considered companies that aligned more with her artistic interests and eventually found one that was a better fit.

Imagine what it would be like if every day you went to work doing what you love. How much more productive do you think you would be? How much more fulfilled would you be if you worked on things that mattered to you? If moving more towards your passion is not a simple exercise for you to do on your own, hire a coach to help you. You can never be disappointed pursuing your purpose by following your passion.

Our lives become meaningful through the impact we make on others, more than living and working just for ourselves. As we grow, our passion inspires others to pursue their passions and dreams[2].

Motivation

You can be passionate about something all day long, but if you're not motivated to do something about it, you cannot and will not achieve your goals or fulfill your purpose. Motivation is the emotion and energy we need in order to choose and pursue specific goals. Most academic theories are based on the assumption that we are all motivated to engage in a specific behavior purposefully and intentionally when we expect a desirable, valuable, and positive outcome as a result.

What motivates you? Is it your passion? Is it desire to be, do, or have something? Could it be your drive to get out of your current situation? What is going to be that thing that gets you out of bed in the morning and pursue your goals day in and day out? List a few of your motivators here.

Our circumstances can motivate us to do, have, or be something more or different than our current reality. When I was in the administrative role, making less than my peers, raising my son as a single mom, and trying to make many ends meet, I knew I had to increase my income if I wanted to create a better life for myself and my son. I was motivated by what I wanted as well as by what I didn't want any longer. When we are motivated enough by what we see or experience or what we don't see or don't experience, we set a goal. The key word is *enough*.

There are two types of motivation. The first is internal or intrinsic motivation, which is having a natural interest and engaging in an activity for the pure satisfaction it provides with no need for an external reward or acknowledgement. For example, I enjoy writing. Although I do write for public benefit, I also keep a journal where I write about my thoughts, ideas, and feelings. I find it to be a good way to ground me at the start of my day and it's therapeutic when I'm trying to work through an issue. Writing is both a personal and professional exercise that I am intrinsically motivated to do. No one has to pay me, beg me, remind me, or threaten me to write. I write for the sheer enjoyment of it.

To be intrinsically motivated in our work, there are three critical psychological states that must be met[3]. First, we have an expectation of what we will get from the behavior or action. For example, when I write, I expect to get joy. Second, we must have control. When writing starts feeling tedious or becomes boring, I can stop. Third, the work we're engaged in is personally meaningful. Writing for the benefit of other women aligns with my passion and, therefore, the work is significant. Intrinsic motivators are thought to be the foundations upon which self-directed, self-determined, and intentional actions are built.

In contrast, external or extrinsic motivation is when a person is motivated by something external, such as a reward, some form of recognition, or fear of punishment. While extrinsic motivation might make a person feel good (or enable them to avoid pain), they are exhibiting the behavior due to an external reward (pleasure) or punishment (pain) and not for the enjoyment of it.

While neither intrinsic or extrinsic motivation is better or worse, good or bad, it's helpful to know what is motivating you to do or achieve something. When you're clear on what motivates you, you can better understand what you need in to do to achieve your goals. Understanding your motivators also helps to clarify what might be getting in the way of you pursuing your career dreams. If you are intrinsically motivated, there's going to be some level of enjoyment in pursing the goal, no matter the reward or lack of.

To figure out whether you are intrinsically or extrinsically motivated at work, make a list of every task you perform in a given day. Then, think about if you would continue to perform each task if you didn't have to, without ever receiving any external recognition. If you would still perform that task, your motivation comes from within. If you'd have to have some external reward, then that is an external motivation.

Here's another example. If someone offered you a million dollars to do something you wouldn't normally do, and you decided to do it for the million dollars and no other reason, you'd be extrinsically motivated to do so. Sometimes, you have to think about the origin of the motivation. Most people are motivated to go to work to care for their families, to contribute their skills and ideas, or to be involved in something meaningful. All of these are intrinsic motivators, however, the pay, an extrinsic motivator, is also present.

We will often stay feeling stuck when we allow fear, the desire to stay in our comfort zone, or a lack of knowledge and ability, to outweigh our desires to do, have, and be more. Getting beyond this place of stagnation requires identifying what's causing it, along with a desire to move forward. Oftentimes, people have the desire, but they don't understand that fear, complacency, or some other negative mindset are keeping them from attaining what they truly desire. The next time you feel stuck, I encourage you to challenge yourself and ask, "How can I move past this place?" And then write out everything that comes to mind without censoring or judging the ideas. If you're determined to truly advance, the answer will come. If you need support, brainstorm with your coach. You don't have to do this alone.

Inspiration

If passion is the flame, motivation is the match that maintains the flame, and inspiration is the spark that lights the match. They all work in conjunction with the other. Inspiration can be considered that burst of creativity and energy you feel when you have an encounter with someone or something that stimulates your inner being. You can be inspired by someone else's work, something in nature, art, a speech, or even a quote. Anything in your environment can breathe that burst into you.

I want to see women thrive more in the workplace as leaders. I believe that having more female leaders will make a significant change on how women are treated overall. More women leaders will change the way we are able to raise our children, care for our families, and better our communities and societies as a whole because women approach decision-making and problem-solving differently than men. Having more women engaged in the workplace will impact our own well-being and our ability to contribute new ideas that will better serve the common good.

While this is my passion, I have had many days, weeks, and months, that I did not feel motivated to work on anything related to my passion. This book, blogging, or even engaging in conversation seemed to be able to get me out of my slump. My focus was elsewhere, like on my home, family, or ensuring as a self-employed person that I was making enough money to live. My passion got put on the back burner.

What sparked my motivation to continue to work in an area I am passionate about over and over again has been inspiration. I've been inspired by what others have written on women in the workplace. The thought of bringing a different perspective as a black woman into the ongoing conversation energizes me. I've also been inspired by those I mentor and the challenges I see them dealing with. The inspiration again ignites my motivation which, in turn, allows my passion to keep burning.

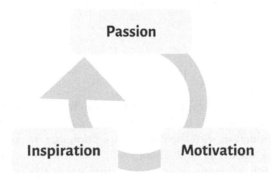

FOOD FOR THOUGHT

1. What are you passionate about? People? Ideas? Technology? Social Issues?

2. What are your intrinsic and extrinsic motivators?

3. How do your motivators show up at work?

4. What inspires you?

TAKE ACTION!

What specific actions can you take as a result of reading this chapter?

Notes

1. https://www2.deloitte.com/us/en/insights/topics/talent/worker-passion-employee-behavior.html.

2. https://www.forbes.com/sites/karlmoore/2015/01/19/the-great-power-of-connecting-passion-with-purpose/3/#5abfe93071fe.

3. Hackman, J. R., & Oldham, G. R. (1980). Work redesign. Reading, MA: Addison-Wesley.

8. Goal Setting

There are four components of goal setting that are often not talked about, but are key to achieving any goal. Two are behavioral strategies: visioning and crafting an action plan; and two are mental strategies: having self-confidence and goal commitment.

Having A Vision

Often, we're able to see ourselves attaining our goals before we take even one step towards them. Intentionally envisioning success is a strategy that serves as a motivator for achievement. A vision is simply a clear mental representation of a likely future event. In our minds, there is overlap between an actual physical image that we see with our eyes and a mental image that we imagine. Therefore, our brains cannot tell if we are actually experiencing or envisioning an event. This provides a strong motive to help us to achieve our goals. Take a moment to imagine yourself in your dream job. Use all your senses to envision yourself being at that point in time of your life. Imagine getting dressed in a full-length mirror as you prepare for work. What is the image staring back at you? Are you in a suit? A set of scrubs? Jeans and a tee-shirt (my favorite when working from home). Picture yourself driving to the office. What are you driving? Where are you going? When you get to work, envision someone wants to introduce you to a new colleague. How are they introducing you? What are they saying? I could go on with this imagery, but I hope you get the picture. Here are few more things to bring to your mind's eye as you dream about your future:

- What does your home look like? Is it a house? Do you live by the beach? In the mountains?

- Who lives with you? Do you live alone, with your children and spouse, or other loved ones?

- Do you have a spouse/partner/significant other? What's that relationship like?

- What is your health like? Do you work out? Are you eating healthy? Getting enough rest?

- Are you on a spiritual path? If so, where are you on that journey?

Use your imagination to the fullest to dream big!

A vision bridges thought and action. It allows us to picture our goals, and plan how to bring them to reality. In turn, this enables us to strategize and problem solve before events occur.

Now, I've heard it said that life happens when you're busy pursuing your dreams. I certainly can attest to that. When God gives us a vision, He doesn't always show us what we're going to go through to accomplish it. Had I known the sacrifices some of my goals and desires would require, I probably wouldn't have pursued some of them. Therefore, in the midst of trials and challenges, the vision serves as a compass, helping us get through difficult situations. If I didn't have a clear vision for my life, I would have given up on a lot of things because they felt too hard to attain. But the vision grounded me and reminded me of what I was striving for and always inspired me when I needed it the most.

There are three ways we can go about enacting a vision; if you can first see it, you can be, do, or have it.

1. You can focus your attention on the desired outcome by mentally envisioning yourself achieving the goal.

2. You can focus on the process of achieving your goal by mentally walking yourself through the steps needed to get there.

3. You can combine the two approaches, as both are needed to build the bridge between thought and action.

In one study, the effects of visioning on thoughts and behavior were examined by training seventy-seven college freshmen how to mentally prepare for a midterm exam[1]. Participants were trained in either envisioning the step-by-step process of how to achieve a goal, the goal outcome, both, or they were not trained at all. The authors found that, in the shorter term, students trained in envisioning the outcome reported being more highly motivated and inspired to study for the exam than the non-trained group and the step-by-step process group. Those trained in envisioning the process, on the other hand, experienced less anxiety the night before the exam and used effective problem-solving behaviors by preparing for the exam earlier and by studying, on average, three hours longer than the other groups. Those in the combined process-outcome group achieved the highest scores on exams, however they had the highest anxiety and worry, and the lowest confidence[2].

The study concluded that those trained in envisioning the process rather than the end result fared the best, as those individuals yielded both high scores (although not as high as the combined condition group) and low anxiety.

What we can draw from this conclusion is that when envisioning your goals, it is more impactful to envision yourself going through the process of attaining a goal than it is to see yourself already at the finish line so that you can anticipate and plan for challenges should they occur.

Let's say your goal is to earn a law degree. If you envision the outcome, you might see yourself on graduation day walking across the stage. If you envision the process, you might see yourself walking through campus carrying a book or backpack, sitting in class taking notes on your laptop or tablet, studying for exams at your dining room table, doing research on the internet for a paper, or receiving your papers back with a nice big A at the top. Envisioning the process enables you to put yourself in the desired environment as well as account for potential obstacles, like how to be a student and work fulltime, before they actually occur.

Crafting An Action-Plan

Once you envision your future and account for potential barriers, the next step is to craft an action-plan to address them. I spend most of my coaching time with my clients discussing the implementation of their action plans for situations such as meetings, difficult conversations, and negotiations. An action plan is simply a pre-planned strategy for a specific situation.

For example, right now I am coaching a client who is transitioning out of one company into another and wants to manage her negative behaviors. She has a tendency to be reactive and respond destructively in stressful situations. She realized she first has to be more aware of when she gets triggered, such as when someone challenges her expertise. Once aware, she brings her observations to our coaching sessions where we discuss how to respond more appropriately the next time so that she can be more effective in her new role and company.

I have found that creating an action-plan has also been a helpful strategy to use when encountering someone else's negative behavior. However, we must keep in mind, the barriers noted in the literature that black women face can be so implicit and systemic, they might be difficult to identify and overcome. Therefore, while crafting an action-plan might not change someone else's behavior, it enables us to choose the best response and take better emotional care of ourselves in and after each stressful interaction.

In 2002, one research group[3] presented the results of a study showing that combining one's goals with a pre-determined action-plan led to more goal progress. A well-crafted action-plan was found to be very useful for more challenging, rather than easily attainable goals[4]. The plan served as a motivator for initiating action when participants were faced with an expected circumstance even when mental stress was high[5]. In other words, the plan became the participant's "coach" by reminding them to act on their intentions even in the face of fear or intimidation.

This strategy could be helpful for those who have a desire to achieve more, but often fall short because of fear or intimidation, and have no other support in place. Other recent research suggests that having an action-plan can greatly enhance success because it links desired behaviors with certain situations and allows for intentional responses. Having pre-determined actions have been found to be less demanding than having to continually make decisions about when and how to behave in the moment[6].

When we are clear on what's motivating us and have a vision and plan for how to attain our goals, it results in the greatest possible progress toward them. Therefore, according to these findings, black women would have a greater opportunity to realize career success when our goals align with our interests and ideals and are supported by action-plans. This is particularly useful when considering obstacles such as a difficult boss or colleague or preparing for an important presentation you don't feel confident in delivering.

Possessing Self-Confidence

Self-confidence (also known as self-efficacy) is defined as our individual beliefs about whether we're capable of succeeding in specific situations or accomplishing specific goals. It is also about how much we believe we are able to control our successes and failures. Self-confidence impacts whether we set easy or difficult goals, the amount of effort, persistence, and commitment we put into achieving them, and our attitude about encountering obstacles, difficulties, and setbacks. Basically, our level of confidence is defined by whether we have a positive or negative mindset.

There are six identified methods that help nurture and increase your self-confidence[7]. They are

- being motivated by your own accomplishments

- observing or reading about others' successes

- having a vision of successful goal achievement

- receiving encouragement from others

- paying attention to how well you do in certain situations

- having the ability to control your emotions in various circumstances[8]

As human beings, we make free-will choices. The outcomes of these choices increase our level of confidence. When our actions and career choices result in personal satisfaction, rewards or recognition, or a higher salary, our self-confidence increases and enables us to set new and higher goals. When our choices and behaviors have negative results, we might not feel as confident to try again. This is where resilience, which we will discuss later, plays a part as we all make mistakes and experience failures. Therefore, when you focus on developing more self-confidence (and thereby decreasing your insecurity), you increase the likelihood of achieving your career goals and realizing your dreams.

Committing to the Goal

No personal goal has ever been achieved without a commitment. Goal commitment is simply your determination to accomplish your goals[9]. Goal commitment acts as a motivator. When we set a high or difficult goal, our commitment to the goal ensures action toward achievement[10]. Commitment tends to be associated with our motivation and passion for the opportunity before us. The higher our motivation, passion, and commitment, the higher the likelihood is of realizing our goals.

FOOD FOR THOUGHT

1. What are you passionate about? Is it data, an idea, some form of art expression like dance or music, or something else?

2. Beyond making a living and supporting your family, what is your "why" for achieving your goals? How does the work you're currently doing, either paid or volunteer, align with your why?

3. Besides family and friends, who are the people you want to positively impact? Is it young people, the homeless, those dealing with cancer?

TAKE ACTION!

If you don't yet know your why, start paying attention to the things that interest you or that you enjoy doing. If you know why you do what you do in your career, write it here:

Ask others to share with you their observations of you and what you seem to be passionate about.

Write out their responses and consider which of them interests you enough to do more research or spend more time doing.

What other actions are you motivated to take after reading this chapter?

Notes

1. Taylor, S. E., & Pham L. B. (1996). Mental simulation, motivation, and action. In P. M. Gollwitzer & J. A. Bargh (Eds.), The psychology of action: Linking cognition and motivation to behavior (pp. 219–235). New York: Guilford Press.

2. Taylor, S. E., & Pham L. B. (1996). Mental simulation, motivation, and action. In P. M. Gollwitzer & J. A. Bargh (Eds.), The psychology of action: Linking cognition and motivation to behavior (pp. 219–235). New York: Guilford Press.

3. Koestner, R., Leeks, N., Powers, T. A., & Chicoine, E. (2002). Attaining personal goals: Self-concordance plus implementation intentions equal success. Journal of Personality and Social Psychology, 83(1), 231–244. Retrieved May 16, 2006, from http://0-web.ebscohost.com.library.alliant.edu/ehost/ pdf?vid=62&hid=114&sid=1a5128b5-89ff-4c2e-8df5-644d83be605a%40sessio nmgr104.

4. Gollwitzer, P. M., & Brandstätter, V. (1997). Implementation intentions and effective goal pursuit. Journal of Personality and Social Psychology, 73(1), 186–199. Retrieved May 16, 2006, from

5. Brandstätter, V., Lengerfelder, A., & Gollwitzer, P. (2001). Implementation intentions and efficient action initiation. Journal of Personality and Social Psychology, 81(5), 946–960. Retrieved May, 16, 2006, from http://0-web.ebscohost.com.library.alliant.edu/ehost/ pdf?vid=103&hid=107&sid=e24542d0-5d2b-4ac4-99ab-771d665137bc%40sess ionmgr102.

6. Koestner, R., Leeks, N., Powers, T. A., & Chicoine, E. (2002). Attaining personal goals: Self-concordance plus implementation intentions equal success. Journal of Personality and Social Psychology, 83(1), 231–244. Retrieved May 16, 2006, from

7. Bandura, A. (1977). Social learning theory. Englewood Cliffs, NJ: Prentice Hall; Williams, S. L. (1995). Self-efficacy and anxiety and phobic disorders. In J. E. Maddux (Ed.), Self-efficacy, adaptation, and adjustment: Theory, research, and application. New York: Plenum Press.

8. Williams, S. L. (1995). Self-efficacy and anxiety and phobic disorders. In J. E. Maddux (Ed.), Self-efficacy, adaptation, and adjustment: Theory, research, and application. New York: Plenum Press.

9. Locke, E. A., & Latham, G. P. (1990). A theory of goal setting and task performance. Englewood Cliffs, NJ: Prentice Hall.

10. Klein, H. J., Wesson, M. J., Hollenbeck, J. R., & Alge, B. J. (1999). Goal commitment and the goal-setting process: Conceptual clarification and empirical synthesis. Journal of Applied Psychology, 84(6), 885–896. Retrieved October 18, 2007, from http://0-web.ebscohost.com.library.alliant.edu/ehost/ pdf?vid=58&hid=114&sid=1a5128b5-89ff-4c2e-8df5-644d83be605a%40sessio nmgr104; Baumeister, R. F. (1996). Self-regulation and ego threat: Motivated cognition, self-deception, and destructive goal setting. In P. M. Gollwitzer & J. A. Bargh (Eds.). The psychology of action: Linking cognition and motivation to behavior (pp. 27–47). New York: Guilford Press.

9. Mindset

Any change in direction relating to your thoughts and actions requires a shift in mindset. You cannot continue to think the same thoughts, act in the same ways, and expect different results. Some consider this the definition of insanity. To go to the next level in anything—your career, a relationship, your health, your education—you get to let go of some old ways of thinking and being. Now, this is easier said than done because we're not initially aware of our blind spots, or we don't know that a certain way of thinking and the resulting action is actually getting in our way.

There's an approach to behavior change therapists use called Cognitive Behavioral Therapy (CBT). The theory behind the approach is that our thoughts affect our emotions which, in turn, affect our actions. So, if you want to affect change in your life, it starts with how you think.

I work with leaders who want to become better leaders, but when we start talking about how they can do that, some start talking about what they can't do because of the company culture. Or why they can't because of how their bosses, colleagues, or direct reports act. Or they start talking about what others need to do. While this might be true, we generally have very little control over anything outside of ourselves. Even if the power has been given to us. Therefore, since the only actual control we have is over ourselves, then we have to look to ourselves—and no one else—to change. We cannot expect our situations to transform if we're not willing or don't see the need to change as individuals. So, if you're ready for something different and see your life going to the next level, keep reading.

The key to shifting your mindset is to take yourself—your thoughts, your actions, and your reactions—off of autopilot. Slow down enough to notice what's happening. Do you have a tendency to think negatively? How is that serving you? How can you shift your thoughts to be more positive? Do you react to someone or something in a particular way that is deemed as disruptive or disrespectful? Even if you don't agree or see it, consider what thoughts preceded your reaction? What past experiences informed it? What was the trigger? How can you change your perspective? How can you move on from the past? What I'm suggesting is not easy by far but yields far better results for you and your relationships.

Change begins with awareness. When we or others are unaware of our blind spots, we remain oblivious and, therefore, don't change. There's no perceived need. Once we recognize the need, through verbal feedback or simply noticing how others' responses to us, we can begin to a different approach, even if we don't know what that is yet. What feedback have you received recently that you haven't paid much attention to? As you slow down your thoughts and take yourself off autopilot, how willing are you to reflect, consider what the person said or did, and be introspective about it?

When we receive negative feedback, our natural and immediate reaction is typically to defend ourselves. Hearing what we're not doing well is rarely fun. Once you get over the initial sting, however, how can you look at things from the other person's perspective? What truth is there in what they said or did? What can you do, behaviorally, to change that person's perception of you or your intention? Do you need to apologize? Adjust a behavior? Communicate your intention more sincerely? This is where you have an opportunity to do something different. What are you going to do with the gift of feedback you've been given?

Sometimes, we're aware of the need to change before others are. Have you ever caught yourself speaking in a disrespectful or condescending tone of voice to your boss or coworker unintentionally, for example? What did you do to correct it? What thoughts did you notice you were having which caused the tone? Taking the time to do an examination of our thoughts, feelings, and behaviors isn't always easy. When we do, however, we're given the opportunity to choose who and what we want to be in the moment, rather than allowing our automatic thoughts to make the choice for us.

Once you've been given feedback, it doesn't mean you've accepted what was said. Have you ever heard the same feedback "all your life" and haven't done a thing about it? Maybe you don't feel like you can—*It's just how I am,* you think. Or maybe you don't see a problem with it—even if others do, it's *their* problem.

To be different and do differently, when given feedback, we have an opportunity to examine whether our current behavior is a problem. You don't have to know what to do just yet. That will come. The fact you are aware and recognize the opportunity is a blessing in and of itself. It's then, and only then, that you can start identifying what steps to take to bring about the adjustments you want to make. Perhaps it's taking a class, going to see a therapist, or reading about a particular topic. There's a variety of ways to learn new behaviors, habits, and attitudes. If you don't know where to begin, start with doing some research. Usually, once you start, one thing leads to another until you get a clearer picture.

Remember, learning is lifelong. While it's possible for you to think, feel, and behave differently overnight, change is typically a process that takes time. If you want to learn something new or do something you haven't tried before, don't expect mastery on your first attempt. Once you learn, you usually practice, then get feedback, then refine your actions, and practice again. Over time, you start to become intentional and your new behaviors become more natural.

I'll use myself as an example. When I was younger, I knew I wanted to do more than the administrative work I started out doing. But in order to do something different, I had to apply for different jobs. When I was denied on the second or third attempt to change positions at the container terminal, a manager pulled me to the side and gave me some very painful, yet helpful, feedback that I remember to this day. He said first, I had to dress the part. If I wanted to be taken seriously and be seen as capable of doing more, I had to look like I was capable. Although my wardrobe was fine for the workplace, it didn't communicate that I was confident and serious about developing my career. So, I had to acquire a new wardrobe. Second, he told me that I had to start taking initiative and not wait for someone to tell or ask me to do something. If I had an idea, I should speak up, share it, and ask for what I wanted instead of waiting for someone to offer it to me. If I wanted to go into a particular role (for me it was Human Resources), I needed to demonstrate in my present position what skills I brought to the table. I was not to wait for anyone to give me permission to be the best I could right then and there. That was certainly a new way of thinking for me as I had become quieter and more compliant being around older, intimidating, and demanding men. Finally, he shared with me the piece that really helped me to break through my mindset: he noted my attendance record at work. If I wanted to be taken seriously as a professional, I had to take my current job seriously before I could expect to be considered for any other role with more responsibility.

At the time, as a single mother, while I had some legitimate reasons for taking time off, the manager saw right through me when he said if I want to be taken seriously by others, I'd have to be serious about how I showed up every day. I wasn't taking my role seriously enough. I was working just enough to not get fired. I wasn't working to set myself up for success. No matter the reason for my absences, I was giving a perception that I didn't care about my job, the company, and, ultimately, myself and how people thought of me. Although none of these behaviors were conscious or intentional, once I received the feedback, I could see the situation from a different perspective. It was then that I decided to make a change.

The first thing I changed was my wardrobe. I wore more appropriate attire for the culture—less free spirit and casual and more corporate. This included paying attention to my hair, makeup, accessories, and nails as well. I also started taking my job more seriously. I began sharing my ideas about how to streamline a process or tackle a problem. I began asking for projects that would allow me to demonstrate and practice new skills and give me more visibility in the organization. I also limited the time I took off to absolute emergencies. If I could find someone to watch my son when he was sick and couldn't go to daycare, that's what I did rather than staying with him myself. Although I hated not being with him when he wasn't feeling well, I started looking at the bigger picture of what I was trying to accomplish. I wanted to build a career and a better life, and to do that I had to start making some sacrifices.

It took a while, but those efforts paid off. They led to promotions and, ultimately, getting into my dream field that I'm in today. It required me to change my approach and mindset around how I was thinking about work, motherhood, and myself. I continued to make mistakes, after all, I'm human; but, over time, I got better in certain areas I was intentionally focused on developing. Skills I once didn't have or were underused, I got deliberate about developing, and they started to become second nature. It takes practice and consistency to get there.

FOOD FOR THOUGHT

1. How would you describe your mindset and the internal chatter (that we all have) going on in your head? Would you say you're more positive and open or more negative and guarded?

2. How does your internal thought process influence your external behavior?

3. How does your behavior impact your relationships and interactions at work?

TAKE ACTION!

Choose 5 people who you trust to give you candid feedback. List their names here:

- Ask each person whether they see you as having a more positive, negative, or neutral disposition. Ask for examples of their experiences that support their perspective.

- Take note of what you learn from each person and identify which behaviors you think help and which get in the way of you being effective, particularly in your professional role.

- Jot the feedback and your thoughts down here:

What other actions are you motivated to take?

10. The Top 5 Personal Traits of Success

Whether I'm working with new leaders or those close to retirement, certain traits and behaviors will set the best leaders apart from others and are essential for being successful in the workplace. The five traits I'm about to share are the foundations of your brand and reputation that we will discuss in more detail in another chapter.

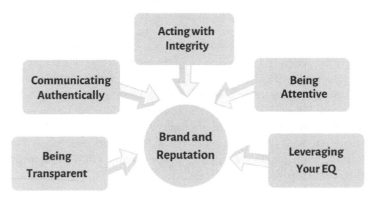

Being Transparent

A transparent object is something that allows light to pass through it so that other objects beyond it can be clearly seen[1]. A window, for example, as long as it's clean, can be seen through. An object that cannot be seen through clearly is considered unclear, indistinct, vague, or ambiguous. If we apply these definitions to communication, to be transparent as a professional means that you are being truthful and openly sharing your point of view. You're not hiding anything like an ulterior motive or agenda and you're not vague about your thoughts or position. Transparency enables trust between people. When you're transparent, others put their confidence in you and are willing to speak favorably about you because you are being real. Without transparency, a genuine relationship cannot be established. This can impact your ability to influence and collaborate with your colleagues, managers, and direct reports.

Transparency can be scary, when you think about it, because it requires you to be vulnerable and let other people into your more private thoughts and feelings. Allowing yourself to be vulnerable can, in turn, invite criticism and evoke the fear of not being accepted. Part of being human is having a longing for acceptance. By this I don't mean being a people-pleaser. Wanting to be accepted can simply mean you wish to feel like you belong.

Being transparent does not mean you are expected to tell all your personal business, but it does means noticing when you have opportunities to share more about yourself, taking the time to do so, thus allowing for a closer, more intimate, relationship with another. Discerning when transparency is appropriate is the harder part of the equation. It involves risk and requires practice. Most women tend to take more calculated risks than men and only act when they're confident their behavior is going to yield a favorable result. I encourage my clients to practice doing something scary, like being transparent, with people who they feel safe with first, so that making a mistake while practicing will be no big deal and will not jeopardize the relationship or how the person views them.

In your effort to be transparent, be sure you use tact. This means being sensitive to how you might come across and choosing words that would be easier for someone to hear. So, instead of saying, *that's the stupidest idea I ever heard!* You might try, *that's an interesting idea but I think we can do better.* See the difference? Many of us, especially as black women, are able to speak our minds. But are you able to speak your mind with a colleague, demonstrating restraint, and keeping your relationships intact? This is what tends to be more of a challenge for a number of us. If this is an area of opportunity for you, try observing or even speaking with someone who uses tact very well and learn a few tips and tricks from them. I tend to be on the quieter side and not always assertive, however, assertiveness is also important. So I have learned to model the behavior friends, family, and colleagues who I consider gifted in the art of telling people exactly what they think without hurting their feelings. Communication really is an art.

In having a conversation with my husband recently, I used a word that came across to him as offensive. While my intent was to be transparent, it wasn't my intent to offend him. When he shared what the impact of the word I used had on him, although I meant what I said, I could see how my word choice put him off. I could have chosen a different word to express the same thing. While I know to be tactful, and I coach others on this skill, I don't always get it right. Again, that's part of being human.

Some people take transparency and equate it to being truthful without forethought of the effect your words are going to have on another. That's not being transparent, that's being thoughtless, careless, and if I'm really being truthful myself, it's being downright hurtful. "Keeping it 100" doesn't mean tearing someone down for the sake of being honest.

Authenticity

A close cousin to transparency is authenticity. Being authentic means to be genuine and trustworthy. When used to describe an object, authenticity means that the piece is an original, it's valid, it's real. The opposite of being authentic is being fake or inauthentic. Being authentic in the workplace means that what you are saying and how you are acting are in alignment with who you are as a person. It also means that your speech and behaviors line up with your beliefs and values.

Have you ever experienced someone who you would describe as "fake"? They act one way but underneath you have a sense (or you actually know) how they really feel or think is contrary to how they're behaving? Sometimes, you can't even put your finger on what's wrong with the picture, but you know something is.

Or maybe you are not always authentic with people. Perhaps you work with someone you don't particularly like but have to get along with to get a job done. Even when we're trying to be our best selves, in spite of how we're feeling, others can sense it. Or, they learn we're not who we present ourselves as being because we can only sustain a façade for so long. When you're authentic, people believe your actions and your words. Like transparency, this helps them to trust you and can strengthen your relationship. A lack of authenticity often results in others' inability to trust you and therefore, erodes a relationship or keeps one from forming at all.

Transparency and authenticity go hand in hand. Transparency is about going beneath the surface of your words and expressing the feelings and thoughts behind the words; authenticity is being truthful about the words you speak. If you're truthful but your conversation is superficial or you speak meaningful words, but you're not being truthful, then you have the potential of confusing the listeners, at best, or losing your professional credibility, at worst.

Integrity

Another close cousin to transparency and authenticity is integrity. To have integrity is to not just be real, but to also be consistent in your character—whether at work, home, church, a family barbecue, at a club, or anywhere else. This doesn't mean that you won't have different social norms you abide by from situation to situation. As a Christian and minister, I sometimes use different words in church to express myself than I do in a professional setting. When you adjust your behavior to social norms and cues, you're not being fake, you're being mindful and aware of the different situations you find yourself in. While my language might change, who I am and my character shouldn't. If I wouldn't lie in church (and risk being struck by lightning), why would I lie at work or at home? What's the difference? Building trust with another human being means to act with integrity 100% of the time.

Being Attentive

A final trait that I continuously have to work hard on is being attentive. By this I mean bringing your full attention to the moment you're in and being with the person or people in front of you instead of allowing your mind to wander to your to-do list, looking at your phone or another device, or pondering what you're going to have for lunch. Being attentive allows you to fully take in the moment and respond appropriately without being distracted by other things. It is a success trait because it is so easy to not be present and attentive, thereby, making you seem distant, inaccessible, uninterested, or inauthentic. With all the distractions we have, giving someone our undivided attention and being present is not only a gift, but it sets you apart from others who might have their heads down and distracted. Dividing our attention has become more of the norm. When you're attentive in a conversation or meeting you're communicating that what is being said or done matters to you.

I often get to work with leaders who are transitioning from an individual contributor role to a position in which they are leading a group of people for the first time. Even experienced managers and executives I work with fall short in their interpersonal, non-technical skills. Most leaders are promoted because of their technical capabilities, know-how, and business savvy; they're able to get the job done, meet goals, complete projects, and impact the organization's bottom line. However, the skills that are required to elevate them to being an effective and transformational leader are often underdeveloped because we don't typically learn interpersonal skills in a classroom. We learn them initially by interacting with our parents, siblings, teachers, family, and friends. And if what we learn doesn't fit with the culture of the organization we're in, it shows. Time and time again, I hear stories of leaders losing great talent because they did not possess the requisite interpersonal skills they needed to retain their top employees and keep them engaged.

Demonstrating Emotional Intelligence

A lot has been written on Emotional Intelligence. If you do a Google search, you'll find many articles and books so I won't go into great detail here. But I think a short discussion would help.

A simple definition of emotional intelligence is the ability to be aware of and control your emotions appropriately while also appropriately assessing and managing yourself in social situations. Let's look at this concept in a little more detail.

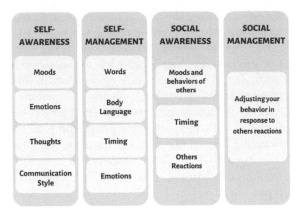

SELF-AWARENESS	SELF-MANAGEMENT	SOCIAL AWARENESS	SOCIAL MANAGEMENT
Moods	Words	Moods and behaviors of others	
Emotions	Body Language		Adjusting your behavior in response to others reactions
Thoughts	Timing	Timing	
Communication Style	Emotions	Others Reactions	

Awareness. Awareness is the cornerstone to being a successful person. Self-awareness requires paying attention to your thoughts, assumptions, beliefs, emotions, and expectations and behaving appropriately and accordingly, considering those around you. Self-awareness also includes having an awareness of what is motivating you to think a certain way or behave in a certain manner. Finally, it entails paying attention to how you're communicating, your words, timing, and tone, as well as your body language when you speak. Self-awareness requires you to slow down long enough to examine these often-unconscious thoughts and behaviors to determine whether there is something you can do differently for the sake of the relationship.

I once worked with a leader whose father raised her to expect people to take responsibility for their actions. When she went to work at a certain company, however, the culture of the organization supported pointing fingers at others and not taking personal accountability for their mistakes. My client had a belief of how people should behave and expected that behavior. So when she started working with people who did not own up to their errors or the part they played in a particular situation, my client called them on it which created a great deal of conflict. Once she was made aware of how her underlying beliefs and expectations were impacting how she was relating to her colleagues, she was able to make different choices of how she showed up and whether this was the right environment for her to be in.

Being socially aware means that you are present to the moods and the behaviors of others. You're noticing what's going on around you and how other people are reacting (or not reacting) to you. Being socially aware requires a level of empathy ("I understand, I've had days like that too!") or at least sympathy ("I can't relate, but I know this must be difficult for her").

Once my client became aware of her underlying expectations, she could begin to see how her behavior was having an impact on others and why they were responding the way they were to her. Whereas before this level of awareness, my client wondered what everyone else's problem was.

Management. Once you become self- and socially-aware, you then can make choices about how you will manage yourself in social situations.

Self-management involves choosing how to act or respond in a given situation, being aware of your moods and mindset. I have found that it's sometimes best to pause before I respond to something someone did or said, especially when I have a more negative emotional reaction.

Managing your responses, body language, and tone when replying to less than positive information gives you a better chance of maintaining any relationship that's important to you. Basing your replies on your emotions is considered more of a reaction—a knee-jerk act or statement that is made without consideration of how it will be received. Self-management involves choosing when and how to have a conversation with someone. It enables you to communicate when you need time before giving an answer or performing a particular act in order to ensure your response will be genuine.

Self-management for my client would look like her being able to manage the external manifestations of her internal thoughts and feelings and, if she can, challenging herself to think more positively so that there won't be such a disconnect between how she's feeling and how she's responding.

Social management is similar to self-management in that you are managing your reactions and responses. With social management, in addition to your own emotions, you're aware of the other person's expressed needs, goals, and emotional cues and interact in such a way that builds rapport and trust. Social management also allows for collaboration, teamwork, and respect. It's important to think about, in advance, how the other person is going to receive the information you have to share. And plan to deliver your message accordingly. Will what you have to say help or harm them? If it will be harmful, is there a better way to share your thoughts that will also ensure the lines of communication stay open?

Yes, it takes a tremendous amount of self-control and practice to develop your emotional intelligence; however, when it comes to the workplace and relationships in general, being self- and other-aware and managing yourself accordingly is a skill that you can apply in meetings, when working with peers, when speaking to your boss, and certainly when delivering a message to a direct report. How you are feeling and the way you choose to express or not express what's going on internally can mean the difference between staying right where you are and advancing to that next career level you want.

FOOD FOR THOUGHT

1. Which of the above traits would you consider strengths and which would you consider development opportunities? Why?

2. How would you rate yourself on a scale of 1 to 10 on each of the above traits, with 10 being you're so good you could teach a class on that trait?

TAKE ACTION!

If you didn't give yourself a 10 in all of the above traits, identify one thing you can do differently to increase your score one point in one area, and who can hold you accountable for following through on what you choose to do.

Notes

1. Oxford Dictionary (2019), https://www.lexico.com/en/definition/transparent

11. Leadership Presence

Most clients I work with are interested in advancing their careers beyond their current roles but can't because they don't know what's getting in the way of that happening. They have been given positive feedback about their skills and the results they achieve; however, they are not perceived as promotable. Leadership presence makes up approximately 26% of others' perceptions of your ability to be a higher-level leader. [1] It also accounts for over 50% of why organizations hire coaches. Forty percent of coaches say that helping someone develop their leadership presence is one of their top two requests they receive[2]. This indicates that while presence isn't the only attribute to have in order to be deemed a leader, it is important.

Leadership presence enables you to demonstrate your abilities in your current role through your behaviors, your communication style, and your physical attire. It starts with having the mindset of a leader, no matter your title, which includes self-awareness, emotional intelligence, a positive attitude, and self-confidence. Developing leadership presence is like baking a cake. You need all the necessary ingredients for it to come out right. It's not a cake if even one component is missing (at least, not a good one). And just as cakes need heat to be complete, presence requires consistency to permeate every aspect of your identity. Let's talk about the recipe for leadership presence in a bit more detail.

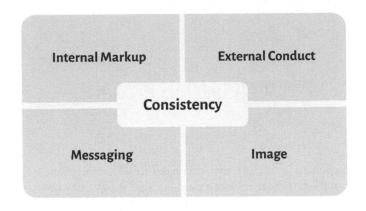

Your Internal Makeup

When considering your presence, it is essential to start with being introspective about your emotional intelligence (EQ), mindset, and self-confidence.

Since we've already discussed what EQ is in the previous chapter, let's talk about how to leverage it for projecting leadership presence. When you have a high EQ, you are able to recognize what you are feeling and how others are responding to you in order to manage situations appropriately. [3] Effective leaders are consistent with using and demonstrating emotional intelligence.

In addition to EQ, the right attitude sets you apart. The combined fifteen women in both my masters and doctorate studies approached work and life with can-do attitudes, and they encouraged everyone around them to do the same. They summoned their courage in the face of fear and were clear about their purpose and their goals. Their sincere and authentic perspectives not only pushed them forward on even the most difficult of days but also energized those around them. Effective leaders leverage their own genuine, positive attitudes to motivate and encourage others.

The third component, confidence, starts internally before it works its way outward. It's about being confident in yourself and your abilities whenever you walk in a room, have a conversation with colleagues, or even write an email. Confidence, coupled with motivation, passion, and inspiration, helps you put your thoughts into action, and without it, few of your dreams will be fully realized.

Once you're clear about your internal makeup, the next dimension to focus on is your external conduct.

Your External Conduct

How people see you act from day to day, is typically more noticeable than the words you speak. Actions tend to speak louder than words. For others to see you as leader-like, your behavior must be authentic and decisive, determined and engaged, confident, and once again, consistent. Those who have presence are also found to be truly approachable and friendly. They're professional, yet good natured, which comes from having a positive inner-attitude.

The first component of your external conduct is authenticity. Authenticity as a leader is important. People want to trust that you are being genuine in every situation. Once they trust your authenticity, they know who and what they're dealing with at all times. Think of those individuals you know either personally or see in the media who come across as leader-like. Whether right, wrong, good or bad, those who are authentic help us to believe that they will be themselves in any situation, which fosters trust (or distrust) in their leadership.

Next, it's important to be decisive. Those who are decisive are able to make decisions quickly and effectively without wavering. If you're one, like me, who needs time to process your thoughts before making a decision, just say so and set a time when you'll get back to a person. There will be times when you will have to make a decision on the spot, however, so do your homework before going into a meeting or discussion. By doing so, you're demonstrating your professionalism and your desire to make an informed decision. When you're armed with the right information, decision-making is easier.

Along with being decisive, it's key to be determined. Determination as a leader is about not giving up no matter the challenge, be it finding an error in a report or having a difficult conversation with a peer. Demonstrating your resolve exemplifies determination. As a leader, it's important to show determination, courage, and confidence, especially under pressure. It's an ingredient of presence that some call "gravitas." It's that seriousness of character in appropriate situations that demonstrates your understanding of the situation. Your confident determination and courage, and being emotionally intelligent enough to understand what behavior is called for in each moment will enable you to work through whatever challenges you face.

As mentioned in a previous chapter, those who demonstrate leadership presence ensure they are present and in the moment. They are able to connect with others in a way that puts them at ease. We often see poor examples of this when we're in meetings where leaders are observed multi-tasking by being on their laptops, tablets, or phones. While this behavior might be the norm for some organizations, being engaged and present in a meeting whether of 2 or 200, will certainly distinguish you from the rest. Especially as a black woman.

I received feedback on behalf of one leader I was coaching who was told by one of her colleagues that she just didn't seem to be paying attention in meetings. They observed her on her phone or with her focus elsewhere. This gave others the impression that she wasn't interested in the discussion and as a result, lessened her stakeholders' opinion of how effective she truly could be in her role. By the time we completed our coaching, she corrected that behavior. The post-coaching feedback I received noted that she rarely pulled her phone, she was less distracted, and more engaged and present in meetings. This shift enabled others to enjoy the gift of her knowledge and perspective and gave others the perception that she was a capable leader.

Leadership presence also requires you to behave consistently for people to recognize you as a genuine, decisive, determined, and engaged leader. You cannot expect others to perceive you as a strong leader if you show interest in one topic but not another. Or to be decisive on some issues and indecisive on others. Inconsistent behavior, no matter what it is, confuses people. They do not know which demonstrated action to trust from you which causes mistrust.

Although leadership presence has been considered an elusive, intangible concept, people know it when they see it. When they don't see it, they might not be able to put their finger on what is missing, but they know something's amiss.

Finally, confidence ties your external conduct together. Most of us have been taught to act "as if" and to "fake it till you make it." This means that even when you don't feel confident, act as if you are and the feelings of confidence will eventually follow.

Your Messaging

Communication is a third vital component of leadership presence. What you convey as a leader is extremely important. How you communicate impacts your influence on others. It's not just what you say, but how you say it. If a leader is unable to communicate, she's not a good leader. Period.

Only 7% of our communication is what we say, leaving 93% to be how we say it (38% our tone of voice and 55% our body language) [4]. Therefore, when communicating:

1) **Use strong and assertive words.** Speak confidently, using language that is not tentative, but definitive and sure. Often women will speak more cautiously, using words like *perhaps* or *maybe*, or apologizing for everything they say or are about to say, or did or are about to do. For example, have you (or someone you know) ever said, "I'm sorry for interrupting, but..." while in a meeting or conversation? While our mothers taught us to be polite, you don't have to apologize for having a thought you want to share. You can say *excuse me*, and share your thought. No apology necessary. It'll take practice so consider doing so in a safe space first, with those you're comfortable with before unleashing your new style in an important discussion.

The next time you're in a meeting, pay attention to the communication styles of the men versus the women and notice if there are any differences. Also, pay attention to your own style and determine if there's anything that communicates caution or uncertainty. Additionally, ensure your voice is loud enough for your entire audience to hear you. Be sure to project your voice but not yell.

2) **Be direct, clear, and concise.** Be straightforward and not too verbose or use words or jargon that others have trouble

understanding. You don't have to go into a long explanation to make your point. Have your backup information available, and if you need to explain, do so. But don't feel like you have to give the history of the world before you explain why you made a decision.

Women in particular have a tendency to make statements that come out sounding like questions? I did that on purpose. When you see it in writing, it doesn't make much sense, does it? It has the same effect when you're speaking. Are you asking a question or making a statement? If you're making a statement, make the statement. Do not put an inflection at the end of your statement as if you are unsure or seeking validation.

3) Be credible. Have a clear point of view. Use your voice (your own thoughts and opinions) and back up what you say with your experience and education. Connect with others using relatable language and stories. One show I used to enjoy watching was *The Apprentice*. When the participants were called into the boardroom to explain why they failed at a task, they were asked specific and direct questions. I would often yell (okay, not yelling but fuss) at the TV (usually at the women) saying, "Just answer the question!" Some people hem and haw and never answer the question asked. Doing so will erode and undermine your credibility. It will communicate you do not have an opinion or point of view, you weren't paying attention in the first place, or you did not grasp what was being asked of you. And if any of these are the case, why would anyone want to hear what you have to say or follow your lead?

4) Mind your non-verbal communication. Those with strong leadership presence can convey their credibility and confidence without saying a word. They look people in the eye when speaking, they offer a genuine smile, they pay attention to their facial expressions and body language to put people at ease, and they offer strong handshakes upon greeting or being introduced to others. As women especially, we have an opportunity to stay mindful of how we are communicating from head to toe. Be sure you hold your head straight. I have a tendency to tilt mine to one side. I caught myself one day on FaceTime while I was talking to a client and saw how distracting that might have looked. Keep your hands comfortably at your sides or on the table in front of you. Do not fiddle with a pen or other item. It conveys nervousness. If you're sitting, do so in a manner that's comfortable, yet not distracting, or communicating lack of confidence. In essence, ensure you are as confident with your nonverbal communication as you are with your words.

Overwhelmed? Practice one thing at a time, and once you feel you have a handle on one nonverbal gesture, move on to another. At times, I have asked or been given feedback about my communication style and I have worked components that require attention. Remember that development is ongoing. We never stop learning. Practice doesn't make perfect, it makes better.

Every woman I interviewed for my studies demonstrated a silent strength and presence that can't be described. It was more of the energy they were emitting that caused me to sit up a little straighter or speak in a more serious tone.

Your Image

The fourth component of leadership presence always seemed so superficial to me, but with experience came understanding. Have you ever heard the expression, "you never get a second chance to make a first impression"? How you present yourself can positively or negatively impact how people receive you and can influence the trajectory of your career. Particularly as a black woman. While some studies say that attire accounts for only about 5% of leadership presence, ensuring you present the right first impression is key to any relationship. We'll talk more about your external presentation in a few chapters when we discuss your brand and reputation, however, here are a few specific tips I've learned from and observed of successful black women.

Wear clothing that is appropriate for the occasion, conveying confidence, yet staying congruent with your personality. As a black woman, I intentionally dress just a little more formal than the occasion requires. If it's a casual event after work and I've been in jeans all day, even if jeans are appropriate, I'll change to a pair of slacks and a nice top. Or I'll make sure I have on a pair of denim jeans that are pressed (and I do not enjoy ironing) and fit well. I wouldn't wear a suit to a casual Saturday meeting when everyone else is in jeans and tennis shoes, but I'd probably leave the sneakers at home and wear some heels or at least a nice pair of sandals (as long as my toes are done). Now, I'm not a fashion expert and you know your style. Some women are more colorful and flamboyant, some are more muted and reserved. Whatever your style, make sure your attire is communicating what you want it to.

Beyond what you're wearing, leadership presence includes the ability to convey your inner grace, sophistication, and elegance through your attire. This includes wearing clothes that fit. They're not too tight or too loose. Recently, I lost some weight rapidly due to illness. Instead of going out and buying a new wardrobe, although that's an option too if you can afford it, I had my clothes tailored so they would fit.

Leaders, both men and women, accent their outer appearance with accoutrements that are enhancing but not distracting. I am not a flashy dresser. While I admire those who do and can, I don't feel I'm being authentic when I wear clothes that catch the eye—even appropriately. Certain looks simply don't fit my personality. However, I do often add accents such as earrings, necklaces, and rings whenever I go out. I also might wear something, like a necklace, as a conversation piece. It's a great way to break the ice with someone new or with who you're less comfortable.

Having an appropriate style (not being over- or under-done) shows attention to detail as well as care and concern for your product (you). If you have the budget, get your hair and nails done regularly. There's nothing wrong with pampering and taking care of yourself. If you don't have the budget, choose a hairstyle that you can keep up and fits with the environment in which you're working.

I recently saw a commercial for a new lipstick line that touted a diversity of vibrant colors like blues, greens, pinks, and oranges. They were beautiful! But I just can't see myself wearing them, first, given my personality and, second, because of the corporate environments I work in. Those colors, for the professional situations I find myself in, wouldn't be considered appropriate. However, I know of an attorney who owns her own firm. Every time I see her, the tips of her hair are a different color, like pink, purple, or blue, and she has the personality to match. She's figured it out.

Dress in a manner that fits your personality and attitude and communicates your savvy as a leader and businesswoman. Pull your outfits together with confidence. Feeling good about how you look ties your leadership presence in a nice little bow.

FOOD FOR THOUGHT

1. On a scale of 1-10, with 10 being the highest, how would you rate yourself overall on having leadership presence?

2. If you were to work on one component of your presence, what would it be and why?

TAKE ACTION!

For thirty days, focus on a specific area of leadership presence: your mindset, your behavior, your communication, or your attire.

Make a note of what you're working on and what you'd like to be different after thirty days.

Write out a plan of what you need to do to get there. If you don't know, ask a friend or colleague who you consider has a strong presence, to help you.

At the end of the thirty days, reflect on how you did and what changes have you or others noticed.

If you don't see as big a difference as you would like, tweak your plan and go another thirty days. Or, if you noticed a change from your efforts, choose another aspect of presence to focus on for the next thirty days.

What other actions can you take after reading this chapter?

Notes

1. Gordeau, Jenna (2012). Do You Have 'Executive Presence'?
    https://www.forbes.com/sites/jennagoudreau/2012/10/29/do-you-have-executive-presence/#73f00bf66358

2. Underhill, B. and McAnally, K. (2015) as cited in Baldoni, J., Presence: Your
    Key to Stronger And Bolder Leadership, https://www.forbes.com/sites/
    johnbaldoni/2015/01/29/presence-your-key-to-stronger-and-bolder-
    leadership/#6d32a0af3f99

3. http://www.theeiinstitute.com/what-is-emotional-intelligence/4-mayer-
    and-salovey-model-of-emotional-intelligence.html

4. Dr. Albert Mehrabian, 1981

12. Speaking Up, Expressing Yourself, Having A Voice

Once you feel confident that you can command a room with your presence, the next thing to think about is sharing your ideas, thoughts, and perspective. As black women, our experiences are unique and can add a great deal of value to any team or organization we're in. But first, it's important to have a clear point of view on topics that concern the work you do.

Don't Be Intimidated

Allow me to share a personal example. Since graduating with my doctorate degree, I've been motivated and encouraged to write this book based on my graduate research of successful black women leaders. I've started and stopped the process too many times to count, usually because life happened or I had writer's block and decided to turn my attention to something else. I'd walk away from the project, but it always called me back. It was something I was compelled to do.

So here I am, over ten years later, still having this book inside of me that I want to share with who could use it. I'm making a go of it once again. This time, even though life continues to happen, I noticed that every time I even thought about sitting down to write—there was some internal resistance happening. I didn't know why. After considerable introspection however, I realized that at the core of my motivation to write was my desire and passion to support women in the workplace, but at the core of my procrastination was fear. And my fear had become more powerful than my motivation.

I love to read, and many of the books I read are about business and leadership. Over the past few years, I've noticed that the authors have typically been older, Caucasian men. They have had a wealth of experience in large, well-known companies as senior executives, and have had experience dealing with a great deal of business challenges. Additionally, the books written for and about professional women are usually written by Caucasian women with similar backgrounds and experiences as the men. Nothing wrong with either. I've gleaned much from these experts and appreciate their wisdom and perspectives. But they couldn't and didn't speak from or to my experiences as a black woman. Because that was missing for me, I decided to write this book to fill the gap.

It can be intimidating when you're trying to do something that others, perceived as more experienced, have already done. At first, I thought, *Who am I to write a book? I've not held any executive positions in big companies. Who's going to want to read this? Do I really have something of value to offer?* Just typing these thoughts makes me cringe as I worry about being credible, in spite of my degrees and certifications. But when I realized I was thinking from a place of fear and intimidation and not giving myself the room to be different and unique as a black woman—not to mention a mom, wife, minister, businesswoman, and a bunch of other identities and experiences I bring to the table. I began to see the value of my perspective to the conversation of leadership development—especially for black women. After all, isn't this the benefit of being in a diverse country—the gift of having different perspectives from which to draw? Once I understood what the fear was about, the writer's block and, the anxiety around writing the book, lessened. They have continued to try to rear their ugly heads throughout this process, but I keep reminding myself that my voice matters. I now approach the project more freely and boldly—identifying what my expertise is and simply writing about that.

Being courageous in the face of intimidation is not about acting without fear but acting in spite of it. Despite my fear of what other people will think or say about my perspective, I decided to keep moving forward in writing this book. It was the only way I was going to be able to see the project, and what I felt God was calling me to do, through to the end.

To encourage myself, I began reflecting on other times I had persevered in the face of obstacles and overcame. I remembered being back in graduate school trying to pass some important exams.

Find Your Voice and Use It!

The first half of my doctoral program was academic, meaning I took a multitude of classes for almost three years after work. The second half of my program was dedicated to getting practical experience in an internship and conducting my research. In between those two halves, were three distinct tests we had to take called the comprehensive examinations, or comps. Comps were three-three hour written exams designed for students to demonstrate their ability to synthesize and apply all they learned in their classes. Comps were only offered twice a year: once in the spring and once in the winter. If you missed one date, you'd have to wait six months for the opportunity to take the tests again, and you couldn't move forward in the program without passing.

After almost three years of going to class from 6 p.m.-10 p.m. once or twice a week, I was excited about being eligible to take the exams and move one step closer to getting my PhD. I gathered my notes from all my classes and scheduled my study times. I did nothing else from January to about April in 2004.

About a month before taking the exams, I found out I was pregnant with my youngest daughter. From the time I found out to the time she was born, I had morning (really, all day) sickness so bad that I could barely study, let alone sit for comps. So I couldn't take them in the spring as I planned. I had to wait until the next time they were offered in December.

Not a problem, I thought. I had more time to study and expected to really be prepared when they came around again. My daughter was born healthy and on time in November of that year, and while I was no longer dealing with the morning sickness, I now had to care for my newborn, along with the three other children we had. Thankfully, this time, I wasn't alone and had my husband's help and support.

Because I was nursing and Joi, my daughter, was so young, I obtained permission to bring her with me on campus to take the exams. Instead of being in a computer lab with the rest of the students, I was provided a private office so I could feed and attend to my baby if I needed to. I think she slept the whole time. We drove forty-five minutes back and forth to San Francisco for three days straight so that I could take the three separate tests. By the end of the week, I was exhausted, but I felt confident I did well and was happy they were over. It would take a few weeks to get the results, so I went on about my life.

In January of the following year, I received a call from one of my instructors. She said I had passed one of the three tests and had two more chances to pass the other two. But remember, I had to wait another six months to do so and couldn't do anything else academically in the interim.

So in the spring of 2005, I once again, traveled back and forth to San Francisco, this time without my daughter, two days in a row, to take the other two exams. Again I came home feeling good about how I performed on the tests. A couple of weeks later, I received another call from the same instructor to inform me I didn't pass either of the exams. It's now a year later from the date I was supposed to take them, and I was no closer to my goal.

In the exams, we were given essay questions to answer, and we were expected to answer using all we had read and learned over the past two-plus years. We were allowed to bring in ten pages of notes. Although ten pages seems like a lot, it wasn't compared to all the books and articles we'd read and the lectures we attended over the course of our academic study. Once I typed all the notes up of what I thought would be important for the test, I then had to condense everything to ten pages. In order to do that, I had to reduce the font to six points and almost needed a magnifying glass to see them. However, by the time I sat down to take the exams, I really didn't need the notes, because with all the time I spent compiling them, they were already committed to memory. The task of combining all of the years of what I learned into ten pages was an exercise and test in and of itself.

While three hours initially sounded like plenty of time to write the answer to an essay question, given the complexity of the multipart question, the thoroughness with which we had to respond, and the editing we needed to do before turning it in, three hours wasn't quite enough. In attacking the two failed tests a second time, the pressure was on.

When I didn't pass the second time, I was frustrated. I started questioning whether I was smart enough. I wanted to quit, but I couldn't. I had spent too much money and time to just walk away with a bunch of debt and no degree. I just couldn't and wouldn't do that to myself or to my family and others who were supporting me. So, I decided to ask an instructor to help me better study for the tests.

When we met, he first asked me to share my thought process and how I was approaching the tests. He identified right away what I was doing wrong. While I accounted for my notes, my audience, and even the time I had, what I hadn't accounted for was my own voice. That's what was missing, why I failed the exams, and the main point of me telling this story.

When I worked with my professor in trying to pass the two tests for the third and final time, he had me focus on my perspective rather than the content of each subject I was supposed to have mastered. He asked me questions such as, how did I view how people behaved at work? What were my ideas on how to motivate people? How did I define leadership? He pulled out of me what was already in me and taught me how to think differently about how to approach a problem. He encouraged me to insert my voice into what I was writing about, no matter what I was writing. Those grading the exams wanted to hear what I thought. They didn't just want me regurgitating data. Working with him not only helped me pass the other two exams (finally!) but it has helped me many times over, both professionally and personally.

It's important to be conscious of and very present to your perspective or point of view on topics and issues. You have one, you just need to get clear about it if you're not. Once I found my voice, what made sense to me, and how I thought about life, the exams were easier to tackle. Rather than responding to the questions using someone else's perspective I read about, I responded to them from my own viewpoint and used the literature to support it. In order to do that, however, I had to silence the voices and opinions of others in my head that would feed into my fear and keep me from speaking up or sharing my thoughts.

As a black woman, I often find myself trying to fit into environments where I stand out. By nature, I don't like bringing attention to myself and prefer to work behind the scenes. However, working behind the scenes doesn't allow me to add anything to a conversation. In the past, when I didn't stand out in some areas and brought nothing to the table, the feedback I received was that people perceived me as being indifferent and not concerned. What a disservice that is to myself and the world in which I'm trying to make a positive difference. What a disservice it is to God not to employ the gifts He's given me and use them in such a way that allows His light to shine through me. My voice, your voice, is not supposed to be diminished. We all have something to contribute while we're here on this earth.

Often, as women and black women, especially, we feel invisible in the workplace. When we try to speak up and bring our ideas and thoughts to the forefront of a discussion, they often get shot down or, worse yet, ignored entirely. I have spoken with countless women of different backgrounds who have had this experience, and I've had my own. While this happens to everyone, men and women, from time to time, it seems to happen more often to women and people of color.

I remember being at a meeting once in which I came up with a brilliant idea that I shared with the group I was meeting with, who were mostly senior executives and men. At the time, I was still in a support role. When I presented the idea, it was like I was on mute because the conversation continued as if I hadn't said a word. I had to pinch myself to see if I was dreaming. Then, no more than two minutes after I shared my thoughts, the man sitting next to me, who happened to be my boss, said the same exact thing I had just said. Everyone reacted as if it was the greatest idea they'd ever heard. *Really?* I nudged my boss and jokingly said, "Hey! That was my idea!" They all laughed and the meeting continued. Although I wasn't angry, offended, expected the credit, or anything else, I would have at least thought there would be an apology or even an acknowledgement from anyone that the idea came from me. Nothing!

My boss, in comparison to me, was also black. But he was a vice president, at least 6'2" (compared to all of my 5'3"), and at least one hundred pounds heavier. I don't know why my voice wasn't heard that day. I doubt it, but maybe I wasn't loud enough. Maybe they heard me, but because of my position in the company, they discounted what I said. There are a number of other maybes that could have contributed, it's really not worth the time to figure out. What's important to know from this story is that this scenario has happened countless times to black and other women. While society should be asking "Why?", our role is to include in our action plans how to prepare for such situations so we're not caught off guard.

Looking back on myself and the situation, I didn't know I had the option to do or say anything. With hindsight being 20/20, I would have asked to have a conversation with my boss about what happened in the room to glean his perspective, advice, and support on what to do if I ever experienced that again. Because another piece of the puzzle that doesn't relate to any of us individually is the unspoken norms of an organization. It was okay for me to joke in the meeting about not being heard and making everyone laugh. It would have not been okay to hold everyone up until we discussed and worked out why that happened in the first place. It would have been equally inappropriate to call my boss out on his behavior in a more serious and aggressive way in front of his peers and others in the room. We'll discuss it in the next chapter, but timing, tone, and tact when delivering a message are very important. There's a time and place for everything. That moment wasn't the proper time or place.

Because I didn't feel like others were open to my ideas and remembered how it felt to speak up, I wondered whether the next time I shared an idea would I be ignored again. This questioning had as much to do with my lack of self-confidence as it had to do with others being willing to hear what I had to say. I have learned that no situation is ever truly one-sided. While we might not be able to control or even influence another's choices and behaviors, we have 100% control over ours.

Our workplaces, society, and the world at large are very complex, and we cannot always pinpoint why something is happening. It could be a combination of many things. Like I said, we only have control over ourselves. If you're in a situation where you find your voice being stifled or ignored, if the moment is not an appropriate time to raise an issue, schedule some time to have a conversation with someone you trust; a boss, a coach, a mentor, a colleague, or the person you feel, specifically, was not open to what you had to say. This fosters open communication and relationship building and builds trust. Ask about how you're perceived in meetings and in the organization at large. Brainstorm the possibilities of doing things differently the next time.

No one is perfect. We don't get it right every time, but when you act with intention and purpose, you'll find you'll have more clarity around what you'll accept or not as the outcome of a situation. Then you'll act in such a way that, to the best of your ability, you are going to achieve the outcome and be heard.

FOOD FOR THOUGHT

Finding your voice might not be easy and can be a process, especially when you have other voices to contend with, like a parent, teacher, or an ex. Take the time to answer the following questions to help you think about your unique point of view:

1. Who are you? How do you identify? How would you describe yourself? I wrote out all the ways to describe myself and was surprised when I came up with over fifty attributes. For example:

- I'm a wife and mother.

- I am black, a woman, and a business owner.

- I love to dance and read.

- I'm a Christian.

Each of these personal attributes inform how I see the world and the vantage point from which I speak and evaluate my experiences. I'm going to have a different world view as a woman than a man, and I'm going to have a different perspective as a black person than a white person. That's the beauty of diversity.

2. What are your beliefs and values? I'm not necessarily talking about religious beliefs, but that's in there too. I'm talking about what assumptions do you make about life? What are your underlying beliefs that inform your thinking?

3. What experiences have you had that support your current beliefs?

4. What experiences can you think of that counter your beliefs? For example, because I had bad experiences with older white men in positions of power, I created a belief that older white men in power acted a certain way, which was not in my best interest. In order to balance that belief, I think of examples of other white men I know who do not fit that stereotype, so that I don't take a perspective that can affect the impact I have on others.

Your identity, beliefs, values, and experiences form the basis of your perspective or point of view. Be sure you're not holding onto outmoded beliefs or values that no longer fit how you want to approach your work and those you work with.

TAKE ACTION!

What actions can you take as a result of reading this chapter?

13. Building Relationships

In order to make the impact you want to make in your role, on your team, or in your organization or community, you have to have strong interpersonal skills. You won't be effective without them. Let's look at some fundamental ideas that can easily cause problems if you're not mindful of them.

Building Trust

Think of a time when you felt you could trust someone you worked with. What made them trustworthy? List those attributes. Now think of a time when you felt you couldn't trust someone. What made them untrustworthy? What is the difference between the two experiences?

Would you consider yourself a trustworthy or untrustworthy person? What makes you one or the other? Have you noticed that once trust is gained and then lost, it is extremely hard to regain, and if you do regain it, it takes a tremendous amount of energy and time? Gaining and maintaining your peers', directs', and leaders' trust is essential to your success. Strong relationships of any kind are built on the foundation of trust. Keeping information confidential and following through on what you say you are going to do are examples of demonstrating you are trustworthy. Using good judgement in knowing when to share what information with who is also an indication. You do not want to be known as a gossip or a flake. If your job, like mine, depends on holding things private, then ensure you do so.

Professionally and personally, integrity is a strong value for me and with that, it's important to keep what I discuss with my clients to myself. I recently worked with a leader whose manager hired me to work with her. As a coach, I established up front with all parties involved that I honor confidentiality and would not be sharing what conversations I had with one leader, with the other, or anyone else. It's important that my clients trust that what we discuss will go no further than the two of us unless they choose to share it with someone.

A couple of weeks into coaching this leader, the manager who hired me asked if she and I could schedule a call for her to hear how the coaching was going. I had to explain to the manager that while I would be happy to talk with her, I was concerned that my client wasn't aware that her manager had reached out to me. If I were to agree to a meeting without my client's knowledge, it not only breaches my promise, but also could greatly erode the trust built between my client and me and negatively impact the outcomes of the coaching. Thankfully, the manager understood.

If you're currently in a situation where you've lost someone's confidence in you and are trying to gain it back, there are some ideas below you can try. Whatever you decide to do, be consistent. I can't express this enough. If you're not consistent, your efforts won't be taken sincerely.

Trust is founded on integrity and honesty: consistently (there's that word again) doing what you say you're going to do and if you say you're not going to do something, you don't. If you make a mistake, don't make excuses and don't blame someone else for it. By owning up to your part in a matter, you'll still be building trust.

Developing trust also involves being reliable. Your peers, directs, and upper management should know they can depend on you. At the most basic level, this means showing up to work and meetings on time, but it also includes keeping your commitments whether you're collaborating on a project, planning a meeting, or completing an action item. Be sure to follow through.

Connecting

The foundation to anyone's success is having good, strong relationships. In order to get there, it means taking time to get to know a person and allowing them to get to know you. While this process might be more difficult for some and easier for others, it's still important. So, let's talk about how to connect with someone.

Imagine that you are new to a position and there are three other people you'll be working closely with. Although they were on your interview panel and chose you as the most-qualified candidate, they don't know anything else about you beyond what's on your résumé and you know even less about each of them. The first step in getting to know someone and, thereby, expanding your network is to choose. Choose the person that's most interesting, that you seem to have the most in common with, or that you click with the most. Or, here's a challenge, choose someone who you think you'd connect with the least—someone who might be different and seemingly the total opposite of you. Get curious about who they are as a person and professional, what they are passionate about and their goals, and what skills and gifts they bring to your team.

When I meet people for the first time whether a client or colleague, a business or social connection—I'm always interested in knowing more about them: their background, where did they grow up, the schools they attended, what made them move to (in my case) the Bay Area, why did they choose their field. If my questions seem too intrusive for your taste, think of questions that you'd feel comfortable asking. How long have they been working for the company, and what does their job entail, are pretty benign questions? When you get to a point of comfort, ask more questions and be ready to tell them about you.

If you tend to be apprehensive about meeting new people, practice with someone you already know, like a brother, colleague, or friend, so you can get comfortable asking and answering questions. It's much easier when you feel an initial connection with someone. Establish a comfort level in conversing with these individuals before venturing out into the deeper waters of talking to a stranger.

Getting to know people can happen in the breakroom at work, having a coffee together at Starbucks, or going to grab lunch nearby. If you want to take it even slower, schedule a "getting acquainted" call or meeting. Draft a list of questions you'd like answers to. The conversation doesn't have to be long. Maybe fifteen to twenty minutes to start. At the end of that time, if you've enjoyed the conversation, plan another. If you haven't enjoyed the discussion or feel like you didn't click, don't schedule another meeting. It's that simple. If this is someone you have to work with and you still don't click, do your best to discover what you have in common and connect on that level. Make it as simple as you please; the relationship will form organically.

While you can be purposeful in starting and maintaining relationships, it does take two. If the other person does not make a mutual effort to stay in touch with you, then decide how important the relationship is. If it's important or vital to your role, continue to work on staying connected—be transparent in why it's important to you. It'll probably put the other person at ease so they can stop wondering, "Why does she want to talk to me?" You can tell them upfront why—because you'll be working together, because their job interests you, because you find that person interesting, or whatever the reason—the more you're transparent, the greater the possibility of creating a connection.

In your interactions, while you're being transparent, be authentic. After all, acting perfect is not being transparent. To the degree that you're comfortable, share your concerns and shortfalls, where you will need support, or what is going on in your life—you have a child starting school soon, a parent that you're taking care of, the degree that you are earning at night—you don't have to get deep, but it is okay to talk about you as a person. That's the only way people will get to know you authentically. Some of my best professional relationships are the result of me and the other person being willing to open up to each other.

Having Mentors and Sponsors

In addition to connecting with colleagues, peers, bosses, and direct reports, it's important to also build relationships with those who have the potential to serve as a mentor or sponsor. I often encourage my clients, to identify individuals, both men and women—those who have the qualities, skills, and traits, they'd like to emulate.

The other day, I was talking to a client whom I had given this assignment to, and she identified Michelle Obama as a model. Great choice! There's a lot we all can learn from Mrs. Obama. She is visible enough that if you wanted to, you could read or watch interviews about her life and identify how she "does it." At the same time, there are also people in our lives who are good at displaying one trait or another. I don't think one person has it all. But you can take a little from this person and a little from another and decide what works best for you. That is what this book intends to offer—not a formula, but options for success.

I wouldn't be who I am without the help and support of the mentors and sponsors I've had in my career. They've supported me through difficult career decisions as well as celebrated with me in my successes. As a coach, I encourage all my clients to identify people who could support them in this way. None of us succeed on our own. While both mentors and sponsors are needed, there's a difference between the two.

A mentor is an advisor: they can be a sounding board, an advice giver, a thought partner, an encourager, and someone to give you a kick in your butt when you need it. They can help you make difficult decisions and problem-solve in a safe environment, and they can also introduce you to others who can be resources for you. Mentors come in all shapes, sizes, colors, industries, professions, ages, genders, career levels, and so on. The best thing I did for my career was have a variety of mentors. Some were black women, some weren't. Some were in the same profession as me, some weren't. Some were older than me, and some younger.

I feel I can learn from anyone, and the one thing that keeps me learning from people is my curiosity. I never feel or think that I have all the answers. But I always know I can find them either through research or, more often, with the help of other people. The beauty in having a diversity of people to talk to throughout your career is that you gain different perspectives. Or because you do share the same gender or ethnicity, or you are the same age, you have someone who can relate to what you are going through, can support you through it, and celebrate with you like no one else can. We all need one another.

When looking for a mentor, one question to ask yourself is, "Who can I talk to that has the skill, knowledge, or experience that I'm looking to have?" Or, Who can help me solve a problem or make a certain decision? First, think of those you either already have relationships with or that you have access to. See about scheduling some time to talk with them and plan for the meeting. Think about what you would like help with and feedback on and how that person can assist you; how much of this person's time do you want for this conversation; is this a one-time meeting or would you like to set up periodic check-ins; is there something you can offer the person in return for their time—treat them to lunch or coffee, offer support in an area you're familiar with, or connect them to a resource you have available to you? In this day and age of countless meetings and no time to do much else, it's important for you to be clear and succinct enough so your potential mentor can understand what you are looking for and tell you if they can help you or not.

Some people get anxious about even the thought of approaching someone they don't know or don't know well for the first time. You might think, *People are busy, they don't have time. They might not be interested.* While all of this could be true, consider why someone *would* be interested: perhaps you can give them a different perspective they don't have, or you're able to keep them up-to-date on different things happening in the market, or maybe they just want to pour into someone as I'm sure someone has poured into them. Imagine how much easier it would be going into the conversation with these more positive assumptions.

If having this understanding doesn't help whatever reservations you have, this is an opportunity to be courageous and reach out anyway. Or decide you're not ready to take this step, but ask yourself, *When will I be ready? What will it require of me?* Either way, you'll make a conscious, intentional decision.

Finally, decide when you will contact this person and do it. Once the meeting is over, you'll be surprised at how much easier it went than you thought it would. You might also be surprised at the person's willingness to support you.

While a mentor helps you to figure *it* out, a sponsor helps to make it happen. Sponsors are those who are in positions to advocate for you, give you project or job opportunities, or give you visibility to other influential people. Sponsors are willing to put their name and reputation on the line for you, believing in your skill set and potential. While mentors are easier to find and, for the most part, you get to choose them, sponsors can be less in supply and ultimately, they choose you. They have to know if they become involved in your career, that you will not let them down. Some sponsors start out as mentors. The relationship shifts to sponsorship when they offer to do something on your behalf that will help you succeed.

If a person you'd like to sponsor you doesn't know you very well or at all, then the first order of business is to connect. This means developing a genuine relationship with that person without asking for anything other than some of their time and sharing of their perspective and knowledge. In order for them to become your advocate, they'll first want to get to know you in order to speak favorably on your behalf. So you have to walk the talk. Ensure your reputation in the organization is strong, that your work is high quality, and that you follow through. Sponsors and more senior leaders, in general, want to observe if you demonstrate in your current role, what it takes to move to the next. If you were in a sponsor's shoes today, would you be willing to put your name and reputation on the line for you? If the answer is no, what do you need to do in order to turn that into a yes? Get to work on time? Actively engage in meetings. Apologize to someone for an error or the part you played in a conflict?

And while you're busy climbing your career ladder and getting mentored and sponsored, don't forget to do the same for someone that's more junior to you in their career. Be sure to lift as you climb.

Communicating

While we all communicate every day with a multitude of people in a variety of ways, our methods of communication matter. In establishing relationships, get to know your audience: their needs, and goals, their likes and dislikes, their personalities, passions, and preferences. When you get to know and understand a person individually, you will also learn the best way to communicate with them.

We have many methods of communication today: e-mail, phone, text, face to face, direct message, and virtual outlets such as FaceTime, Skype, Google Hangouts, Zoom, etc., not to mention social media. When deciding the best way to speak with someone, first understand your own preference. While I used to enjoy talking on the phone (running my mouth as my mother would say), I find that my time doesn't allow for lengthy conversations like it used to. E-mail or text are currently my preferences for quick communication. If, however, I text a client for example, and they call me back, I know that their preference is to talk by phone, so the next time I reach out, I accommodate their style, pick up the phone, and call them. I used to become irritated thinking, *If I texted them, it's obvious I couldn't or didn't want to talk, why did they call me back?* However, I have learned it's not obvious to some and to be a great leader, sometimes I have to lead by following.

When meeting a client for the first time, I often ask, *What's the best way to communicate with you?* While their method might not be ideal for me, I have learned in order to really connect with someone, interacting according to their preferences brings me one step closer to not only meeting their needs but mine as well. As long as communication is happening, all is well.

Timing, Tone, and Tact

Understanding the channel of communication is just the beginning of being effective with people. The next thing to consider is *what* message you want to send *and how* you want to send it. I'm not just talking about the content or the words you use—while they are important too—but I'm inviting you to consider *how* you're saying what you're saying. What's your tone of voice and body language (if you're speaking face to face)? Although my teenage daughter doesn't get this yet, there's a big difference in how she says "okay" depending on her mood and if I'm to be honest with myself, how I ask or tell her to do something can influence how she responds. If I tell her in a calm voice *go clean your room*, even adding please on the end of it to sound more pleasant. If she says, *okay*, but doesn't do it right away, my voice volume will eventually go up, and my tone will get harsher the more I have to repeat myself. My daughter's response also changes from a bright, *okay!*, to a more exasperated, *Okayyyyyyy-ya!*, with an eye roll and, God forbid, a neck roll (which is a different subject for a different book). Now we are at odds with one another all because of how she said, *okay*. One of my mantras is, *It's not what you say, but how you say it.* It's important to be mindful not only of your words, but your tone and body language as well.

Let's talk about words. While *how* you say something comprises about 93% of our message, the 7% of the communication that is truly verbal is still important. I can often be in a discussion and hear one word that triggers me and then I'm stuck on that word for the rest of the conversation, not hearing anything else a person says after that. I'm sure you can think of a few words that would stop you in your tracks and cause you to turn and say, *What did you say?*, even though you're not really asking a question.

When speaking with others, being tactful with the words we choose to express ourselves goes a long way in helping you to be an effective communicator. Think about the words you tend to use that could be considered unprofessional or off-putting. Then think of, or ask someone to suggest what new words you can use instead. It can take a lot of practice, but over time, you'll get it.

If you're not entirely aware of the impact of your style on others, ask a handful of people what their experiences of you has been. When you start hearing similar things from different people, you've hit on a common thread.

Another thing to consider when you're communicating is your timing. In this fast-paced world we live in, there's a million things going on at once—in our minds and in our external environment. You and the person(s) you're speaking to both have other thoughts running in the background of your minds while you're with one another such as other work priorities and issues as well as possible health, family, or financial concerns that might be weighing on either of you at any given time. A conversation can go poorly if initiated at the wrong time; therefore, it's important to check in with yourself before you start a discussion to ensure you're in the right headspace, and also notice or ask if it is a good time for the other person to talk. If you had picked up on what else was happening around you, then you might have provided information that could have been shared at a better time.

Years ago, I remember being at church, and a young lady had just finished a spoken word piece in front of the congregation. At the end, she threw the mic down and ran out of the sanctuary, clearly upset about her performance. When I went to find her, she was in the bathroom crying. I said, "You did a great job! The only thing you did wrong was throw the microphone down." Although my intention was to give her helpful feedback, my timing was way off. I could have commented in a different way at a different time. I hadn't even realized that I inflicted more hurt on her than she already was feeling until another person brought it to my attention about an hour later, because the young lady told them what I had said and done. I felt horrible and went back and apologized for being so insensitive. Unfortunately, however, the damage was already done.

Since then, I've learned to be more tactful and aware of what's going on before I speak up. While you might or might not find yourself in this type of situation at work, there will be times when you will have to give feedback to a colleague, subordinate, or manager. Or you might have to have a difficult conversation with someone. Being mindful of your timing, tone, and tact will be useful in assuring you honor the relationship with that individual.

Collaborating

Now that we've talked about the foundational skills that are important in being successful in your professional life, let's discuss a competency that relies on and builds upon the foundational skills: collaboration.

Those in the workplace are increasingly finding themselves in positions in which they are having to collaborate on something with someone in order to accomplish a common goal. Collaboration can also be considered teamwork, but it's teamwork with a purpose. The assumption is that, a) you have a common goal you're trying to achieve, b) you are both/all open to hearing other perspectives and points of view and, c) everyone is coming to the collaboration effort as equals even if you're teaming up with a higher-level manager or subordinate.

When you have a respectful and comfortable relationship with the person you're working with, where you're able to communicate your ideas in a way they can receive and understand what you are saying, then collaboration can be easy. At other times, when these elements are absent, teaming with others can be more difficult and that isn't always apparent.

Beyond getting the job done and your goals accomplished, collaboration has many benefits. It enables you to build relationships with others in and outside of your workplace, either those you already know or those who you haven't met before, which in turn strengthens your professional network. Collaboration also exposes you to a diversity of others' skills, talents, and ideas you might not have had access to otherwise. Furthermore, it helps you to break up the work, make it more fun, and is a great opportunity for you to develop new competencies.

Collaboration isn't collaboration, however, if you're not open to others' ideas in how to solve problems or approach a task. The blessing in being a black woman is that we have the opportunity to bring a different perspective to a situation if we're listening for what is being said, and even what is not being said. Everyone brings their experiences, backgrounds, biases, and values to the table, and when we're open to hearing and sharing our thoughts (appropriately in a business setting), then ideas tend to form that wouldn't have been possible without those specific voices.

The great thing about collaboration, at least as a concept, is that it levels the playing field. Whether you're a high-level manager working with someone just starting their career or you're in a support role working with someone who is a leader at your company, when truly collaborating, all parties are agreeing to take off their labels of "boss" and "employee," put on their thinking hats, and bring all their skills and knowledge to the table. Each of you having something to contribute. When collaborating, it means that someone has something valuable (a skill, a connection to someone else, some knowledge) that you don't have and vice versa.

FOOD FOR THOUGHT

1. Which of the above relational skills do you consider yourself strong in?

2. Which of them would you like to develop?

3. How will developing these skills help you in your current role?

4. How could developing these skills help you with future opportunities?

5. Who do you know that demonstrates your targeted skill well?

6. What is it about what they do that you admire?

7. How can you emulate that behavior?

8. How can you help others develop in the areas you consider a strength?

TAKE ACTION!

What actions can you take as a result of reading this chapter?

14. Self-Analysis

SWOT

Over the years, through life, schooling, and career, I've been challenged from time to time with the question: Who are you? Not what roles do you play such as wife, mother, or businesswoman, but who are you as a person if you strip those roles away? Who are you as an individual working within those roles? Is the essence of who you are consistent across roles, even to a greater or lesser degree, depending on the context? To answer to this question, and I encourage you to ask it periodically as you develop in your career, there are a few key things that you will need to identify. The first are your strengths, weaknesses, opportunities, and threats. This assessment is known as a SWOT analysis.

I often use electronic assessments to gather multi-rater feedback for my clients. When I sit down with them to debrief what people said about them, their eyes immediately dart to and then fixate on the more "negative" responses. I often have to redirect them and juxtapose their weaknesses to their strengths. It's not wrong to pay attention to our flaws, but solely doing so not only tends to distract us from enjoying the positive feedback provided, but also, focusing on our limitations is not a helpful strategy to start with. Instead, begin by considering your strengths. Where are you good at? What topics do you have considerable knowledge? Which of your many attributes give you an advantage over others in your field?

One area I once saw as a weakness or disadvantage—being black, female, and being a black female—I have reframed and now see as a strength. As I stated above, as black women we bring a unique perspective that is often missing from problem-solving and decision-making conversations. Leveraging your strengths can position you to make an even bigger impact in the lives of others.

While knowing your strengths is important, understanding what your weaknesses are is significant as well as they help you to identify your development opportunities and what resources you have to minimize them – like asking a colleague (a resource) to edit a document for you. If you're not clear about your strengths or weaknesses, ask a handful of others for feedback—and be prepared to be open to what they have to say.

Let me give an example from my experience. When I first started my business, I knew what I wanted to do: teach people how to be strategic in their careers and as leaders, but I didn't know how to go about doing it. I floundered for a few years until I took the time to do a SWOT analysis. To understand my strengths, I wrote out what I considered them to be, and then I asked a few close friends and colleagues to share what they saw my strengths as. I did the same with my weaknesses. They were harder to look at and hear about compared to my strengths, but it was important to know what they were. When looking at your weaknesses, consider what skills you can develop, what type of tasks you should completely avoid, and what feedback you've received from others. Then think about who you know that has a strength in an area you would call a weakness. What can you learn from them? Can they mentor you or can you offer your strengths in an area the other person isn't as strong?

Once you bring your strengths and weaknesses to your awareness (although some of my weaknesses I don't even want to think about), the next step is to evaluate what the external opportunities and threats are. The goal is to learn to leverage your strengths, minimize your weaknesses, capitalize on the opportunities, and maneuver around, if not, eliminate the threats.

After I took a hard look at my strengths and weaknesses, it was time to consider the opportunities and threats in my profession and industry. Who was doing what in the market? What advantages did I have because of my knowledge, skills, abilities, attributes, and unique perspective? How could I use my strengths to create opportunities? I considered what was going on socially, politically, economically, and technologically. I started getting targeted news feeds that spoke to my specific focus.

Finally, I considered the threats. I identified what, externally, could possibly threaten my ability to be successful. Again, I looked at the social, political, economic, and technological forces but I also looked at my own weaknesses.

For example, a potential threat to the coaching industry at the time of this writing is Artificial Intelligence (AI). If someone could program a computer to do the same thing a human can do, which I don't think can fully be done, then the longevity of the profession is in danger. Therefore, as a coach, I must ask myself, how do I continue to stay relevant in the market and compete with technology? And what is my competitive advantage that will enable me to turn the threat into an opportunity? I could offer my own on-demand coaching app for example. The entire profession is grappling with this challenge. Looking at threats keeps us from being blindsided, helps us to stay ahead of the game, and, if we're smart, keeps us ensuring our knowledge and skills are current and relevant.

Conducting a SWOT analysis should not be a one-time event. Periodically scanning the external environment for opportunities and threats while staying mindful of your strengths and weaknesses and continuing to develop your knowledge, skills and competencies, is a powerful tool for career advancement.

Values

One analysis I don't see companies or individuals do enough of or often is take the time to look at their values. Our values are simply those things that we govern our behavior by. Integrity, my relationship with Christ, friends, and family are some of my top values and inform how I live my life, run my business, and interact with every person I engage with. Over the years, I have become more aware and conscious of my values which have helped in decision-making, goal-setting, and prioritizing.

When what we are doing, saying, or experiencing is in alignment with what we believe, we feel comfortable; life is going well, and we feel happy. When what we are saying, doing, or experiencing is incongruent with what we truly believe, we feel a disconnect that can cause a great deal of discomfort and unhappiness. Having an understanding of your values allows you to live a more intentional, focused, authentic, and purposeful life. When you become more mindful of your values, you will find that you become clearer about why you do what you do. Our values drive us whether we're aware of them or not; becoming more aware of them gives you more options.

The first step in becoming more aware of your values is to list what your values are. If you already know what they are, great. List them at the end of this chapter and your top 10. If you don't know what your values are, take this free assessment to find out.

Once you have your values prioritized, examine them against the work you're doing, the relationships you have, your goals, etc. If everything is in alignment, you're on the right path! What else can you incorporate to make the journey even better? If your values and life choices do not coincide, what do you need to do to create better harmony? What one thing can you do within the next thirty days to get more in alignment? What will be your plan of action over the next three months, six months, twelve months, and eighteen months? You can use this planning worksheet to help guide you.

Understanding *Your* Value

Have you ever thought about the value you bring to your organization, team, or role, or the impact of your specific knowledge, skills, and abilities on business results that help the company make money? Being able to articulate your value to a potential customer or employer via your LinkedIn profile, résumé, bio, etc. allows them to see the impact you can make on or for them.

I used to have a hard time articulating my value. It was uncomfortable to do. I felt like I was bragging or coming across as arrogant. It can be hard because we often take our strengths for granted. They come so easy to us that we don't recognize that not everyone can do what we do the way we do it. Sometimes, others have to bring something I've done that they felt was valuable or helpful to my attention. Getting feedback is one beneficial way to uncover your value if you're not clear. Sometimes you're too close to see it yourself.

Another way to understand your value is to reflect on moments that you have helped someone or accomplished something. Perhaps it was delivering a persuasive presentation or you solved a difficult problem. Whatever it was and no matter how small or insignificant it seemed, take a step back and look at the situation from a different perspective. Identify the specific situation and think about the details: what was the issue, who were you working with, etc.; what were obstacles you faced: limited time or money or working with a difficult client for example; what were the actions you specifically took; what was the outcome? This process of identifying the situation, obstacles, actions, and results is called crafting a SOAR story. Writing out a handful of situations like this, putting yourself in the heroine or star of the story, helps you see your value on paper and identify some themes. SOAR stories can be used in interviews or when having a conversation with your boss, for example, when you're sharing a success story with them.

Your Brand and Reputation

If you haven't received feedback in a while, are you aware of how people see and think about you — either positively or negatively? How you approach your work, what your consistent results are, and/or the services you provide, are all examples of what is considered your brand. Your brand is based on decisions you make and behaviors you demonstrate that others can observe. Your brand, in turn, informs your reputation, which is the bigger impression you leave on others and generally, what people say about you to others. Your brand is what you want to be known for, while your reputation, is what others know you for. Ideally, for you to be successful professionally, the two will align.

When someone hears your name or sees your work, what image do you think comes to their mind? What image do you want your name or work to conjure? For me, I want people to think of me as knowledgeable and capable of helping them achieve their professional goals. I want them to speak favorably about me to others in such a way, that they strongly recommend working with me, see me speak, or read my books. When you meet someone for the first time, do you think about the impression you're making and what they will walk away with thinking about you? While you cannot control others' thoughts, at all, you can control how you present yourself and what behaviors you want them to see. And when you are consistent in your presentation and actions and couple those with your knowledge, skills, and abilities, you are better able to influence your reputation.

However, if you have a poor attitude and treat people horribly, no amount of style or competence will keep your reputation from being tarnished. It's great if you can solve all the problems of the world, but if you do it in such a way that you alienate everyone around you, how likely will the longevity of your success be? Those who are very accomplished, but leave bodies in their wake, are the ones who do more damage than good for themselves, their teams, and their organizations. You might be able to impact the bottom line and business results, but how are you impacting morale and the people who work with and for you? While you might be a superstar on your own, imagine how much more you can accomplish if you had people working with you because they want to rather than out of fear of losing their job or you losing your temper.

If you're unsure of your reputation, conduct short, "multi-rater" interviews. Coaches and other human resource and talent development professionals use this process to gather feedback on a leaders' behalf. Those you interview can be anyone who has worked with you (peers, bosses, direct reports, customers, vendors, etc.) and can speak to your strengths, weaknesses, development opportunities, and threats. When choosing colleagues to interview, be sure to choose those who truly care to see you develop, thrive, and succeed and are willing to, not only, tell you how great you are, but also tell you the areas where you could be better. While positive feedback can be supportive and flattering, it's not always the most helpful. Whereas constructive feedback might sting at first, it will truly help you to grow into the professional you desire to be.

In preparing for the interview, draft two to three questions that you'd like to ask each stakeholder you talk to about their perceptions of you. And while you're talking with them, take notes you can refer back to when needed.

Keep in mind, sometimes even the most well-intended people might not share their opinions of your performance in a way that is palatable. However, if you set aside your feelings, how can you see things from that person's perspective? It will require you to take a step back and be objective. If you trust this person, then trust the truth in what they're saying, even if it's not your truth.

We all create our own reality out of our childhood and adult experiences, as well as our beliefs, assumptions, and expectations, If you can remember that others simply have a different perspective than you, not right, wrong, better, or worse, just different— then you have an opportunity to glean from their point of view and be a more effective leader.

After collecting the information, be sure to thank those who participated and let them know not only that you appreciate their input, but that you're taking what they shared into consideration for your development. This doesn't mean you have to do anything with it, you're just saying you are willing to reflect on it. Finally, once you've conducted all the interviews, put your notes away and take a day or two to let it all digest before doing anything. Once you're ready, look at your notes again, and decide where you want to go from there.

If you identify something you can work on immediately, do it. Don't wait. If it's something that's going to require a little more thought, figure out when you'll take the time to really think about it. If it's something that will require more resources, identify what those are and make a plan to address it. If you receive conflicting feedback—one person says one thing about you and another person says another—ask yourself how two people are seeing two different things. How are you showing up in one context that you're not in another? Can you go back to each person and get more clarity?

When collecting feedback for my clients, I often get conflicting opinions about the same person. One stakeholder, let's say a leader's direct report, might see that person as delegating too many of her responsibilities. While another stakeholder, the leader's boss, for example, might not see her delegating enough. Which perspective is accurate and true? They both are. That client is simply being viewed from two different perspectives. While the direct report feels that their boss, my client, gives more than she should, my client's manager sees she has an opportunity to delegate more so that she can focus on more strategic issues.

It is my client's job to reconcile the conflicting information. Perhaps she is delegating and the boss isn't aware of it, which is a communication and visibility issue. In this case, my client has an opportunity to share more of what she and her team are doing, to her bosses. On the other hand, she could have poor communication with her direct reports, not sharing the bigger picture or explaining why she's giving the tasks that she is. Often, my clients have more control than they think over others' perceptions. While you cannot always control perception, you can certainly influence it.

When I was a trainer at a large fast-food chain in California, we taught about the impact of delivering a bad product or poor customer service. We'd start with a simple illustration of a person buying a hamburger meal. To make the math easy, let's say the meal costs $10. If that customer buys that meal and gets poor service or the food is bad, what do you think she would do? Well, in addition to possibly throwing the meal away and complaining to the manager about the order, she'd also likely share her poor experience with those she knew. She might not do a group text or anything (or she might), but in individual conversations, she could share her negative experience. I know I've done that, haven't you? Let's say she tells ten people, more if the service is really bad, and those ten people decide not to eat at that chain. That one bad experience cost the company ten customers and $100. If we multiply that experience by a year of one bad experience per day, millions of dollars would be lost because of a few dissatisfied customers. And now with the magic of social media, this little illustration pales in comparison to the number of people you could truly influence and increases the costs exponentially. This doesn't mean that the company doesn't also have its loyal customers, however, their reputation will continue to be impacted unless the company focuses in on what they want the customers' experience to be, which means that they have to hone in on their brand.

If we apply this concept back to you as a leader, can you see how your presentation, performance, and attitude can impact, positively or negatively, your reputation, your relationships, your influence, and even your career opportunities? So what is your brand and what do you want it to be? Identify the areas that need developing—presence, performance, or attitude—and create a plan to develop in those areas. Hire a coach or find an accountability partner that will support you.

FOOD FOR THOUGHT

What is your current reputation?

TAKE ACTION!

Choose five people you trust and will give you honest feedback about how they see you. List their names here:

Ask them the following questions:

a. What do they perceive as your strengths that you should continue doing?

b. What do they see as your weaknesses and your development opportunities that you should learn how to start doing?

c. What behaviors do they see you exhibit that you should stop doing before they derail your career?

d. What other actions are you motivated to take after reading this chapter?

15. Being Authentically You

I often work with women who question whether they belong in their leadership roles. *Am I smart enough, good enough, or competent enough?* are some of the questions they ask themselves. This struggle is known as the imposter syndrome. It's the idea that you feel like a fraud as a professional woman—especially if you're black or another woman of color. It comes with a concern that one day someone is going to figure out you don't belong in your position or learn that you're incapable of succeeding in your role. Although this feeling is common, it is one of the factors that keeps us from advancing as we'd like. One of the many lessons I've learned is that there is only one me in the world, my flaws and all. No one else has the exact same way of thinking or looking at things as I do. So I've learned to do me since it's all I can do. Everyone else is taken. So, I encourage you to do you too!

Blaze A Trail

As I said in a previous chapter, I felt intimidated from reading all the business books that were written by authors who didn't exactly share my experiences or perspectives. Since I hadn't seen many books like what I'm writing on the market, I didn't have many models I felt compelled to follow. The lack of information out there was actually what inspired me to write this book.

What has become a theme for me, and possibly you, too, is feeling like I'm always creating a new path. A path that has no map to follow. I continue to forget and relearn the lesson of being unique and the benefit of standing out rather than the comfort of blending in.

The black women that I interviewed for my research, they were often the trailblazers. They were the first black woman or the first black person to do whatever it was they were doing. They often felt quite alone and were unaware other women who were having similar experiences.

I share this to encourage you to blaze those trails and find others who are blazing their own. You might be pursuing your goals in different ways, but you can relate to and support one another as you climb. I have many friends and colleagues who aren't in the same field as me, but we celebrate one another and hold each other up when we need.

Being a forerunner is not always easy, but when you open the way for others, your gifts are being used tremendously. Even if you aren't entering unfamiliar territory for black women or women in general, you can still be, and are, that role model to other young women coming up behind you. Someone is always watching.

Leveraging Your Uniqueness

When I did my inventory of who I thought myself to be and what I brought into the world when I arrived, I recognized that my point of view was unique. At the time of this writing, I have fifty years of life experiences, I grew up in a racially diverse, middle-class suburb of San Francisco, I'm cis-gendered, raised as an only child in a large multicultural family by both parents, and I'm passionate about leadership, particularly black and other women leaders. I am, what society considers, educated, and I've never lived more than one hundred miles away from my hometown. I see the world through all of these lenses, and while my perspectives intersect many other individuals', I can say that I've never met anyone who is just like me—and I know you haven't either. We're all exceptional and bring a valuable perspective to any table.

Arguably and speaking very generally, simply by virtue of being female, your communication style is inherently different than that of a man. If we layer on culture, age, upbringing, who and what influenced you as you matured, etc., we have a very unique way of communicating. If you can identify how your different perspectives impact your communication style, and keep in mind that the person or people you are communicating with has a unique style as well, then you can become more effective when speaking with different individuals.

I've learned (mostly) to get over the fear of "doing me." We're often bombarded with messages of how being different is "bad" whether you're female, a person of color, a mother, gay, poor, and the list goes on. But instead of embracing those negative perceptions, why not turn them into superpowers? Speak confidently from the position of being a mother. You're bringing something different to the conversation. Share your experiences as a woman, as a black woman, as a black woman who is gay...you are sharing information with others who more than likely, don't think like you or even considered your point of view. This in and of itself adds value. Even if you find someone with similar characteristics as you, you're still uniquely and wonderfully made. Not even twins are exactly alike. They're individuals as well. I'm not a twin, but I've met enough to know this to be true.

FOOD FOR THOUGHT

What unique perspectives do you have to offer as a woman, a black woman, a married woman, a younger or older woman, etc.?

TAKE ACTION!

Formulate your perspectives into a point of view about the work you do or how you approach the world that can bring value to any discussion.

What other actions can you take after reading this chapter?

16. Managing Change and Being Resilient

Accepting Change

As you develop as a professional, the road to your goal is not going to be easy or straightforward. If it is, you haven't set a big enough goal. Like everyone else, in the course of my lifetime, I've had big life events happen like getting married and getting divorced, having babies, dealing with physical and mental health challenges, having dear loved ones pass away, experiencing financial difficulties, losing jobs and job opportunities, and going through relationship ups and downs. While you can't always plan when change is going to happen—like a layoff, death, or a financial challenge—you know it will. Life is seasonal. We might not know the exact day when summer, for example, is going to start each year, but we often start preparing for it by planning vacations, buying summer clothes, or making summer arrangements for our kids when school is not in session—well in advance of the season arriving. So while we have no control over some things, we do have some control over others.

As I've said before, the only thing we have 100% control over is ourselves, our choices, our thoughts, and our behavior. If there's something in your life that is not working, don't look outside of yourself, like to a boss or a colleague, expecting them to change when the power is within you to decide to do so at any time, even if the change doesn't happen overnight.

When altering behavior, we first have to be made aware of what we're doing that's not working or can be done differently. We then have to accept and agree that the behavior is happening. Sometimes we can be in denial of or blind to our own actions. And then, we must acknowledge that change is needed. Without any one of these three components, change is not going to happen.

When we don't recognize we have things to change that are within our control, nothing changes, everything stays the same, and we blame others (e.g. "such and such made me mad") for our own choices and actions even though we have total control. Once we become aware of our shortcomings, we have the power and the opportunity to do something different. In an instance, you can choose to not only transform your life but the lives of everyone around you. *That's* powerful.

Making Mistakes and Being Resilient

I've often tried to behave perfectly, giving myself no room for errors and to learn and grow. Because I'm more of a strategic, big-picture thinker, one challenge that I've always had is not being able to pay keen attention to detail. Even when I try my best to not err in drafting a document, for example, I inevitably miss a mistake that becomes glaringly obvious once it is brought to my attention. I'm always embarrassed when someone else catches it, and I do a good job of beating myself up when it happens.

I want to share two things with you about trying to be perfect, if this is a challenge for you. First, do yourself a huge favor by acknowledging and accepting that you're not going to be good at everything. You can acknowledge you're not perfect, but do you really believe and know that you're not? Second, ask for help in the areas you're not strong. For a long time I knew, intellectually, that I can't be good at everything, but somewhere outside my intellect I did not accept that I was imperfect and continued to try to think a certain way or do particular things that I wasn't designed to think or do. The result? I made lots and lots of mistakes that could have been lessened if I had just asked for help. In more recent years, I've come to be more accepting of my shortcomings and, as a result, when I have a task to complete that is outside my skill or knowledge set, I ask someone who is good in that particular area for their assistance.

For example, although I've always enjoyed math and science and am good at both, I can make small mistakes like putting the wrong number on a spreadsheet or the right number in the wrong cell (it's embarrassing to even admit!), which throws the entire document off. Given that exactness isn't my strong suit, no matter how hard I try, I've learned to ask someone to give the document a review. While it takes longer to get the task complete, I'd rather it be right than send it out with errors. I've had to learn to shift my mindset from wanting to be fast and efficient, first, to wanting to be accurate.

FOOD FOR THOUGHT

1. What change is happening in your life right now that's causing you to feel off balance? What can you do to be more accepting and relieve any stress or anxiety you might feel around the issue?

2. What thoughts or behaviors are getting in the way of you being your best? If you don't know, ask someone. If you do, what can you do to start to make changes?

3. Are there any tasks you're supposed to complete that you're simply not good at? What can you do to get help in these areas (consider including your boss or a thought partner in this)?

TAKE ACTION!

What specific actions can you take as a result of reading this chapter?

THE HOW

17. Goal-Setting and Strategic Planning – Putting It All Together

Throughout this book I've invited you to take action on some of the ideas you generated as you read. This chapter will help you bring all those ideas together into one strategic plan.

When you hear the term *strategic planning*, what comes to mind? What initially came to mind for me was that strategic planning is something that those in the top levels of an organization do: they set the strategic direction for the entire company that everyone else has to follow. But through the visionary leadership class I spoke of in an earlier chapter, I learned that strategic planning and thinking are not just for executives of big corporations. Being strategic is a skill any professional can learn and employ whether they're at the top of their organization, they lead a team, or they are just starting their career as an individual contributor. As I started being more intentional about pursuing my career goals, I became more strategic in my thinking about what I really wanted and how I was going to get it.

I broaden my thinking to be more strategic by reading books like this, attending conferences and events, and talking with other colleagues and professionals. I gather ideas and information that I think will be useful and I start noticing trends and themes. I read articles about my topics of interests and take notes with the intention of doing something immediate with the information. I then schedule time, either alone or with a friend, to look at all I've learned in a given period of time, say, the last three months, and decide what, if anything, I want to do with what I've learned within, say, the next three, six, nine, and twelve months. I then make a plan to get it done.

It's a fun, engaging, and motivating process that has enabled me, time and time again, to achieve my goals, and I'm excited to share it with you. I encourage you to modify this process to make it work for you.

First and foremost, you have to make planning a priority and a regularly scheduled event in your schedule. If you don't, it's not going to happen or something else is going to get in the way. Whenever my clients don't complete an assigned task, it's usually because of time, not desire, that it doesn't get done. I recommend reading through the following steps and pausing between each one to complete first before moving to the next.

Step 1.

First, envision the desired future you want—what does it look like? What will you be doing? Who will be with you? What will you have achieved? If you were to reflect back on as if you already realized the vision, what will you be most proud of? What point of time are you in? How old are you? Is it a year, ten years, or more away?

In some of my workshops, I have participants interview each other using the above questions, as if for a magazine or news article of their choice. I tell them to project themselves ten years into the future and answer the interviewer's questions as if they'd already realized their vision and achieved their goals. Remember, we're imagining the future, so the questions will be framed in the present tense, such as: what were the major steps you *took* to get to where you are today? What advice do you have for those women coming up behind you? What *were* the major obstacles you faced, and how did you overcome them? What lessons have you learned along the way? Going through this exercise helps you to envision the experience of what it feels like to be successful before you even take the first step towards it. Take your time going through this exercise. Create questions of your own you'd like to answer and, if possible, have a friend ask you the questions so you can just dream. The clearer you can get the vision in your mind, the clearer you can be on how to achieve it.

I like creating vision boards. They can be a powerful daily reminder of what you're working towards. The materials I typically use are a poster board, scissors, a glue stick and now, thanks to technology, Google images, or just plain old magazines. I flip through the pages or do a search using words that are a part of my vision such as "best seller" or "women leaders." I print or cut those images out, in color, and add them to my board. And I don't limit my vision board to just my career, although you can. I have my vision for my home and family, and even the puppy I want to get some day. He's so cute. I can't wait to meet him!

At this step, you're simply thinking things through and gathering ideas you will eventually copy over to a document for your use and reference.

Step 2.

With your vision clearly in your mind or on a poster, decide on you short-, medium-, and long-term goals which for me, are thirty-, sixty-, and ninety-days and six-, twelve-, and eighteen-months. Because my life and schedule change so quickly, I do not plan beyond a year and a half, even if I've imagined my life ten years from now. Again, make this process work for you. If you are planning a longer-range goal, like getting a particular certification or working on a longer-term project, thirty, sixty, and ninety days might be too short a timeframe.

Step 3.

Ensure that your goals are in ORDER: Organized, Realistic, Directed, Engaging, and Recognizable.

Organized: just as with visioning, make your goals as clear and specific as possible so that there is no doubt about what you are trying to accomplish. For now, at a high level, organize your goals and thoughts in such a way that you know the exact details of who, what, when, where, why, how, and how much.

For example:

Who: your support system and resources

What: the specific goal you want to accomplish, the specific resources you'll need

When: the timeframe you want to get started and the time frame you want to complete the goal

Where: the location you're to be in to achieve the goal (at home, in another city, at another company)

Why: your purpose and motivation for accomplishing this goal

How: the specific steps you will take (see #4 below)

How much: what type of an investment do you need to make?

- **Realistic:** You want to have a stretch goal, something that's challenging and just a little out of reach. At the same time, it shouldn't be so out of reach that it's not attainable. Be realistic in setting your goals, asking yourself, whether the goal, timeline, or anything else is really attainable. Do you have the time? Will you have the support you need at this point in time? Is there anything else you need to do first (like take a beginning or general ed class before taking something more advanced)?

- **Directed:** Ensure the goal flows from your vision and that it aligns with who you want to become.

- **Engaging:** Remember, this is YOUR goal and not what someone else has told you you should do. Working towards a goal might be challenging and not always fun or easy, but you are willing to commit to and engage in the process because you want the prize at the end.

- **Recognizable:** You should be able to measure your goal achievement either quantitatively using a particular number, such as getting ten new customers in 60 days or qualitatively, like getting approval to move forward on a project or getting accepted into graduate school. Decide how you will recognize you're successful.

Step 4.

Create your plan with a timeline of the specific actions you will take that you identified in Step #3 including:

- *who* will you need to involve that will help provide information, or hold you accountable?

- *what* specific steps do you need to take? Can you break any steps down into smaller actionable steps? *what* resources (money, time, people, and things) will you need to accomplish your goal?

- *when* do you plan to start and complete each action? *When* will you review your plan, track your progress, and ensure it's still aligned with your vision and how often will you do it?

- *where* do you need to go to get more information or where do you need to be to accomplish the goal?*how* will you measure your progress and what will you do to course correct if you get off course?

- *how much money*, if anything, and time do you have to invest? How much is needed?

While the four steps above are really the strategic thinking and planning piece, there's no point in thinking and planning if you're not going to execute. So, the fifth step is to get into action by implementing your plan. Get your calendar out and to do list out and schedule the specific activities you are committing to during the time frame you identified (e.g. in the next week, month, or coming year).

Keep in mind that while you're pursuing your goals, be flexible and patient with yourself and others, remember to practice self-care, and be sure to enjoy the process! Planning for the future can be fun, pursuing it is the journey, and getting there and seeing how far you've come, is the reward.

References

Bandura, A. (1977). *Social Learning Theory.* Englewood Cliffs, NJ: Prentice Hall.

Banks, C. H. (2006, February). *Career Planning: Towards a more inclusive model for women and diverse individuals.* Paper presented at the Academy of Human Resource Development virtual conference. Retrieved November 10, 2007, from http://www.eric.ed.gov/ERICDocs/data/ericdocs2sql/content_storage_01/0000019b/80/1b/df/8d.pdf.

Baumeister, R. F. (1996). Self-regulation and ego threat: Motivated cognition, self-deception, and destructive goal setting. In P. M. Gollwitzer & J. A. Bargh (Eds.). *The Psychology Of Action: Linking Cognition And Motivation To Behavior* (pp. 27–47). New York: Guilford Press.

Bell, E. L. J. E., & Nkomo, S. M. (1998). Armoring: Learning to withstand racial oppression. *Journal of Comparative Family Studies,* 29(2), 285–295. Retrieved November 10, 2007, from http://0-web.ebscohost.com.library.alliant.edu/ehost/pdf?vid=15&hid=114&sid=1a5128b5-89ff-4c2e-8df5-644d83be605a%40sessionmgr104.

Bell, E. L. J. E., & Nkomo, S. M. (2001). Our Separate Ways: Black And White Women And The Struggle For Professional Identity. Boston: Harvard Business School Press.

Bell, E. L. J. E., Nkomo, S., & Hammond, J. (1994). *Glass ceiling commission: Barriers to workplace advancement experienced by African-*

Americans. Retrieved November 22, 2006, from http://digitalcommons.ilr.cornell.edu/key_workplace/118/.

Betz, N. E. (2002). Explicating an ecological approach to the career development of women. *The Career Development Quarterly, 50,* 335–338. Retrieved December 2, 2006, from http://0-web.ebscohost.com.library.alliant.edu/ehost/pdf?vid=99&hid=107&sid=e24542d0-5d2b-4ac4-99ab-771d665137bc%40sessionmgr102.

Bova, B. (2000). Mentoring revisited: The black woman's experience. *Mentoring and Training, 8*(1), 5–16. Retrieved October 18, 2007, from http://0-web.ebscohost.com.library.alliant.edu/ehost/pdf?vid=24&hid=114&sid=1a5128b5-89ff-4c2e-8df5-644d83be605a%40sessionmgr104.

Brandstätter, V., Lengerfelder, A., & Gollwitzer, P. (2001). Implementation intentions and efficient action initiation. *Journal of Personality and Social Psychology, 81*(5), 946–960. Retrieved May, 16, 2006, from http://0-web.ebscohost.com.library.alliant.edu/ehost/pdf?vid=103&hid=107&sid=e24542d0-5d2b-4ac4-99ab-771d665137bc%40sessionmgr102.

Brown, D. (2003). Career Information, Career Counseling, And Career Development (8th ed.). Boston: Pearson Education.

Burlew, A. K. (1982). The experiences of black females in traditional and non-traditional professions. *Psychology of Women Quarterly, 6*(3), 312–236. Retrieved October 18, 2007 from http://0-web.ebscohost.com.library.alliant.edu/ehost/pdf?vid=28&hid=114&sid=1a5128b5-89ff-4c2e-8df5-644d83be605a%40sessionmgr104.

Burrell, G., & Morgan, G. (1979). *Sociological paradigms and organizational analysis.* Burlington, VT: Ashgate.

Butler, M. E. (Ed.). (1997). *Black Women Stirring The Waters.* Oakland, CA: Marcus Books.

Campbell, D. B., & Fleming, J. (2000). ."Fear of success, racial identity, and academic achievement in black male college students." *Community Review, 18,* 5–18. Retrieved June 29, 2006, from http://0-web.ebscohost.com.library.alliant.edu/ehost/

pdf?vid=107&hid=107&sid=e24542d0-5d2b-4ac4-99ab-771d665137b
c%40sessionmgr102.

Canavan, D. (1989). Fear of Success. In R. C. Curtis (Ed.), *Self-Defeating Behaviors: Experimental Research, Clinical Impressions, And Practical Implications* (pp. 159–188). New York: Plenum Press.

Canavan-Gumpert, D., Garner, K., & Gumpert, P. (1978). *The success-fearing personality.* Lexington, Massachusetts: Lexington Books.

Cassell, C., & Symon, G. (2004). Essential Guide To Qualitative Methods In Organizational Research. London: Sage.

Catalyst (2004). *Advancing African American women in the workplace: What managers need to know.* Retrieved January 20, 2006, from http://www.catalyst.org/bookstore/freematerials.shtml#woc.

Center for the Study, Education and Advancement of Women. (1981). Black working women: Debunking the myths: A multidisciplinary approach: Proceedings of a research conference to examine the status of black working women in the United States. University of California, Berkeley.

Chambers, V. (2003). *Having It All? Black Women And Success.* New York: Doubleday.

Citrin, J., & Smith, R. (2003). *The 5 Patterns Of Extraordinary Careers.* New York: Crown Business.

Coleman, J. (1992). "Black American women administrators in higher education." *Hardee Center Collection of Papers on Women Administrators,* 1.

Cook, E. P., Heppner, M. J., & O'Brien, K. M. (2002). Career development of women of color and white women: Assumptions, conceptualization, and interventions from an ecological perspective. *The Career Development Quarterly, 50,* 291–305. Retrieved December 2, 2006, from http://0-web.ebscohost.com.library.alliant.edu/ehost/pdf?vid=32&hid=114&sid=1a5128b5-89ff-4c2e-8df5-644d83be605a%40sessionmgr104.

Cooper, H., & Tom, D. Y. H. (1984). Socioeconomic status and ethnic group differences in achievement motivation. In R. Ames & C. Ames

(Eds.), *Research On Motivation In Education: Vol. 1. Student motivation* (pp. 209–242). Orlando, FL: Academic Press.

Covington M. V., & Beery, R. G. (1976). *Self-worth and school learning.* New York: Hold, Rinehart & Winston.

Creswell, J. W. (1998). Qualitative Inquiry And Research Design: Choosing Among Five Traditions. Thousand Oaks, CA: Sage Publications.

Creswell, J. W. (2003). Research Design: Qualitative, Quantitative, And Mixed-Method Approaches. Thousand Oaks, CA: Sage.

deCharms, R. (1976). Enhancing Motivation: Change In The Classroom. New York: Irvington.

Deci, E. L., & Ryan, R. M. (2000). "The "what" and "why" of goal pursuits: Human needs and the self-determination of behavior." *Psychological Inquiry, 11*(4), 227–268. Retrieved February 16, 2006, from http://0-web.ebscohost.com.library.alliant.edu/ehost/pdf?vid=114&hid=107&sid=e24542d0-5d2b-4ac4-99ab-771d665137b c%40sessionmgr102.

Denzin, N. K., & Lincoln, Y. S. (Eds.). (2000). *The Handbook Of Qualitative Research* (2nd ed.). Thousand Oaks, CA: Sage.

Diener, E., Suh, E., Lucas, R., & Smith, H. (1999). "Subjective well-being: Three decades of progress." *Psychological Bulletin, 125*(2), 276–302. Retrieved October 18, 2007, from http://0-web.ebscohost.com.library.alliant.edu/ehost/pdf?vid=21&hid=115&sid=ffaf3454-e7ed-4c15-bd97-69722b7fc36a%4 0sessionmgr102.

Dubion, E. J. (1983). "Women doctoral students in higher education administration: Lifestyle aspirations and multiple role commitments." *Journal of NAWDAC, 20*–24.

Dubois, D. D. (2000). *"Training & development, 54*(12)," 45–50. Retrieved October 3, 2005, from http://0-web.ebscohost.com.library.alliant.edu/ehost/pdf?vid=15&hid=115&sid=ffaf3454-e7ed-4c15-bd97-69722b7fc36a%4 0sessionmgr102.

Dweck, C. S. (1996). Implicit theories as organizers of goals and behavior. In P. M. Gollwitzer & J. A. Bargh (Eds.). *The psychology of action: Linking cognition and motivation to behavior* (pp. 69-90). New York: Guilford Press.

Edwards, A., & Polite, C. K. (1992). *Children Of The Dream: The Psychology Of Black Success.* New York: Doubleday.

Ehrhart-Morrison, D. (1997). No Mountain High Enough: Secrets Of Successful African-American Women. Berkeley, CA: Canari Press Books.

Emmons, R. A. (2005). "Striving for the sacred: Personal goals, life meaning, and religion." *Journal of Social Issues, 61*(4), 731–745. Retrieved February 7, 2006, from http://0-web.ebscohost.com.library.alliant.edu/ehost/pdf?vid=118&hid=107&sid=e24542d0-5d2b-4ac4-99ab-771d665137bc%40sessionmgr102.

Fassinger, R. E., & Richie B. S. (1994). "Being the best: Preliminary results from a national study of the advancement of prominent black and white women." *Journal of Counseling Psychology, 41*(2), 191–204. Retrieved June 16, 2006, from http://0-web.ebscohost.com.library.alliant.edu/ehost/pdf?vid=42&hid=114&sid=1a5128b5-89ff-4c2e-8df5-644d83be605a%40sessionmgr104.

Fay, D., & Frese, M. (2000). "Self-Starting Behavior At Work: Toward A Theory Of Personal Initiative." In J. Heckhausen (Ed.), Motivational psychology of human development: Developing motivation and motivating development (pp. 307–324). Amsterdam: Ensevier.

Fleming, J. (1978). "Fear of success, achievement-related motives, and behavior in black college women." *Journal of Personality, 46*(4), 694–716. Retrieved June 29, 2006, from http://0-web.ebscohost.com.library.alliant.edu/ehost/pdf?vid=125&hid=107&sid=e24542d0-5d2b-4ac4-99ab-771d665137bc%40sessionmgr102.

Fleming, J. (1982). "Fear of success in black male and female graduate students: A pilot study." *Psychology of Women Quarterly, 6*(3).

Fleming, J., & Horner, M. S. (1992). *The motive to avoid success.* In C. P. Smith (Ed.), *Motivation and personality: Handbook of thematic content analysis* (pp. 179–189). New York: Cambridge University Press.

Gallagher, C. (2000). Going To The Top. A Road Map For Success From America's Leading Women Executive. New York: Penguin.

Goldberg, L. R. (1990). An alternative description of personality: The big-five factor structure. *Journal of Personality and Social Psychology*, 59(6), 1216–1229.

Gollwitzer & J. A. Bargh (Eds.), *The Psychology Of Action: Linking Cognition And Motivation To Behavior* (pp. 219–235). New York: Guilford Press. Gollwitzer, P. M. (1996). "The Volitional Benefits Of Planning." In P. M. Gollwitzer & J. A. Bargh (Eds.), *The psychology of action: Linking cognition and motivation to behavior* (pp. 287–312). New York: Guillford Press.

Gollwitzer, P. M. (1999). "Implementation Intentions: Strong Effects Of Simple Plans. American Psychologist, 54," 493–503.

Gollwitzer, P. M., & Brandstätter, V. (1997). "Implementation intentions and effective goal pursuit." *Journal of Personality and Social Psychology*, 73(1), 186–199. Retrieved May 16, 2006, from http://0-web.ebscohost.com.library.alliant.edu/ehost/pdf?vid=50&hid=114&sid=1a5128b5-89ff-4c2e-8df5-644d83be605a%40sessionmgr104.

Gollwitzer, P. M., & Moskowitz, G. B. (1996). "Goal Effects On Action And Cognition." In T. E. Higgins & A. W. Kruglanski (Eds.), *Social Psychology Handbook Of Basic Principles* (pp. 361–399). New York: Guilford.

Graham, S. (1994). "Motivation in African Americans. Review of Educational Research," 64(1), 55–117.

Hackett, G., & Byars, A. M. (1996). "Social cognitive theory and the career development of African American women." *Career Development Quarterly*, 44(4), 322–340. Retrieved July 3, 2006, from http://0-web.ebscohost.com.library.alliant.edu/ehost/detail?vid=129&hid=107&sid=e24542d0-5d2b-4ac4-99ab-771d665137bc%40sessionmgr102.

Hall, D. T. (2002). *Careers In And Out Of Organizations*. Thousand Oaks, CA: Sage.

Harackiewicz, J. M., & Sansone, C. (1991). "Goals and intrinsic motivation: You can get there from here." In M. L. Maer & P. R.

Pintrich (Eds.), *Advances In Motivation And Achievement: Vol. 7. A Research Annual* (pp. 21–49). Greenwich, Connecticut: Jai Press.

Harlander, S. K. (1996). "Breaking through the glass ceiling: An industrial perspective." *Journal of Animal Science 74*(11), 2849–2854. Retrieved November 24, 2006, from http://jas.fass.org/cgi/reprint/74/11/2849.

Heppner, P., & Heppner, M. J. (2004). Writing And Publishing Your Thesis, Dissertation, And Research: A Guide For Students In The Helping Professions. Belmont, CA: Brooks/Cole-Thompson Learning.

Hersey, P., Blanchard, K. H., & Johnson, D. E. (1996). *Management Of Organizational Behavior* (7th ed.). Upper Saddle River, NJ: Prentice Hall.

Hofstede, G. (2003). "Geert Hofstede cultural dimensions." Retrieved September 1, 2007, from http://www.geert-hofstede.com/.

Hofstede, G. (2003). "Geert Hofstede cultural dimensions: United States." Retrieved September 1, 2007, from http://www.geert-hofstede.com/hofstede_united_states.shtml

Holland, J. (1973). *Making Vocational Choices: A Theory Of Careers.* Englewood Cliffs, NJ: Prentice Hall.

Judge, T. A., Higgins, C. A., Thorensen, C. J., & Barrick, M. R. (1999). "The big-five personality traits, general mental ability, and career success across the lifespan." *Personnel Psychology, 52*(3), 621–652. Retrieved June 6, 2006, from http://0-web.ebscohost.com.library.alliant.edu/chost/pdf?vid=54&hid=114&sid=1a5128b5-89ff-4c2e-8df5-644d83be605a%40sessionmgr104.

Karoly, P. (1999). "A Goal Systems Self-Regulatory Perspective On Personality, Psychopathology, And Change." *Review of General Psychology, 3*(4), 264–291. Retrieved May 15, 2006, from http://0-web.ebscohost.com.library.alliant.edu/ehost/pdf?vid=135&hid=107&sid=e24542d0-5d2b-4ac4-99ab-771d665137bc%40sessionmgr102.

Katz, I. (1967). "The Socialization Of Academic Motivation." In D.

Klein (Ed.), *Nebraska Symposium On Motivation*. Lincoln, NE: University of Nebraska Press.

Klaesges, R., (2004). African American women's career transition experiences: Choosing to leave corporations for self-employment. Unpublished thesis, Alliant International University, San Diego, CA.

Klein, H. J., Wesson, M. J., Hollenbeck, J. R., & Alge, B. J. (1999). Goal commitment and the goal-setting process: Conceptual clarification and empirical synthesis. *Journal of Applied Psychology, 84*(6), 885–896. Retrieved October 18, 2007, from http://0-web.ebscohost.com.library.alliant.edu/ehost/pdf?vid=58&hid=114&sid=1a5128b5-89ff-4c2e-8df5-644d83be605a%40sessionmgr104.

Koestner, R., Leeks, N., Powers, T. A., & Chicoine, E. (2002). Attaining personal goals: Self-concordance plus implementation intentions equal success. *Journal of Personality and Social Psychology, 83*(1), 231–244. Retrieved May 16, 2006, from http://0-web.ebscohost.com.library.alliant.edu/ehost/pdf?vid=62&hid=114&sid=1a5128b5-89ff-4c2e-8df5-644d83be605a%40sessionmgr104.

Lawrence-Lightfoot, S., & Davis, J. H. (1997). *The art and science of portraiture*. San Francisco: Jossey-Bass.

Lee, T. W., Locke, E. A., & Latham, G. P. (1989). Goal-setting theory and job performance. In L. A. Pervin (Ed), *Goal concepts in personality and social psychology* (pp. 291–326). Hillsdale, NJ: Lawrence Erlbaum.

Lightfoot, S. (1983). The Good High School: Portraits of character and culture. New York: Basic Books.

Locke, E. A., Frederick, E., Lee, C., & Bobko, P. (1984). "Effect of self-efficacy, goals, and task strategies on task performance." *Journal of Applied Psychology, 69*(2), 241–251. Retrieved October 18, 2007, from http://0-web.ebscohost.com.library.alliant.edu/ehost/pdf?vid=5&hid=109&sid=8af1260c-0629-4cdc-a853-96061bb389c8%40sessionmgr109.

Locke, E. A., & Latham, G. P. (1990). *A Theory Of Goal Setting And Task Performance*. Englewood Cliffs, NJ: Prentice Hall.

Locke, E. A., & Latham, G. P. (2002). *Building A Practically Useful*

Theory Of Goal Setting And Task Motivation: A 35-Year Odyssey. *American Psychologist, 57*(9), 705–717. Retrieved February 3, 2006, from http://0-web.ebscohost.com.library.alliant.edu/ehost/ pdf?vid=5&hid=103&sid=0a822701-8556-4332-9bf9-07c08d86c84b %40sessionmgr102.

Marshall, C., & Rossman, G. (2006). *Designing Qualitative Research* (4th ed.). Thousand Oaks, CA: Sage.

McClelland, D. C., Atkinson, J. W., Clark, R. A., & Lowell, E. L. (1953). *The Achievement Motive.* New York: Irvington.

Miles, M. B., & Huberman, A. M. (1984). *Qualitative Data Analysis: A Sourcebook Of New Methods.* Beverly Hills, CA: Sage.

Mischel, W. (1996). "From good intentions to willpower." In P. M. Gollwitzer & J. A. Bargh (Eds.), *The psychology of action: Linking cognition and motivation to behavior* (pp. 197–218). New York: Guilford Press.

Morrison, A. M., White, R. P., Van Velsor, E., & The Center of Creative Leadership (1987). *Breaking The Glass Ceiling: Can Women Reach The Top Of America's Largest Corporations?* Reading, MA: Addison-Wesley.

Murphy, S. E., & Esner, E. A. (2001). "The Role Of Mentoring Support And Self-Management Strategies On Reported Career Outcomes." *Journal of Career Development, 27*(4), 229–246. Retrieved October 18, 2007, from https://library.alliant.edu/patroninfo~S6?/0/ redirect=/wamvalidate?url=http%3A%2F%2F0-web.ebscohost.com.li brary.alliant.edu%3A80%2Fehost%2Fpdf%3Fvid%3D9%26hid%3D109 %26sid%3D8af1260c-0629-4cdc- a853-96061bb389c8@sessionmgr109%2522%2520HYPERLINK%252 0%2522http%3A%2F%2F0-web.ebscohost.com.library.alliant.edu%2F ehost%2Fpdf%3Fvid%3D9%26hid%3D109%26sid%3D8af1260c-0629- 4cdc-a853-96061bb389c8%2540sessionmgr109%2522

Nauta, M. N., Epperson, D. L., & Kahn, J. H. (1998). "A multiple-groups analysis of predictors of higher-level career aspirations among women in mathematics, science, and engineering majors. *Journal of Counseling Psychology, 45*(4), 483–496. Retrieved February 20, 2007, from http://0-web.ebscohost.com.library.alliant.edu/ ehost/

pdf?vid=9&hid=103&sid=0a822701-8556-4332-9bf9-07c08d86c84b
%40sessionmgr102.

Nichols, J. C., & Tanksey, C. B. (2004). "Revelations of African American women with terminal degrees: Overcoming obstacles to success." *The Negro Educational Review, 55*(4), 175–185. Retrieved June 16, 2006, from http://0-web.ebscohost.com.library.alliant.edu/ehost/pdf?vid=13&hid=109&sid=8af1260c-0629-4cdc-a853-96061bb389c8%40sessionmgr109.

Noe, R. A. (1988). "Women And Mentoring: A Review And Research Agenda." *Academy of Management Review, 13*(1), 65–78. Retrieved October 18, 2007, from http://0-web.ebscohost.com.library.alliant.edu/ehost/pdf?vid=13&hid=103&sid=0a822701-8556-4332-9bf9-07c08d86c84b%40sessionmgr102.

Orpen, C. (1994). "The Effects Of Organizational And Individual Career Management On Career Success." *International Journal of Manpower, 15*(1), 27–37.

Pervin, L. A. (1989). "Goal Concepts In Personality And Social Psychology: An Historical Introduction." In L. A. Pervin (Ed). *Goal concepts in personality and social psychology* (pp. 21–49). Hillsdale, NJ: Lawrence Erlbaum.

Pintrich, P. R. (2000). "The Role Of Goal Orientation In Self-Regulated Learning." In M. Boekaerts, P. R. Pintrich, & M. Zeidner (Eds.), *Handbook Of Self-Regulation* (pp. 451–502). San Diego, CA: Academic Press.

Pintrich, P. R., & Garcia, T. (1991). "Student goal orientation and self-regulation in the college classroom." In M. L. Maehr & P. R. Pintrich (Eds.). *Advances in motivation and achievement: Vol. 7. A research annual* (pp. 371–402). Greenwich, CT: Jai Press.

Poole, M. E., Langan-Fox, J., & Omodi, M. (1993). "Contrasting subjective and objective criteria as determinants of perceived career cusses." *Journal of Occupational and Organizational Psychology, 66,* 39–54. Retrieved October 11, 2005, from http://0-web.ebscohost.com.library.alliant.edu/ehost/pdf?vid=17&hid=109&sid=8af1260c-0629-4cdc-a853-96061bb389c8%40sessionmgr109.

Povey, R., Conner, M., Sparks, P., James, R., & Shepherd, R. (2000). "Theory of planned behavior and healthy eating: Examining additive and moderating effects of social influence variables." *Psychology and Health, 14,* 991–1006. Retrieved May 16, 2006, from http://0-web.ebscohost.com.library.alliant.edu/ehost/ pdf?vid=21&hid=109&sid=8af1260c-0629-4cdc-a853-96061bb389c8%40sessionmgr109.

Powell, G. N., & Mainiero, L. A. (1992). "Cross-Currents In The River Of Time: Conceptualizing The Complexities Of Women's Careers." *Journal of Management, 18*(2), 215–237. Retrieved November 14, 2006, from http://0-web.ebscohost.com.library.alliant.edu/ehost/ pdf?vid=17&hid=103&sid=0a822701-8556-4332-9bf9-07c08d86c84 b%40sessionmgr102.

Rawsthorne, L. J., & Elliot, A. J. (1999). "Achievement goals and intrinsic motivation: A meta-analytic review." *Personality and Social Psychology Review, 3*(4), 326–344. Retrieved February 5, 2006, from http://0-web.ebscohost.com.library.alliant.edu/ehost/ pdf?vid=25&hid=109&sid=8af1260c-0629-4cdc-a853-96061bb389c8%40sessionmgr109.

Recker, G. T., & Wong, P. T. P. (1988). ."Aging as an individual process: Toward a theory of personal meaning." In J. E. Birren & V. L. Bengtson (Eds.), *Emergent Theories Of Aging* (pp. 214–246). New York: Springe.

Richie, B. S., Fassinger, R. E., Linn, S. G., Johnson, J., Prosser, J., & Robinson, S. (1997). "Persistence, Connection, And Passion: A Qualitative Study Of The Career Development Of Highly Achieving African American-Black And White Women." *Journal of Counseling Psychology, 44*(2), 133–148. Retrieved June 12, 2006, from http://0-web.ebscohost.com.library.alliant.edu/ehost/ pdf?vid=21&hid=103&sid=0a822701-8556-4332-9bf9-07c08d86c84 b%40sessionmgr102.

Rosen, B. C. (1959). Race, Ethnicity, And The Achievement Syndrome. American Sociological Review, 24(1), 47–60.

Rubin, D. F., & Belgrave, F. Z. (1999). "Differences between African American and European American college students in relative and mathematical time orientations: A preliminary study." *The Journal of black Psychology, 25*(1), 105–113. Retrieved November 20, 2007,

from   http://0-web.ebscohost.com.library.alliant.edu/ehost/
detail?vid=29&hid=109&sid=8af1260c-0629-4cdc-
a853-96061bb389c8%40sessionmgr109.

Ryan, R. M., Sheldon, K. M., Kasser, T., & Deci, E. L. (1996). "All goals
are not created equal: An organismic perspective on the nature of
goals and their regulation." In P. M. Gollwitzer & J. A. Bargh (Eds.),
The psychology of action: Linking cognition and motivation to behavior
(pp. 7–26). New York: Guilford Press.

Salkind, N. J. (2000). *Exploring Research* (4th ed.). Upper Saddle River,
NJ. Prentice-Hall.

Schank, R. C., & Abelson, R. P. (1977). "Scripts, Plans, Goals, And
Understanding." Hillsdale, NJ: Lawrence Erlbaum.

Schein, E. H. (1978). Career Dynamics: Matching Individual And
Organizational Needs. Reading, MA: Addison-Wesley.

Shepard, H. A. (1984). "On The Realization Of Human Potential: A
Path With A Heart." In M. B. Arthur, L. Bailyn, D. J. Levinson, & H.
A. Shepard. *Working With Careers* (pp. 25–46). New York: Columbia
University School of Business.

Shields, C., & Shields, L. C. (1992) Work, Sister, Work: Why Black
Women Can't Get Ahead And What They Can Do About It.
Secaucus, NJ: Carol.

Spradley, J. P. (1979). *The Ethnographic Interview.* Orlando, FL:
Harcourt Brace Jovanovich.

Super, D. E. (1957). "The psychology of careers: An introduction to
vocational development. New York: Harper."

Swiss, D. J. (1996). *Women Breaking Through: Overcoming The Final 10
Obstacles At Work.* Princeton, NJ: Peterson's Pacesetter Books.

Taylor, S. E., & Pham L. B. (1996). "Mental simulation, motivation,
and action." In P. M.

Taylor, S. E., Pham, L. B., Rivkin, I. D., & Armor, D. A. (1998).
*Harnessing The Imagination: Mental Simulation, Self-Regulation, And
Coping. American Psychologist, 53*(4), 429–439. Retrieved February, 13,
2007, from http://0-web.ebscohost.com.library.alliant.edu/ehost/

pdf?vid=25&hid=103&sid=0a822701-8556-4332-9bf9-07c08d86c84
b%40sessionmgr102

Tesch, R. (1990). Qualitative Research: Analysis Types And Software Tools. New York: Falmer Press.

Thomas, D. A., & Gabarro, J. J. (1999). *Breaking Through: The Making Of Minority Executives In Corporate America.* Boston: Harvard Business School Press.

Tresemer, D. (1977). *Fear Of Success.* New York: Plenum Press.

Turner, C. (1983, February). "Psychosocial barriers to black women's career development." Paper presented at the Stone Center for Developmental Services and Studies, Wellesley College, MA.

United States Census Bureau (2004). "The black population in the United States" (PPL–186). Retrieved June 29, 2004, from http://www.census.gov/population/www/socdemo/race/ ppl-186.html.

Weathers, P. L., Thompson, C. E., Robert, S., & Rodriguez, Jr., J. (1994). "Black college women's career values: A preliminary investigation." *Journal of Multicultural Counseling & Development,* 22(2), 96–105. Retrieved February 20, 2007, from http://0-web.ebscohost.com.library.alliant.edu/ehost/ detail?vid=29&hid=103&sid=0a822701-8556-4332-9bf9-07c08d86c 84b%40sessionmgr102.

Webb, T., & Sheeran, P. (2005). "Integrating concepts from goal theories to understand the achievement of personal goals." *European Journal of Social Psychology, 35,* 69–96. Retrieved March 18, 2006, from http://0-web.ebscohost.com.library.alliant.edu/ehost/ pdf?vid=33&hid=109&sid=8af1260c-0629-4cdc- a853-96061bb389c8%40sessionmgr109.

Weiner, B. (1992). Human Motivation: Metaphors, Theories, And Research. Newbury Park, CA: Sage.

White, B., Cox, C., & Cooper, C. (1992). *Women's career development: A study of high flyers.* Cambridge, MA: Blackwell.

Wiese, B. S., & Freund, A. M. (2005). "Goal progress makes one happy, or does it? Longitudinal findings from the work domain." *Journal of Occupational and Organizational Psychology, 78,* 287–304.

Retrieved   February   2,   2006,   from
http://0-web.ebscohost.com.library.alliant.edu/ehost/
pdf?vid=32&hid=103&sid=0a822701-8556-4332-9bf9-07c08d86c84
b%40sessionmgr102

Williams, S. L. (1995). "Self-efficacy and anxiety and phobic
disorders." In J. E. Maddux (Ed.), *Self-Efficacy, Adaptation, And
Adjustment: Theory, Research, And Application.* New York: Plenum
Press.

Wrigley, B. J. (2002). "Glass ceiling? *What* glass ceiling? A qualitative
study of how women view the glass ceiling in public relations and
communications management." *Journal of Public Relations Research,*
14(1), 27–55. Retrieved November 24, 2006, from
http://0-web.ebscohost.com.library.alliant.edu/ehost/
pdf?vid=37&hid=109&sid=8af1260c-0629-4cdc-
a853-96061bb389c8%40sessionmgr109

Notes

.

About the Author

Dr. Julianna Hynes, Ph.D.

Professional Development Strategist, Author, and Speaker

"Action is the foundational key to all success." – Picasso

Dr. Julianna Hynes is Professional Development Strategist, Author, and Speaker. She partners her clients to create business and career strategies that align with their professional and organization's goals.

With a focused yet personable demeanor, Dr. Hynes challenges her clients to shift their thinking from auto-pilot to a more purposeful and deliberate mindset. She's successful in helping leaders refine their existing skills while also developing the competencies that will enable their future success. As an expert in women's leadership, Dr. Hynes is known for helping her clients navigate the nuances of being a woman in the workplace.

Dr. Hynes earned a Ph.D. in Organizational Psychology from the California School of Professional Psychology, where she studied successful Black women leaders.

Combining her academic, personal, and professional experiences, Dr. Hynes has found that having a success mindset, being results-oriented, taking time to reflect, and being interpersonally savvy are keys to successful leadership.

While Dr. Hynes enjoys working with a diversity of people, because of her early career experiences, she's passionate about helping women and emerging leaders elevate their leadership skills with greater clarity, focus, and awareness.

Dr. Hynes lives in the San Francisco Bay Area with her husband of 22 years and the two youngest of their five children. She enjoys spending time with friends and family and loves to dance. As long there's a good beat, Dr. J will move to it.

Made in the USA
Coppell, TX
24 August 2020

Living and Loving
After Divorce

Living and Loving
After Divorce

by Catherine Napolitane
and Victoria Pellegrino

Rawson Associates Publishers, Inc.
New York

Library of Congress Cataloging in Publication Data

Napolitane, Catherine.
    Living and loving after divorce.

    1. Divorcees—United States. 2. Single women—
United States. I. Pellegrino, Victoria Y., joint
author. II. Title.
HQ834.N27 1977   301.42′84   76-50506
ISBN 0-89256-007-X

To my children, Nick and Christina
CATHERINE NAPOLITANE

To my parents, Elsie and Steven Yurasits
VICTORIA Y. PELLEGRINO

Acknowledgments

We'd like to thank all the Nexus groups for their wonderful help. Special thanks goes to Marilyn Fleisig, Doris Annenberg, Bernese Sobel, Marion Lucchesi, Lydia Ritchkoff, Hellie Wolf, Grace Landon, Enid Hameroff, Jeanine Oster, Janet Shaiman, Carol Stier, Muriel Pearlman, Shirley Carduner, Louise Burton, Phyllis Borger, Holly Hollender, Millicent Fox, Audrey Gelzer, Pam Mahl, Sue Zalon, Iris Klein, Belle Steinberg, Carol Chandler, Jo Plaut, Mimi Harris, Dorothy Oppenheim, Gloria Vise, Barbara Morselli, Annette Nober, Ginny Richardson, Eileen Knickman, Natasha Lubin, Fran Mott, Roz Blattman, Sandra James, Gail Goldfarb, Anne Denning, Jeannette Buckholz, Anita Morse and Cathy Delaney. Also to Fran Liebow, Gina L'Hommedieu, Diana Furco, Claire Loerch, Charlotte Kogan, Carla Pomerico, Nea Scholey, Sandy Tauber, and Norma Getler. All have contributed invaluably to the book—giving advice, their stories, their insight. Without their help, we couldn't have done the book.

Thanks also to Elliott M. Epstein, Esq., and Gabriel Cohn, Esq., and Joseph R. Damon, Esq., Assistant Attorney General of the State of New York. Also to Hy Asheroff, Leon Brown, Dr. Richard Ozahowsky, Jerry Berg, Zim Barstein, and William Kaufman.

John Pellegrino contributed many valuable suggestions

to the book. Our typist, Anne Gordon, gave us thoughtful comments all along the way, and Herb Baltuch helped us with many details of putting the book together. Andy Napolitane acted as a sounding board many times, and we thank him. And, of course, special thanks goes to Bill Roeder of *Newsweek* who brought us together.

We are also ever so grateful to have such a warm and supportive editor as Eleanor Rawson, who guided us every step of the way.

We also want to express our warm appreciation to Rhoda Weyr, our agent, who has worked untiringly in our behalf.

Contents

PART ONE

1

Breaking Up

Divorce, an accepted fact of life today, is still one of the most emotionally upsetting life crises a woman ever goes through.

My divorce, seven years ago, left me reeling from all the changes I had to make in my life, and all the problems I had to confront. I was scared; I was lonely; and I had to take care of two young children all by myself. I had little money, no job, and I was bitter about the fact that my husband had told me he was in love with another woman. Added to that was the unpleasant realization that my married friends wanted no part of me and that I had no one to talk to about my anxiety and pain. How I wished I had never married in the first place! And how I wished I would find another man quickly who would be kind, heal up my wounds, love, honor, and protect me forever.

Gradually, however, I got my life together and I did not marry again. Two and a half years after my husband packed his suitcase and moved out of our house, I began an organization for separated and divorced women. I wanted to reach out. I reasoned that since we were all in the same boat, we could help each other to get through the bad times and celebrate the good.

Today Nexus is over five years old. Thousands of women have passed through its doors and have been helped by its program. And through working so intensely with divorced women for so many years, I have come to see how we all share many of the same problems and feelings, and how misguided society is about who we are and what we need. For example, I've found very few therapists who have not been divorced themselves who can really understand the agony the divorced person undergoes, the enormous sense of dislocation that often takes several years to heal. Society has little place for singles in its two-by-two world, and we are often reduced to seeking each other out in sleazy bars and singles resorts that sometimes seem more like meat markets than civilized adult social settings. I've found, too, that there is still an enormous stigma attached to being a divorced woman.

When a widow loses her husband, everyone gathers round to sympathize. When a woman divorces, however, people stay away from her as if she had the plague. The phone doesn't ring, and, rather than being sympathetic, most people seem embarrassed. You have "failed." The aftermath of a divorce can be a wretched, isolated time.

Yet enormous growth can come out of the divorce crisis. I know scarcely one woman who has been divorced for three years or more who wouldn't say, "How much I've changed since my divorce." Today I am neither for nor against marriage, but I do know that marriage is a disappointment to many people. Even people who do have happy marriages often don't experience as much growth as the single person who is fighting for control over his or her life.

Studies now show that those women who are the most

happily married are those who are the most submissive and conventional, the least able to be self-indulgent or assertive. When marriage is the most important part of a woman's life, her quest for personal identity is often given short shrift because of the demands made on her by husband and children alike. The single woman, on the other hand, has many more options for pursuing a meaningful personal identity, for becoming more her own woman.

Moreover, learning the ropes of living as a single woman can be both exciting and rewarding. I have become more outgoing, more confident, and more sure of who I am and what I want. I have made many wonderful friends, both men and women, and I've had the satisfaction of seeing my children develop and grow in a way that's been pleasing to me. Most of all, from a frightened, dependent, starry-eyed woman, I've become self-sufficient, resourceful, and, I think, creative. I like myself.

Nexus has been responsible essentially for developing my strength and optimism, for as the organization grew, I grew. I knew in my gut that there was a tremendous need for a program for separated and divorced women, but when I had my initial belief corroborated over and over again, it was like a dream come true, like being reborn.

That divorced women are sometimes in desperate straits for any kind of help can be seen from some of the letters I have received.

One woman wrote me, "I know I have to cope with being myself, but I don't know where to begin." Another wrote, "I'm a soon-to-be divorced woman, and, boy, do I need moral support!" And a third wrote, "I have been divorced for three years now, and have two children. I spend all my time at home. All my friends are advising me to get involved with your organization."

Members have ranged from women in their early twenties to women in their fifties and sixties. We have rich women and women on welfare, women from different life-styles and backgrounds.

What united us all was the desire to cope with our problems, overcome them, and create new and better lives for ourselves. From the first, our philosophy, which we ran in our first newsletter, went as follows:

> The Nexus woman is not a stereotype.
>
> She shares one condition with her sisters; she is a single woman. The fact is that a woman in the single state, whether she be separated, divorced, or widowed, can be anybody, anytime. She may have children or not, she may be under thirty years or over fifty. She may have been working all of her life, in an office or in her home. Other than that, she may be anywhere from completely liberated, activist feminist to totally conformist "Pussy Cat"; politically she may be anywhere from extreme left to far out. Emotionally, she may be a well-adjusted, positive-thinking, outreaching mature woman, or she may come on as an emotionally torn-up, hurting, bewildered little girl.
>
> The Nexus woman does have an edge on other single women in one respect. She has recognized the importance to herself of relationships with other women. She has recognized the pressure of society to separate her from her sisters, by isolation, competition, and jealousy, and is trying to reject that pressure. She is trying to penetrate her isolation, forced on her by a world of doubles and couples, of which she is no longer a part.

What I want to do in this book is to tell you my story and the stories of other women I've come to know. I want to share with you what I've learned and the struggle I've been through.

My father was a lieutenant colonel in the army and I was brought up in an army atmosphere. The stress was on protocol—on being proper. However, my father did not live a very proper life. He ran around with women and he drank.

My parents broke up when I was fourteen. I helped my mother raise my two brothers. I don't remember being allowed to be a child.

I met my husband at the University of Denver. His parents were first-generation Italian-Americans. Andy was an only child. He'd had a scholarship to The Juilliard School of Music and was scouted for minor league sports, but he decided to go into advertising. He was a junior when I was a freshman, and when he graduated, I left school without a degree, married, and went east. I wish that someone had advised me *not* to leave school. I was running away from one household to another. But my mother told me I would lose Andy if I didn't marry him right away.

I originally wanted to be a fashion designer. I wanted to go to school at Parson's in New York. That was my burning desire. But it literally flew out of my mind when I married. In fact, only recently did I remember how much I wanted that.

Andy is an authoritative, charming, gregarious man, but the making of money took over his personality. He wasn't able to enjoy the comfortable married life-style he helped to create. I did everything Andy wanted. He wanted to visit his parents every weekend, so we visited his parents every weekend without fail.

In the seventh year of our marriage, Andy had an affair with his secretary. My son, Nicky, was then two and a half. I picked up my son and went back to Denver, but my family wasn't much help. I was totally devastated. I believed in being faithful, in loving one man and one man only. I didn't know what I had done wrong, why this had happened to me. I finally found a minister in Denver, and he suggested I return and try marriage counseling. And that's what I did. From that point on, until the breakup of our marriage, it seemed as if Andy and I were continually with either marriage counselors or psychiatrists.

Meanwhile, I had a daughter, Christina. Andy and I both thought another child would bring us together. I was doing what I thought was right, but I was not comfortable. I had a very difficult pregnancy. I didn't have enough confidence in myself at the time, or enough guidance, to realize that we were in a situation that wasn't workable.

After about three years, I said I was going to find a psychiatrist. I needed better help. I think my doctor helped me mature a great deal. He helped me have the courage to break away from my marriage. My husband blames the psychiatrist for our breakup—he thinks he caused it, that it was the psychiatrist's fault. I've heard many other men say that.

When I took the step to go to a psychiatrist, I felt that there was no communication between Andy and me. I would say something and it would just bounce off him; I had no feeling that he cared or that he could understand my feelings. He was wrapped up in business, and he was wrapped up in himself. He was a sportsman and he had his own schedule. If he wasn't working, he was playing handball or golf. On the weekends, he loved to party. He resented our children and the time I spent with them.

I did volunteer community work during this time, and Andy was proud of it but jealous of it. He wanted me to be there for him, to cater to him. My desires as to what to do on a weekend really didn't count for much. If we did what

I wanted to do, he would pout and sulk. He hated my painting (I had taken art lessons from the time I was in school), even though I didn't let it take time away from him.

One night I told Andy that I was extremely unhappy. I said I didn't know if I loved him. I said I wanted him to work with me and that perhaps a trial separation would do us some good.

The next night he didn't come home until five in the morning. From that point on, until two years later, when we divorced, he did not come home until he pleased. He gave himself carte blanche. Later he told me that he felt totally justified because I had said I didn't know if I loved him.

We still went out on the weekends together. We played the role of the happily married couple, as a lot of people do.

I remember pacing one night, all night, because I needed to talk to him, but he slept peacefully. In the morning he was dressed in a new suit; he always was a snappy dresser. His parents were coming in that evening to spend the Christmas holidays with us. He stood by the stairs and said, "By the way, I won't be home tonight. There's a party." The milkman had just delivered the milk, six bottles. I opened the door, picked up the bottles of milk, one at a time, and threw them at him. Yet he didn't raise his voice to me. He just went upstairs, changed his clothes, and left.

One night, after the bottle-throwing incident, Andy said he'd be home by dinnertime. He called about six-thirty from a bar. There was the usual noise and tinkling glasses in the background. He said he'd be late, that he and his friends were going to have a few drinks together. It seemed to me that all anybody in the advertising world did was drink.

I had been to a lawyer two years before, and I called him

that night and told him I wanted a divorce. I did not see our relationship getting any better—it was just deteriorating more and more. I felt like one of the walking wounded, and I wanted to have some happiness and dignity in my life. I, who had married so hopefully and innocently, was about to join the growing number of divorced women in America.

I was not prepared for divorce and how it would affect my life. I had no concrete plans, although I thought I'd probably remarry. I was not prepared to cope with the loneliness, the anger, the fear. Here, for example, are some excerpts from the diary I began keeping about six months after my husband left.

Excerpts from my diary, beginning September, 1969

September 22—What a lonely, depressing day . . . Decided not go to the hospital [volunteer work] today, but to stay home and make some calls about getting a job. (I hope someday, someone will want me—working or as a wife or something.)

October 4—I am having a lonely, anxious, disoriented day. I was wishing for Al to come by, just someone to help allay the fears. Picked up Chrissy at a party. Thinking about that talk with Andy . . . about money . . . sort of sad . . . touching him and still the hostility. Went upstairs to change my clothes and saw Al's car pull up. I was so happy I thought I would die.

October 14—Had an argument with Al. The beginning of a very depressing time. Listening to the Vietnam Moratorium. What a despicable war. The White House is ringed by pickets and I am ringed by my emotions. Will my emotions ever be worked out satisfactorily? Seems unlikely . . . I don't know what is happening to me . . . my calculat-

ing self is not working very well. I need discipline.
I resolve to put my life in order.

October 15—Somewhat calmer. Will begin job soon
with Peerless, but I'm scared. I look at all the nice
little housewives and I'm envious. They don't have
to work . . . But . . . I'm excited also, a challenge. Something different to do. Make some money
. . . that is the thing! ! ! !

October 26—Dr. Z says brinkmanship is no good.
I've decided that prevention, or is it discretion, is the
better part of valor. Better get some contraceptives.
Resolve this day to THINK. Do things calculat-
ingly and with more thought given to planning my
life. I'd like to see this diary in a year. Will I be different? Went to Charley Brown's Friday nite . . .
what a scene.

A year later

August 27, 1970
Had the party last night. I feel terrible today, depressed, upset with myself for feeling so bad about
Al and Andy and the divorce. I hope someday I will
feel good again and secure.

September 24
Ironic that I've spent a whole year trying to do
something with my life, and I am still almost in the
same boat. Didn't I move?

September 25
Andy called this morning. I heard that little kid
crying in the background. I felt so jealous of him
having a mate to wake up with . . . I was so angry.
Then I thought of T.H. and H.B. [husbands of
friends]—all upstanding men. Are all men susceptible to extramarital affairs? If I believed that, I

couldn't go on. Part of my problem now is feeling bad about sex, but a lot of the feelings are about not having anyone for a lover, husband . . . I really believe I am unlovable . . . what a terrible feeling . . . I seem to be so careful about who I go out with. I am so afraid of being promiscuous!

Looking back and rereading my diary, I can feel compassion for myself. I was so confused then! So dependent upon men! So unsure if I could make anything of my life. And out of my loneliness and pain grew the desire to begin an organization that would help me and help other women. And that is how Nexus was born. Now I'd like to share with you what I have learned, what other women have learned.

2

The Case against Lawyers

About two years before Andy and I separated from each other, I went to see a lawyer. While I wasn't ready for a breakup, I wanted to find out what I could expect when and if Andy and I did divorce.

I think this was a good move, and I'd advise any woman thinking about divorce to do the same. The more concrete information you can get, the better off you'll be.

The lawyer I chose was recommended to me by a male friend, my insurance agent, and the only person I could confide in at the time. My lawyer was just out of law school and very understanding. I liked him and, in fact, had fantasies about falling in love with him. I was still looking for a man who was going to be my savior and take care of me forever.

When choosing a lawyer, it is important to choose someone whom you like and trust. But it's also important to choose a lawyer who is experienced in matrimonial law. The lawyer I chose wasn't, and that was my first mistake.

He told me I had no legal grounds for divorce. I couldn't

prove cruel and inhuman treatment, and Andy was not in an adulterous relationship at the time as far as I knew. He added that, even if he were, adultery was hard to prove, and detectives were usually prohibitively expensive. He said that if I wanted a divorce, I should make life so miserable for my husband that he would move out.

I had been worried about not being able to get any monetary support from Andy if I requested the divorce and he opposed it, but this lawyer told me some good news—that I could expect Andy to pay the legal fees and that I could receive one-half to one-third of his income if we divorced. He let me know that I had some rights at a time when I wasn't sure I had any.

Yet, because he was inexperienced, he neglected to tell me to start keeping a financial diary of all our expenses in order to substantiate the kind of money that Andy was making. That's what I should have done, and if I had, I might have received a larger divorce settlement.

Two years later, when my marriage had only deteriorated further, I went back to this same lawyer. By this time, Andy was having an affair, yet the lawyer never suggested that I get a detective to consolidate my suspicions —which he should have done.

He suggested instead that I ask Andy to leave our home for a four-to-six-week temporary separation. Andy did this after much haggling, but I was left high and dry without any money. The lawyer never suggested that Andy agree to provide me with alimony and child support during this period. Several months later, we finally had to go to court to petition for funds.

Six weeks after Andy moved out, he came to the house to pick up his summer clothes and golf clubs. He was going on a little trip to Puerto Rico with his girlfriend. The lawyer then should have suggested I hire a detective to corroborate adultery, which would have been grounds for divorce. But he never suggested doing this, and like most women, I was too naive to go against my lawyer's strategy.

After six months, this lawyer told me that my case was too complicated for him to handle and that he was turning it over to another lawyer. At that point, I should have said, "Hey, wait a minute. I'll pick my own lawyer, thank you." But again, I was too naive, trusting, inexperienced, and dependent to do anything that assertive. I meekly went to meet my new lawyer—a slick, high-priced Madison Avenue attorney who greeted me with the words, "Now tell me what kind of a bastard your husband is. I'm going to help you get the son of a bitch."

This lawyer finally told me to get all my bills and financial records together, and he got me a temporary alimony settlement—which, as it usually does—turned out to set the precedent for what I was finally granted when my divorce came through.

By this time, Andy had left the job he'd been in and gone into business on his own—now earning about half of what he'd previously made. My support was based on the smaller sum, and it has never been changed, even though he subsequently sold his business and went back to a job that paid him as much as, and even more than, he was first making.

Because Andy did not want a divorce, this second lawyer also suggested that I should force him to grant me one by acting like a shrew—by throwing his clothes out, by calling his family and business associates and telling them what a bastard he was. But I refused to act this way. I felt that I knew my husband pretty well, and that if I pushed him too hard or made him too angry, I would pay for it in the end. In retrospect, I think my instinct was right, even though my lawyer chided me for being "too ladylike."

I finally got Andy to sign a legal separation agreement

by waiving the money he owed me—namely, the legal fees, the money I'd spent on maintaining our home and paying the bills during those months we'd been separated. I never should have waived my right to any of that money. I should have waited Andy out—eventually he would have wanted to remarry and I could have had the divorce more on my terms. Yet, because the lawyer wanted to wrap up his case in order to collect his fee, he advised me to do something that actually was not in my best interests. Again, because I didn't know any better, I did as I was told.

This is my own case against lawyers, and I have heard many, many others—terrible stories of women who have been exploited and hurt. My advice to any woman who has to deal with a divorce is, don't go to a lawyer naively and put your life in his or her hands. Prepare yourself and learn as much as you can. Don't be trusting; don't be naive; don't be self-effacing. You can be polite and businesslike, but you don't have to be overly grateful. Remember, a lawyer is being paid to serve your needs.

SOME HARD FACTS ABOUT LAWYERS

The following are some conclusions I have come to regarding lawyers. I might add that there are lawyers who do not exploit women and who have high ethical standards. I am simply listing here what to watch out for. Wherever possible, I have tried to get corroboration from lawyers who are eager to see women treated ethically and decently. Special thanks here go to the Honorable Joseph R. Damon, Assistant Attorney General of the State of New York, formerly a matrimonial specialist with whom I've discussed this chapter.

1. *Divorce lawyers often push for divorce, to your detriment.*

Many lawyers will not be interested in helping you reconcile, if that is a possibility. They may not suggest to you that your case sounds as if your differences might be helped by counseling, and they may pressure you to take certain steps before you are ready. The reason—they do not make money from a reconciliation.

2. *They want to wrap up your case as soon as possible so they can collect their fee.*

A lawyer says, "The first thing a lawyer is concerned with is who is going to pay him. Usually the fees for the wife's lawyer are the obligation of the husband. The fee situation lies at the bottom of the whole thing. The longer he works for the woman, the more fee he accumulates. There are very few women who can pay their lawyers. Therefore, the lawyer has to petition the judge to have the husband pay the fee. Because he is not sure whether the bench will award the kind of fee that is commensurate with the time involved, he doesn't want to gamble too far, and he is eager to wrap up the case. Would he push a woman to make a settlement that he feels in his heart is not quite as good as she should have in order to "wrap it up" faster? Absolutely. A lawyer's time is his stock in trade."

3. *Divorce lawyers fail to give you the correct information or all the information you need.*

One woman I know had been married to her husband for nineteen-and-a-half years before she was divorced. Because she had not been married to him for the full twenty years, she lost Social Security benefits she would have been entitled to. If her lawyer had warned her about this, she would have postponed her divorce.

Another woman I know did not get the necessary help she needed from her lawyer. As she tells it, "My husband had a very shrewd lawyer, and he demanded trial by jury. The jury was all-male, composed of blue-collar workers. My husband's lawyer set out to prove that I was a Jewish princess who had everything—a large home in a very affluent area, jewels, furs, and a full-time maid. The lawyer brought up all kinds of evidence to prove that my husband was a good guy.

"I wanted my lawyer to point out that my husband had neglected me emotionally. But my lawyer, being the inadequate person that he was, was totally unprepared. He said to me, 'Oh, don't worry about that.'

"Charles kept bringing in witness after witness, his brother, his sister, to say, 'Yes, Charles did all these things for his wife. He is a devoted father.' So I said to my lawyer, 'Let's bring in my mother and my sister to say what my husband was really like.' And my lawyer said to me, 'Oh, now, don't get excited! It isn't necessary.' I can only say that I felt like a lamb going to slaughter. I was frustrated and completely sick to my stomach. I often wonder today if he was in collusion with my husband. As a result, I did not get my divorce. He was permitted to move back into the house—where he proceeded to try to torment me to death."

I've heard of other lawyers in some states neglecting to put in a dollar alimony clause—which gives a woman who has not asked for alimony the right to petition later for it, should need arise. There are all kinds of precautions that should be taken and often are not!

A lawyer, too, may not fully warn you to look carefully toward the future. I didn't insist that Andy pay for college or for orthodontists' costs. My children were pretty young then and I thought I'd soon marry again. Now, seven years later, I'm still unmarried and I wish I'd asked for those things. If a man resists agreeing to such costs, a compromise is possible. He can say, "If I'm making X amount of money, and the child wants to go to school, I'll do what I can." This at least is some form of written commitment and better than nothing.

4. *A divorce lawyer may proposition you.*

One evening, my lawyer came to my home to bring some papers for me to sign. As he was leaving, he kissed me. I was so surprised and unprepared that I kissed him back. I think I would have felt too guilty to tell him off then. After all, wasn't he helping me? Shouldn't I be grateful to him for all he was doing for me? At the time, I was frightened and felt I had little control over my life. So I kissed him, even though I wasn't attracted to him.

A week or so later, as I was leaving his office, he got up from his desk, walked me to the door, and said to me, "Jane, I know you need some clothes. Go to a place called ——————, on the Upper East Side, and charge whatever you want to me. I want you to enjoy life."

I walked out of his office with my face burning. It was humiliating to have a man make such a bold proposition—I wasn't *that* naive. I knew that if I charged clothes to him I'd end up in his bed the following week.

I was smart enough to know that this was a bad idea I wanted no part of. But the fact that he had the nerve to prey on my fears of being alone and powerless, and possibly broke, still angers me to this day.

Whatever you do, don't become involved. A lawyer who propositions you knows that you are vulnerable, lonely, frightened, and defenseless, and he is not above taking advantage of your situation. This may be easy for you to fall into, because chances are your lawyer is the first new man you're meeting as a single woman. Moreover, you trust him a little because he's taking your case and helping you.

But sleeping with your lawyer confuses your entire legal picture. If he's doing something you don't like and you're sleeping with him, it won't be easy to disagree or refuse to go along.

Carla had an affair with her lawyer, and because she felt she was in love with him, she didn't protest some of the nasty things he did. However, her husband became so bitter at her lawyer's obnoxious treatment of him that he fought hard not to give Carla as much as he otherwise would have.

The last two people you should be sleeping with are your brother-in-law and your lawyer!

5. *In an effort to get the case wrapped up, a divorce lawyer may suggest you behave in a way that can alienate your husband and be detrimental to you in the long run.*

Here's a case that came to my attention recently, which is not atypical. Joan, who had three young children, wanted a divorce from Harold, because he was having an affair. Harold was a government worker earning $18,000 a year.

Joan's lawyer advised her not to allow her husband to see the children until he agreed to her demands for alimony and child support. She did as her lawyer suggested; her husband consequently kidnapped the children and went into hiding. The children were found after several weeks had gone by—but by the time the case was settled, the lawyer's fees totaled some $20,000.

I believe it would have been in the best interests of this family to have tried to work out an amicable settlement, and to have put that money toward the children's education, rather than into a lawyer's pocket.

Yet, by coaxing tempers to run high and by suggesting hostile acts which can only antagonize the other party, divorce lawyers escalate the marital conflict and thereby justify their high fees.

What can you do to protect yourself? You have to be prepared to play a role at least equal to your lawyer's in your divorce. Don't be so quick to let your lawyer guide you and make decisions. There is a learned timidity on the part of many women when dealing with such male authority figures as lawyers, but you have to resist it. Be prepared to tell a lawyer what you want and to say, "I don't like what you're doing," when you don't.

Look for a matrimonial specialist and visit three before you make your choice. Ask each how he or she would handle your case. You may be able to get an initial interview at no cost, or the fee may range between $25 and $100, although this varies considerably.

Don't choose an inexperienced lawyer. Find out what you will be charged and how.

Many women, by the way, are so intimidated by their husbands that they allow them to choose their lawyers for them and to dictate the terms of the divorce just as they dictated the terms of the marriage. Don't let yourself be bullied. Get yourself a lawyer who will work in *your* best interests.

Word of mouth is usually the best way to get a lawyer. Don't choose a friend. Talk to other women and men who've been divorced. Parents Without Partners also has a legal referral service.

Use your instincts. You don't need a high-powered, expensive lawyer unless there's a lot of money involved or your husband is fighting for custody of the children. Moreover, if your husband is a gentle man and you hire a pugnacious lawyer, he may antagonize your husband so much that you may lose in the long run. On the other hand, if your husband has a high income but won't be fair, he may choose a tough lawyer and you must do the same.

If you're calm enough, read all you can about the divorce laws in your state. Any local chapter of the National Organization for Women can help you get information. Read books and talk to other divorced women. Don't assume that lawyers know everything they should know, because they often don't.

Try to gather as much financial information as you can. Many husbands, especially those who are in business for themselves, hide their earnings. Income is rather difficult to prove because even though the courts do have investigative powers, some men do know how to hide money. Therefore, a woman's settlement often will not be based on her husband's real salary. If a man claims he earns $10,000 a year, but your records show he was *spending* $25,000 a year, the judge will have more to go on when deciding on a divorce settlement.

Be as businesslike as you can. It may help if you bring a friend or relative with you—someone who is calm. If you're crying and frantic, this will not help your case.

I think you should expect compassion and empathy from your lawyer. However, a lawyer is not a counselor or psychiatrist, and you shouldn't expect him to be.

When you want to call your lawyer, think twice. You're paying for every minute he or she talks to you. Your first impulse may be to call when anything goes wrong, but perhaps you can call someone else first. If you're depressed, call a friend or therapist—not your lawyer.

From the beginning of your separation, if you have your eye on divorce, it is usually best to obtain written property, support, and custody agreements. The reason for signing a written legal agreement is that it protects everyone—especially women and children.

On the other hand, in some few cases, it is not in your best interests to sign a legal agreement as soon as possible. If you think your husband will acquiesce to your wishes the longer you put off signing, that's the way you should go. You need expert legal advice here.

Sharon was separated from her husband for two years

without any legal agreement. Every month her husband would come by the house and scream over the bills that had accumulated. Sharon had to put up with this because she had no legal agreement about the money she'd receive. She put a great deal of energy into dealing with his moods, energy that could have been used to rebuild her life.

A woman who has a legal separation is usually much freer to live her own life. As impotent as courts are, a written agreement is your legal implement.

If your husband doesn't want to sign, figure out why. It may be a clue that he wants to be back in the marriage, or it may be he is stalling. On the other hand, if he wants the divorce and you don't, you can use your signing as a bargaining tool to win better terms.

Try to get an agreement that somewhat pleases you both. What a man gives you in the beginning sets a precedent, so don't accept less than you need. It's best to keep a diary of all expenses for a few weeks so that you can be as accurate as possible. Include everything from manicures to car costs to money spent on birthday gifts. Many women who want divorces often feel so guilty that they relinquish their rights to any of the family possessions, but they regret this later.

ALIMONY

Today there is great confusion about alimony. More and more men are reluctant to pay alimony, and statistics show that fewer women are asking for it, in spite of the fact that the divorce rate is increasing. The new thinking seems to be that now that women are "liberated" they can fend for themselves.

However, in my opinion, this is a fallacy, and I think alimony is justified in many cases. There is still job discrimination against women, and most women who have worked in their homes do not have the ability to begin earning the same salaries as their husbands. Says lawyer Emily Jane Goodman, "The reality of our economic and social structure is that women have been made economically dependent on men. It is the exceptional situation where women have achieved economic independence." She prefers to call alimony severance or retirement pay, while lawyer Diane Black prefers to think of alimony as a deferred compensation for contributions to the home.

I might add, too, that, contrary to myth, there are very few women who are living idly on alimony and child support while their husbands are having a hard time surviving. According to a 1976 report in the *Chicago Tribune*, in a recent survey of 1,500 women across the country, only 14 percent said they had been awarded alimony.

Moreover, statistics show that only 38 percent of child-support orders are fully complied with during the first year, and by the tenth year after divorce, the figure falls to 13 percent. Legal action slides from 19 percent in the first year to 2 percent in the eighth year.

Research conducted by a New York Assembly subcommittee highlighted the incidence of men who "took off" after their wives worked to get them through school and into professions. This usually happened when the woman was in her forties and her children were half-grown.

Diana Du Broff, a matrimonial lawyer, says that many more divorced women would be on welfare if they were not "thrown back into the arms of their parents."

Moving out of state is a common ploy men use—so is quitting a job. Often, when a man remarries, the courts must take into consideration the income and needs of both families.

"No fault" divorce is now becoming more common; yet according to a study done by the National Organization for Women, the decision about assets in such a case often does not take into account the contributions of the wife. Her stocks and bonds, her entire financial investment, all her employee benefits, her social security were all vested in her husband and her role as wife and homemaker. If this investment is given no value in court, the newly divorced older wife is wiped out.

Lawyers are now seeing more and more women, even those with young children, refusing to ask for alimony and even child support because they consider it "demeaning." They see it as being owned by the husband.

Yet I've seen women later regret that they did not ask for what they were entitled to. I believe that until women achieve an equal place in society, they should not shoulder all the monetary burdens in a divorce.

Emily Jane Goodman adds, "I see incredible stuff in the courts: desperate women getting fifteen dollars a week, judges who act as if economic equality is an accomplished fact of life."

And it is clear that economic equality is not a way of life: women earn 59 percent of what men of comparable skills and education earn.

The general rule of thumb today: women rarely get 50 percent of a husband's set income. Even when there are children, the payment will frequently be as low as 30 percent. One lawyer in New Jersey said he considered a woman lucky if she could get 10 to 15 percent of the husband's take-home pay. Courts give the husband the edge today, on the assumption that he may want to remarry.

Moreover, the working wife can expect relatively little alimony. She has to concentrate on getting child support, and she should get together as many bills as possible to show the court what it costs to raise the children.

If you and your husband are able to settle your money affairs without a bitter fight, you will be a rare, lucky couple. In the majority of divorces, the money fight becomes the last battleground. It may have less to do with real need and more to do with emotions. Each person—man and wife—tries to manipulate so that he or she wins. Winning assuages the hurt a little bit.

However, the more unemotional and logical you can be when deciding on the division of the spoils, the better.

If he's paying you alimony, you may not be able to get full custody of the house—you may have to share custody. On the other hand, if he's reluctant to pay you, and he makes the bulk of the family income, you probably should fight for the house, for it may be the only item you'll have that can be converted into cash if you need it. If he's getting the stocks and bonds, you may have the right to the house. A good lawyer can advise you here.

Check out with the lawyers you consult what is realistic for you to expect from the divorce. Many women, say lawyers, are unrealistic in their expectations. Gabriel Cohen, a lawyer, offers the following advice:

"A very typical example is that a man leaves home for another woman, and the wife comes in and says, 'There are three of us to support, and my husband earns $50,000 per year. I think I should get $35,000 of it, because I need it.' Perhaps it is true that she does need it, but that is the standard of living she was used to when she was married. After taking taxes into consideration, the man has to be left with enough money to live on or else he will lose his incentive, his job, or want to leave town.

"The courts are going to look at it in that light. This is hard for the wife to understand when she has been so badly mistreated morally, ethically, and emotionally. She feels she should get everything she needs first and he should live on whatever is left."

Lawyer Elliott Epstein gives another example. "A woman in her thirties with two children makes $17,000 and her husband makes $13,000. She wants him to pay her over half of his income for child support. However, this is not realistic. The courts will not allow this because this will not leave the man enough money to give him the incentive to go to work each day. My obligation as the wife's attorney is to do the best for her, I also have to leave the man with enough income so that he has the motivation to go to work and be able to continue to support the wife."

I've heard men bitterly complain, "My wife thinks I'm rich," when they are really just average wage-earners who went into debt throughout their marriages in order to support a life-style they really couldn't afford. Since there is always less money after a divorce, it is unrealistic to expect this kind of life-style to be continued.

On the other hand, I am always surprised at the number of women who do not know what their husbands earn and who do not have property or stocks and bonds jointly in their names. This leaves a woman in a weakened position when she is fighting for a just settlement.

A woman cannot afford to be naive when it comes to bargaining with her husband. I know one woman whose husband told her, after twenty-five years of marriage, that he had been a homosexual for many years and that he wanted a divorce so that he could live with a male companion. She felt so sorry for him that she asked for very little money. "I knew I'd have to go to work after all these years, and I wasn't prepared," she said. "But I felt that he was worse off than I was—that he had to deal with all kinds of emotional problems caused by his condition."

Three weeks after his divorce, this man married his twenty-two-year-old secretary. The alleged homosexuality had been a ploy to win sympathy from his wife.

Another lawyer tells this story: "I know a case right

now of a man who wants out of his marriage. His secretary is pregnant and he wants to marry her. The wife came to me—they were married for fifteen years. He had signed a separation agreement that was so sweet that she couldn't refuse it. But her lawyer had no safeguards built into the agreement. After the divorce, he paid her nothing. It was the old hoax, 'Promise her anything, but give her Arpège.'

"There are ways to safeguard a separation agreement. Her lawyer could have had the agreement bonded, and if he defaulted, the bonding company would be responsible. The attorney for the wife was blinded by the husband's generosity. This wife would have been better off staying married until she could get exactly what she wanted. Some cases don't call for an immediate divorce."

If you think your husband may get tired of paying you, consider a lump-sum settlement. Another thing that is becoming more accepted today is payment for a wife to get "job training" and schooling. The man agrees to put a woman through school and to pay her until she gets on her feet and is able to earn a certain income. Naturally, such arrangements depend on a lot of factors, such as the woman's age, aspirations, and educational background.

I don't believe in pushing a man to the wall and trying to get every last penny you can from him. He may then feel justified in fighting tooth and nail to give you the least he can get away with.

Mary accepted $110 a week from her husband as child support even though she felt he could afford to pay her more. "I knew," she says, "that he was the kind of man who needs to win. So I let him pay me what he wanted, and because he came out on top, I get more from him—extras that aren't part of our agreement." He bought her a car and loaned her money for a down-payment on a summer home.

This isn't too unusual. Some men like to feel their ex-wives still need them, but they want to feel that it's their decision—that everything they're doing is because they wish to, not have to.

Many lawyers won't suggest this kind of approach. But lawyers often offer bad advice. Your lawyer may urge you to fight your husband for everything, down to who gets the permanent-press sheets. And his lawyer may suggest the same. But is this the kind of battle you really want?

A lot of bizarre behavior is started because of lawyers—people who were normally pretty nice start behaving like monsters, changing locks on doors, issuing threats, burglarizing homes. Often, as I've said, lawyers encourage this kind of behavior so that things will build to a head and the case can be concluded.

Because the fight isn't over when a marriage breaks up, money and children usually become the last two battlegrounds.

The maintenance of goodwill, when possible, is the best thing a woman who is still financially dependent on a man can do for herself. The ex-husband of a friend of mine remarried, moved to another state, and had two children by his second wife. In the meantime, my friend came into a rather large inheritance. Yet her husband still continues to send child-support payments because he values the relationship with his children and because he and his ex-wife are able to be civil to each other to this day. She tried to be fair in her dealings with him and this has paid off for her.

On the other hand, don't be a pussy-cat either. If you have a husband whom you have to fight, get the best lawyer you can and fight. Often the woman in a divorce feels so demoralized and depressed that she doesn't have the energy to fight.

Marion hadn't worked outside the home since the early years of her marriage, when she worked as a secretary to put her husband through school. Fifteen years later, her husband met another woman and told Marion he wanted a divorce. He said he didn't feel alimony was justified since Marion was young (thirty-six) and could get a job.

Marion accepted his rationale. Deep down, she felt that it was somehow her fault that he left—if she'd been a "better wife" he might have stayed. She also felt he was right—she could get a job. Therefore, she was ready to accept only small child-care payments.

However, Marion neglected to perceive that while she could get a job, she couldn't get one that would support her in the life-style she was living. Moreover, she had been working in the home while her husband was building a career and his earning capacity. Her time in the home had eroded her earning capacity. What she should fight for is alimony or a lump-sum payment until she can earn what she could have been earning all those years. This is her right, and she doesn't have to feel guilty about asserting it.

I also want to give a word of caution here about payments. Many a man promises to pay X number of dollars initially. However, as the years go by and he gets involved in his own life, his incentive to pay sometimes diminishes rapidly, especially if he has little contact with the children or if he is very bitter about the settlement. Many women spend a great deal of time trying to get a man who won't pay, to pay. Yet if he lives out of the state or can show a lessened income, your case is a difficult one. Therefore, if you can get some built-in guarantees in the agreement, such as bonding, you're better off.

Will he pay? Look at his past record. Does he usually pay his debts? Does he love his children? Does he take his responsibilities seriously? Does he usually do what he says he'll do? Does he gamble? Is he an angry, vindictive person? Does saving face with his family matter to him? Does he have friends who don't pay or who put women down? Asking yourself these questions can help you to assess your situation realistically. If you don't think he'll continue to pay, you can also try to get a block of stock or a piece of real estate held in escrow by an attorney.

The court system as it presently works is not in the best interests of women, and attorneys' fees can be outrageously high. Several women's groups, including FOCUS and the National Organization for Women, are working to get more equitable treatment. You may want to join these groups in their fight.

NOW has drafted a model marriage and divorce bill, working with Hofstra University's Associate Dean Judith Younger, her law students, and NOW members who have experienced divorce. Describing marriage as an "equal partnership," the bill calls for equal division of property. In a divorce, there would be "equitable" alimony and child support, with cost-of-living increases, "no fault" or not.

Before the trial, the dependent spouse would get money for legal fees, so both parties could retain lawyers of comparable ability. A security bond equal to one year's projected payments of child support and maintenance would be required.

Financial disclosure would be compulsory and payroll deductions could be made for support payments. A financial investigation and enforcement bureau would be set up. Training and vocational guidance would be offered for separated and divorced persons, and a widow or widower would be guaranteed half the assets of the marriage.

I also advise women who have to go to court, and who are frightened of going, to sit in beforehand and watch a few cases. When I had my divorce hearing, two friends went with me. One of them later divorced, and she told me how glad she was she had been to court with me. She was prepared.

Joe Damon points out, "Many people approach a lawyer with a degree of inferiority. People see their lawyer's diploma hanging on the wall and acquiesce quickly to the dictates of the attorney.

"Lay people should feel more secure. People with average educations and average incomes should not feel that they are overpowered in the law office. The lay person should go in and ask questions and discuss the case with family, friends, and counselors. This is an important step."

It can be easy for a lawyer to take the lead because most people seeking a divorce are in great emotional turmoil and want someone to lean on. But don't put your life in your lawyer's hands.

3

You and Your Ex-Husband

A formerly married woman's feelings about her ex-husband are usually terribly complex. I've seen many women feel very guilty about this—whether they wanted to murder their husbands or whether they wanted them back. I think it's important to explore these feelings, to analyze them and see what they really mean.

Many women find that after time has passed, and bitterness and anger subside, a wellspring of loving, caring, positive feelings for their ex-husbands emerges. Unfortunately, most women have been taught to feel guilty about having these kinds of caring, loving feelings. Marsha related at a meeting, "My therapist told me I was deliberately being destructive by thinking about my husband, since we'd been separated for a year and a half. He said I was wallowing in my misery." Yet when Marsha discussed her feelings at a meeting, every single woman in the room had experienced the same yearnings and longing she had. I, therefore, disagree with therapists who insist that these feelings are destructive, childish, foolish, or neurotic. The fact is—they're normal! If you have lived with a man and perhaps had children by him, you *do* have feelings toward that man. And just because you may want them to vanish, doesn't mean they will.

The emergence of positive, caring feelings for one's ex-spouse is a stage that practically every divorced woman I've ever talked to has experienced. Ann Marie, for instance, had been married for seventeen years. When she and Jim split up, he got their business and she got custody of their two sons. She and Jim had a nasty separation and only spoke to each other through the children.

Liberation was Ann Marie's new icon. She rejected everything in her background—all the values that had once been important to her. She threw out her dresses and began to wear jeans and tie-dyed tops. She tried every conceivable sexual experience—with groups, with other women, with men from different racial and religious backgrounds. She refused to go on conventional dinner dates and preferred whatever was way-out and different. One night, however, about three years after her separation, she arrived at a meeting dressed in a conservative dress and announced that she was going to church with her two children that Sunday. She also admitted that she was having second thoughts about her divorce and about her real feelings toward her husband. All this from a woman who was sure she hated her husband and her conventional marriage.

While Ann Marie's story is extreme, it corroborates what I'm saying—your feelings change with time. In her case, her reaction to her marital breakup had been an extreme breaking of all the rules that had run her life. This was such an overreaction to who she was and had been that there was a natural swinging back of the pendulum. And this is common too—most people don't move that far from the way they were reared and have lived. What Ann

Marie's story shows is that time heals—perhaps not completely, but to some degree.

ARE YOU THINKING ABOUT A RECONCILIATION?

Janice is another member of our group who talked about reevaluating her feelings toward her husband. She was twenty-seven years old and, after being married five years, decided she was bored and "wanted out." Her husband wasn't a good lover and their sex life was "as bland as pablum without honey." In the beginning of her separation, she was euphoric and did a lot of running—she went to singles bars, met a man and went to Venezuela with him for a long exciting weekend, and got a luxury apartment in the city. However, after months of running, she began to become depressed and thought about going back to her husband. "This life seems to be empty," she said.

For many women who've had a few disillusioning experiences—a love affair that's ended, a disappointment in a person she'd counted on—marriage may seem like a safety zone, a port in the storm. A substantial number of women seem to want to go back with their husbands at some time or another. Yet, it is worthwhile to examine these feelings.

Just because you have loving feelings toward your husband and yearnings to go back to the marriage doesn't mean that you have to act on those feelings. (Assuming that you can.) A lot of us have feelings for people, but that doesn't mean we want to live with them. You may love your brother, or sister, or mother, or friend, but not want to share daily life with them. And the same may be true for your husband, too.

Since going back to your husband is such a big decision, you have to evaluate it carefully. You can't act too hastily or you may regret it later. Here are some questions you can ask yourself.

1. *Why are you thinking of going back with your husband?*

Try to be honest with yourself. Is it for the money? For the children? For the security? Because you don't have another man right now? Because you've had a few disillusioning experiences? Because the single life has been a rude awakening and hasn't lived up to all your fantasies and expectations? Or because you really love your husband and feel you can live with him?

If you are lonely, or feel overwhelmed by money or child-rearing problems, you may yearn for the comfort and security of your marriage. But these aren't very good reasons for making a marriage work. Later on, you may find that you resent your husband and that you wish you'd given yourself more time to get your own life together.

2. *Why is he thinking about reconciling with you?*

Is he trying to seduce you back? If so, why? Is it because he genuinely loves you and is willing to make a real commitment? Is he open to changing? Or is he simply determined to win you back to meet his own needs? Is he the kind of man who has to win? Is his ego or pride making him act this way? Does he want to reconcile for legal reasons? Some men who aren't happy with what they agreed to in their legal separation agreements move back in with their wives so that the separation agreement can be declared null and void. Later, they can separate again and this time try to get a better agreement *for themselves.*

3. *Has he changed?*

I've found that there's a very large fantasy element that often operates when reconciliations are being considered. You so much want to believe that your husband has changed that you come to believe he has changed. Dull old Charlie who spent all his weekends in front of the TV has changed into a fascinating blend of Clark Gable and Gary

Cooper. (Women say things like, "Oh, he's so much fun now," or, "He's so romantic," or, "He's so sexy now.") However, you had better tread carefully because, while people can change to some degree, you can't make a new package out of anybody.

Beatrice was a fifty-year-old member of our group who'd been absolutely euphoric when she and her husband separated. "He dragged me down all those years," she said. "He was so dull, so lethargic, so depressed." She was thrilled to be free.

However, the day that her divorce papers came through, she experienced a different set of feelings. "My friends and I were all going to a singles bar," she said, "and I was excited to go. Then I opened my mail—it was late because I'd been out all day—and I saw those papers and started to sob. I couldn't stop. I went out with my friends anyway, but I cried all the way there."

Two ill-timed events added to her depression—she lost her job and her child ran away from home. She interpreted this running away as a signal that he wanted his parents to reunite. She began to see more of her husband—he wined and dined her as if they'd just met. Soon, she told her friends that she was going back to Jerome—that she was madly in love with him and that their sex life was "fantastic." This lasted for two months. Then they separated again, and this time they did divorce. "We just seemed to go right back to our old patterns," she said. "I thought he'd really changed, but he hadn't."

What had happened? Several things. Beatrice had gone back to Jerome when she felt particularly vulnerable and needy—she had lost a job she cared about and her son was giving her a lot of problems. She had a strong desire for an intact family. She also had had enough of a breathing space from her husband to permit the fantasy to operate that he had changed—that he was different from what he'd been all those years before. And his wining and dining her was very seductive—as it would be to most women.

However, in their case, neither one had changed very dramatically from what they'd always been, and therefore they faced the same problems they had faced before. And because their way of communicating hadn't changed either, once the seduction part of their courtship was over they were back fighting again.

This is not to say that reconciliations aren't possible, because in a small number of cases they are. However, the fantasy that an ex-husband has changed into an entirely new person is unrealistic.

4. *Have you changed?*

In order to save your marriage, both of you have to work at it. And that means *you* have to do some growing and changing too. So ask yourself if your expectations of your husband have changed? Of yourself? Of marriage? You may feel that you've been through so much and learned so much that you can make the relationship work now. However, this may be an intellectual idea but not an emotional reality.

For example, intermittently I have felt that I could go back with Andy and accept who he is without becoming upset. But eventually something would happen that would show me I was wrong. One time, I gave Andy some tickets for an event at Nicky's school—he was responsible for selling or buying his five tickets, as I was responsible for my five. He began to complain about this and I became angry—secretly angry. All my old feelings about him— that he was selfish and inconsiderate, that he put a damper on things by his complaints—served to remind me that not only had Andy not changed but that I hadn't either.

5. *What bothered you about your husband?*

Try to remember. His inertia? His lack of caring? His

inability to communicate with you? His attitude toward the children? His selfishness? Did he work too much or too little? Did he care too much or too little about money? Was he cheap or always in debt? Did he drink too much? Hit you? Gamble? Go out with other women?

Many of these characteristics, or behavior patterns, aren't very easy for a person to change—unless he's in therapy or has a strong motivation to change.

6. *Why did you break up?*

When you're thinking about reconciling, you don't usually think about those reasons that caused you to break up in the first place. But they're important to face because the same problems you've had will probably come up again.

7. *Are you reconciling because you feel guilty? Or he feels guilty?*

Guilt often plays a role in reconciliations, especially guilt concerning your children. When Marsha's youngest son came down with cancer, she began to want her ex-husband back—even though he was living with another woman. Because he felt so sad about his son's illness, he was susceptible to the idea. Soon, he was living with Marsha again. However, this didn't last very long, for he and Marsha really didn't love each other. It was his guilt dictating his decisions, but that wasn't a strong enough reason to make a marriage viable.

8. *Are you reconciling because you want to win?*

Do you want to prove you can get him back so you won't feel so rejected? Could this be the motivation? If you find that the reconciliation picture looks negative, but you still want it, see if you can remain in the "just thinking" phase a little while. You may long for the security of your marriage now, but two weeks from now, when things are looking up, you may be delighted by your freedom and independence. Often those longings for your marriage have less to do with your feelings for your ex than with your needs for security and familiarity And these needs may change or you may find another relationship that is more satisfying.

If you decide to try once more and it doesn't work, you may be in for a pretty low period. Many women report that they feel more despairing when their second try doesn't work than when they first broke up.

Bernice said, "It was worse than when we first broke up because it seemed so final. And I really had hoped that we both could change—I was in a kind of romantic haze for the first week we were back together. But when the fighting started again and we both realized there was no way we could live together, that was terrible—that reality."

On the other hand, if a reconciliation attempt doesn't work, you can at least have the satisfaction of knowing that you did everything you could to give the marriage a chance and you'll be more certain of where you stand emotionally vis-à-vis your husband. Now you can be sure that your marriage is over.

Think carefully about what a reconciliation attempt will do to you. Think, too, how an attempt at getting together again will affect the children. If your children get their hopes up and it doesn't work, will they be confused? Will it hurt them even more?

If you still decide you want to try for a reconciliation, do it with a minimum amount of exposure. Don't announce to the whole world that you're going back.

Perhaps you can date secretly in the beginning. See how it is to be with him. There's often a strong need to tell the world. "Look, we're not such failures after all. We're getting back together. Everything's all patched up." But if it doesn't work, and you've told everyone you thought it would, you may feel pretty humiliated.

If you can, try to go for some counseling before you

date Resist having sex with your ex for a while. Sex is a big pull.

If you do feel that you have to tell the children, explain that you don't know if the reconciliation is going to work. Help them from getting their hopes up too much. This is *the* biggest fantasy most children have. They long for a home that is all together—mother and father and kiddies, and this dream sometimes never dies completely. My own children, after seven years, still hold out some bit of hope— I can tell by remarks they make.

Handling the progress of your relationship in secrecy is far better for your children than trying to explain that "even though we are dating, it may not work." In their heads, it is a "fait accompli," and they are already dreaming of the wonderful, together, happy family. This is not only true for ten-year olds but for twenty-year-olds as well.

GAMES MEN AND WOMEN PLAY

If Andy doesn't see me for a while, he'll find a reason for seeing me. The same is true for me. And I know many couples for whom this holds true.

I believe that's because the marriage bond is so strong that there's an enormous need to maintain contact with one's spouse even after divorce. The need springs from a variety of feelings—including the need to express one's anger and to score points against the other person. These needs produce a lot of game-playing.

Game-playing can be extremely destructive. I've seen many women terribly upset by what I would call classic games men play. And I know I used to be distraught over some of the games Andy would play.

Here are some of the games I've found to be the most common between ex-spouses:

Game 1: Look who I've got with me.

One Saturday, after we'd been separated about a year, Andy came as usual to pick up the children. Only this time he had a woman with him—a young woman in hot pants who proceeded to parade around my front yard. I looked out the window and couldn't believe my eyes.

I later found out that this is not at all unusual behavior. Men frequently bring their women friends around. A man does this to show you he's still virile, to hurt you, to make you sorry you gave him up. Or he may be bringing her around because he can't be alone, even with his children.

In Andy's case, I think he simply wanted a reaction from me. And he got it. I screamed at him to "get that woman off my lawn." I was furious and hurt, and I lost control.

Today, however, I can see the humor in the situation. Moreover, I feel I could have handled the problem in a different way. Now, rather than throw a tantrum, I would wait until later and tell him privately that he was upsetting me. I think this would have been a more mature way to handle the situation, and I also think it would have saved my children some confusion and embarrassment. I know that Nicky felt he was being disloyal to me after the four of them drove off, leaving me to stew.

I see this kind of situation all the time. The first or second time it happens, you can be furious and bitter, especially if you aren't seeing anyone you like. You may be very jealous that he's off having a marvelous life while you're sitting home lonely and depressed. However, while he may be trying to show you that he *is* having a marvelous life, it may not be that great. He may be having problems with the woman he's seeing, or he may not really like her either. He may be just as confused and scared as you are.

When Andy married again, about a year after our divorce was final, I was very upset and jealous. In my fantasies, they had a marvelous relationship, while I had no one. However, I later found out they had many, many problems, and they were divorced after about a year. So my jealousy was to a large extent unfounded.

If your ex is going to parade women around, perhaps he should pick up the children somewhere else so that you don't have to be part of his game-playing. At the same time, I certainly don't feel that you can stop him from seeing the children because of this. That will be destructive to your children and to your relationship with them.

Jealousy is one of the most devastating emotions to experience, and I've experienced intense jealousy, anger, and bitterness. But I also know that as you get more satisfaction from your own life, the jealousy does diminish.

Game 2: Look how I've changed.

Andy once bought a pair of baggy, mustard-colored corduroy pants. He wore them around the house every weekend. I hated them, and I used to think he wore them just to spite me. Once we'd been separated for a while, he began to wear tight European-cut pants, French jeans—he became a much snazzier dresser.

This is very typical of the kind of changes men make after they're divorced. Dull old Harry was overweight and used to sit in front of the TV all weekend long. Now he's lost weight, has acquired a tan and three smashing new suits. He tells you he's learning to dance and to ski—things you wanted him to do while you were married. Or Bill will pull up into the driveway with a new car and a spruced-up image, while you're having trouble paying the electric bill.

Many women react very violently to changes of this kind in their husbands. You may feel furious that he wouldn't dress up during your marriage and that now he looks so nice. You may be bitter and disappointed, and it's perfectly understandable that you feel this way. I was very angry that Andy looked like a man on the town at times when I felt like Hilda the Housewife. I was furious that I had two young children constantly in tow while he was free to play the gay blade.

However, what I realize now is that many times we accept these outward changes as an indication that this man has changed into a marvelous new person. This "new" persona most likely is a way for him to handle his pain, keep busy, and make him feel better about himself.

We may be furious that he didn't care enough about us to make these changes while we were married, but you have to realize that before he was in a safe place. He wasn't insecure enough *to have to make* changes.

I believe the way to deal with your jealousy is to concentrate on your own life and what you are doing to improve yourself in every way. Recount to yourself the REAL reasons you got out of your marriage—even if he left you—because the pain of that should be enough to bring you back to seeing what is really important instead of some surface changes. Remember, clothes don't make the man.

I remember one weekend when Andy came in looking great and announced that he was going on vacation—I took a look at myself and decided that I needed some improving, too. So I picked up the phone and called the hairdresser and made an appointment.

Game 3: See if you can get the money.

My husband never played this game with me. He's always been on time with his payments, and I am extremely grateful for that.

However, many men are not as responsible. Or, because they are in control of the money, they try to manipulate you, threaten you, or frighten you.

Ask yourself *why* he's doing what he's doing. Is he holding back the money to prove he's still the boss? Is he trying to maintain contact? Does he feel overburdened with payments? Does he want to ruin you? Once you know his motives, you'll be in a better position to handle this.

You can always involve your lawyer and take your ex-husband to court. Many women do this because they have no other choice. The courts are your legal weapon, and your ex-husband may shape up if you take this route. You can also appeal to his family or his boss for help; perhaps he'll pay you to save face. But if he really doesn't want to pay you, he won't.

On the other hand, the better the relationship you have with your ex-husband, and the more he is involved with the children, the more readily he'll pay.

It's easy to stop paying an enemy, but if a man is concerned about his family, he will pay. Guilt or responsibility or genuine caring feelings, or a combination of these, will keep him paying. Being nice to him may go against your grain, but if you're not financially self-sufficient, I would think twice about ventilating all your hostile feelings.

One man I used to date periodically withheld the money he owed his wife. He said he fully intended to pay her eventually, but he wanted her to sweat it out. He justified his behavior by saying that she was hostile to him, that she didn't allow him in the house, and that she'd threatened to call the police if he so much as put one foot on her lawn. Withholding the money was his way of getting even with her. He made her call him again and again, and he relished her panic. He knows exactly what he's doing.

While his behavior is deplorable (as is a system in which a woman has to be subjected to this), I think it would be in this woman's best interests to establish a more cooperative arrangement with him so that she doesn't have to suffer this way. I would try to put all my emotions aside and treat the matter as a business relationship. In business, you have to be polite to people you dislike. In the case of a divorce it often pays to be polite to the husband you despise.

It's best to make a strong appeal to the man, e.g., "I need you to be a father and the kids need your support." This is a sound approach and one that has worked for many women. Unfortunately, few lawyers will give you this kind of advice. They may tell you to make scenes, call his parents, tell lies about him to his friends and co-workers.

But all of this venom may make him so embittered that he'll feel justified in using every dirty trick against you. Most people want to be liked—and that includes your ex-husband. If you can allow him to see himself as a good guy, you can benefit in the long run.

Game 4: The kids love me more than you.

In many divorces, each parent wants to prove he or she is the best parent—and children become the grounds for playing out the competition.

The ex-husband of one of my friends bought clothes and toys for his son but insisted he only wear the clothes (and use the toys) when they were together. Little Jimmy would go to his father's in his old clothes, put on his new clothes for the day with his dad, then put on his old clothes when he was going back to his mother. The father bought Jimmy a bike, but Jimmy could only ride it when he was at his father's house.

My friend dealt with this by sending Jimmy to see his father in the worst clothes he had. His father was so humiliated he finally agreed to let his son wear his good clothes all the time.

Another way my friend could have handled this would have been to say to Jimmy, "This is a silly game and I'm sorry he's involving you in it. I wish you could bring your nice clothes or your bike home, too. But Daddy's angry with me now, so we'll have to accept this situation for a while."

She also might have tried getting a third party to help her husband see that his game-playing could hurt their son.

Some fathers use money as a tool to win their children over. The same man I dated who was postponing paying his wife played this game too. One day, he and I and all our children went to a playland for kids. He has two daughters, aged fifteen and eleven. He probably spent between $150 and $200 that day. Whatever his daughters wanted he gave them. He indulged them to the point of absurdity; even after a late dinner, when they could hardly keep their eyes open, he insisted on buying each of them one more stuffed toy apiece.

My feeling is that he buys them so much in order to annoy his wife and score points with the children. I think he loves his daughters, but I also think he's playing a game of "Look how much more I can give you than Mommy can."

If you are in the same kind of situation, try not to let your child see how angry you are if he receives a present from his father. Say something like, "That's nice, I bet you love it." Your anger will confuse your child and make him feel guilty.

Do something nice for yourself so that you don't feel so deprived. Let your anger out to a trusted friend. If you want to talk it over with your ex-husband, you can say something like, "You know I'm strapped for money and it upsets me when I see you giving Charlie and Jane those expensive presents. If you'd like to buy them something, fine, but it would help if you would consult me first because they need some clothes."

Game 5: Let's see if she's still interested in me.

Andy still flirts with me. If I say something like "I need a vacation," he'll say, "Why don't you take me along?" He teases me about my looks and about the phallic symbols in my paintings.

He also tantalizes me with bits of information about his life. He'll mention where he had dinner with his "lady friend." He'll let me know he's tired because he came in from a party at six-thirty A.M. Recently he gave Nicky some silky bikini underwear he didn't want anymore. I felt he was subtly letting me know that he was now wearing sexy bikini pants and not his married boxer shorts anymore!

I believe part of this game is an effort to get the message across: look at what you're missing—other people want me! It also seems important for Andy to know that I'm still interested in him, but I don't know why. If this were a few years ago, I might look on this as a sign that there was hope for a reconciliation. But now I see this as a game. I don't think there is any hope for a closer relationship, although I do think our friendly relationship will last.

I think that all of this is relatively harmless, although I also wonder if the small amount of dependency I have on this relationship makes it more difficult for me to find a second husband. I don't think so, but I can't be totally sure.

This is the point at which this kind of game—which is a very common one—can be destructive. Many men who play this game allow their ex-wives to cling to the hope of a reconciliation when that isn't possible.

For instance, one relatively new organization member lives only two blocks from her ex-husband, who has since remarried. She is extremely dependent on him; he helps her with the storm windows, with her car, and she spends a lot of time talking to him on the phone. Often she won't decide on her plans for the day until she's talked them over with him.

She believes that he still loves her. However, it looks to me as if he loves his new wife but feels guilty and concerned about his first wife. He also may enjoy the attention and dependence of two women.

I'm 100 percent for cooperation between an ex-husband and wife if it's possible. But I think the above relationship is not a healthy one, and her extreme dependence on this man is preventing her from building a more real and satisfying life.

Some men who are involved with another woman try to assuage their guilt by signaling to their wives that they're still in the running. Some women delude themselves ("I think he still loves me, or why would he have come over yesterday morning?") into thinking he might come back when he won't. If you want to badly enough, you can build a case for anything. It will help you if you can talk over your feelings with a trusted friend who will be honest with you. Don't choose a person who will say "Yes, he still loves you," just to make you feel better.

Of course, women can play games too. Some days when Andy came to pick up the children, I used to walk around in my old bathrobe with my hair uncombed. The message I was giving him was, "I think so little of you, I won't even run a comb through my hair."

However, on other visitation days, I would sashay around in my tennis dress. First, I knew Andy liked the way I looked in it, so I was playing the game "Look what I've got." But I also knew that it would aggravate him to see me in my tennis dress because I had refused to play tennis with him during the last years of our marriage. (He had been too critical of my playing, so that tennis with him wasn't fun for me.)

Some women play the game of looking as seductive as they can when their husbands come to pick up the children. "I wanted him to know what he lost," said one friend. Some women make a habit of being as nasty as possible all the time—on the phone and in person, constantly reminding the ex what a dope he has been and still is.

They impose ridiculous rules, such as making the husband call at an appointed hour or pick up the children and bring them back at a certain hour, and if the husband does not follow the rules exactly, then he cannot see the children for a while. He lives in constant fear of being late or doing the wrong thing. The woman who plays this game doesn't consider he might be late because of an unexpected delay in traffic or simply because he is enjoying the children so much that he lost track of time.

I consider these stringent and strict rules to be very harmful for all—for the mother who imposes them, as well as the rest of the family. Everything is tense all day, too. Women play this game because they're angry and because they want control. However, I don't think the benefits of the game are worth the enormous price you pay.

Many women set a whole stage on the day the ex-husband comes to pick up the children, carefully leaving a cigar butt or a man's hat around to let him know that she's seeing other men and that she's still an attractive and desirable woman. This can be harmful if a woman puts an enormous amount of energy into seducing her husband when there's really no hope for a reconciliation.

I've found that with time, the game-playing lessens. Moreover, you can stop the game-playing to some degree by the attitude you take. If you feel that your relationship with your ex is giving you too much pain, you may want to decrease the contact with him. Or perhaps you can make an effort at a more businesslike approach. Game-playing often keeps the relationship alive when we should close that chapter in our lives.

DEALING WITH YOUR ANGER

The enormous anger that so many of us secretly feel is perfectly normal, and I think it's healthy to admit to it. Many times we try to cover up our anger and this leads to bitterness and depression.

At the beginning of our separation, I was so angry with Andy that many times I found it hard to be civil. I can remember one particular day when we had been separated for about four months. We were in the living room talking about the possibility of a reconciliation. He told me that he loved Barbara, the woman he was living with, and he loved her child, too. I think he could see the hurt in my eyes, and he was particularly gleeful about it. On his way out the door, he picked up a potato chip from a bowl on the dining room table and tossed it up into the air and caught it in his mouth. He was very happy because he had the upper hand.

I began to cry when he walked out the door—and then I became furious. But a little later I was able to see how ridiculous his behavior was, and I could actually laugh a little about it.

Today, seven years later, I could still find much to be angry about if I tried. When Andy came to see Christina ride in a horse show recently, he brought his girlfriend's child along, which really irked me. He brings up the subject of his "lady friend" as much as he can. If I wanted to, I could be angry with him all the time.

However, from the beginning, I felt it was important to keep a cooperative and, if possible, friendly relationship with him. I have worked at this, and I think it has benefited me and my children.

There are a variety of ways of handling complex emotions. You can remain locked in anger and bitterness, and who am I to say that you're not justified in feeling this way? But even if you're justified, it's worth questioning whether it's healthy for you to live this way. After all, it's not good for you to feel angry all the time.

Marge, a woman in her early thirties, was embittered because she wasn't getting what she felt she deserved from her husband. She'd expected her husband to pay her more than he'd agreed to in court, even though she had agreed to the sum, and even though she'd been the one who wanted to end the relationship. She had been raised to be taken care of, and during her marriage she'd expected that she'd continue to be taken care of in the same way. Two years after her separation, she was still bitter. Yet Marge's expectations were unrealistic. In fact, after discussing her feelings at a meeting, several women in the group were compassionate but told her that her anger was destroying her—that she had to get over it and get on with her life.

Often, when we are angry, we are sure we are justified in our feelings. This is why it's sometimes helpful to ask a friend: "Do you think I'm overreacting?"

Denise was furious with her husband because he called a woman friend from her house. Yet, if we look at the situation objectively, here is what we see: her husband lives in California, while she lives on the East Coast. He came to visit the children, and Denise left him in her house with the children for the weekend. While at her house, he called his girlfriend, reversing the charges. Denise would not have known about the call if her child hadn't mentioned it. She and her husband had been separated for about two years, and she had had some affairs herself.

Knowing all that, do you think she was overreacting to his phone call? Was it necessary for her to make an issue out of it? Was this really such an affront? I think she was overreacting, although I sympathize with her feelings. And this story is very typical of what people get angry about.

I know a couple, Bob and Suzanne, who have a young

daughter. They once owned a lovely California home. When they split up, Bob (like many just-separated men) had severe emotional difficulties. He quit his job, his part-time business went downhill, and he agonized over what he was going to do with his life. Suzanne was furious when he didn't make the payments he'd agreed to (she was living with her parents), and she told him he couldn't see their daughter until he started to pay up. "I cried on the phone, I was so miserable and guilty," Bob said. "I love my daughter and I wanted to see her."

Suzanne says, "Eventually I realized that my behavior wasn't helping his situation any. I realized that if I helped him, he might be able to get his life together and start helping support us." Suzanne got a job in a beauty parlor, and she started cutting down on her expenses. She let Bob spend time with his daughter and tried to be supportive. She knew she didn't want to live with him again, but she still had feelings for him and she also felt it was in her daughter's best interests to help Bob get on his feet. Sure enough, Bob found a career he likes (the hotel business) and is now sending payments regularly. And he's very grateful to Suzanne for being supportive during a very difficult time in his life.

A friend of mine, Helen, was very upset one day when her husband didn't show up for the children as he had promised. "Fred told me he was coming over to see the children at eleven and they were sitting out on the porch all excited ten minutes before," she told me. "It got to be twelve, then one, and he wasn't there, and when I tried to call him, he wasn't home. I wanted the kids to come inside, but they wouldn't move from the curb. Finally, by two, I made them go to a movie with me."

Instead of screaming at him when he called, she said, "Gee, the kids were so disappointed you didn't show up, and I was upset and disappointed and angry too. Jimmy said to me, 'I had a special hockey stick ready to show Daddy' and he was crying."

This kind of information may come as a complete surprise to many fathers. Fred told Helen, "I didn't know he felt that way." The message that he'd gotten from Jimmy was that Jimmy often would rather have been with his friend Tommy than with him.

Often, divorced men are so into their own lives and so removed from their children that they don't realize how much what they do affects their children. If you can enlighten a father, he may feel more responsible. It's better not to attack, e.g., "You did this or that." Even if that's very hard to do! Talk about how the kids feel instead.

Sometimes, controlling your anger can seem almost too much to ask. One woman I met had a husband who deserted her and her children. About eighteen months later, he returned. She was against him ever putting a foot in her house again, but to her surprise, the children, who had told her they hated him, insisted on seeing him. She gritted her teeth, but she allowed them to see him because she didn't want them to resent her.

I think this was a wise decision. Unfortunately, the most bastardly men get defended by the children. If they don't get a lot of love and attention from their father, they'll fight for the little bit they can get. And they may feel they can risk your anger because they are secure in your love.

In this case, when the children became teen-agers, they realized how irresponsible their father was. The mother says she worked out some of her anger by "pounding veal and talking to friends." Eventually, she said, "I wanted to put what had happened behind me and try to enjoy the time in life I had left."

I'm very much in favor of learning to express your anger—through physical activity such as tennis or pounding a baseball bat . . . through gardening or any other constructive activity. You have to let your anger out or you will be depressed. And I think asserting your rights and needs as a former wife and newly single woman is mandatory, for many men will walk over you if they can.

In the beginning, when you are so angry, find some people to talk to about how you feel. Loud screaming and pounding pillows help. And don't be ashamed of your anger—you probably have very good reasons for it.

After the first few months, however, you can decide how you want to handle your anger. Many women, for instance, have channeled their anger into a positive force for changing the social system that discriminates against women. Activism is always a good way to channel your anger.

For me, letting off steam to friends is a big help. Sometimes I talk my angry feelings into my tape recorder or paint and express my rage on canvas. Doing anything with your hands is a great help.

I have seen many women suffer badly at the hands of men. I have seen the court system used against women, and I have seen women manipulated, hurt, and cheated by sadistic men who were out to win at all costs. For these women, it is necessary that they fight for what is rightfully theirs. But I also believe that you have to look at your anger every once in a while and see what it's doing to you. Is it destroying you?

I had made a decision that I was not going to become bitter and let any man get the best of me. At times it's difficult, but I've tried my best.

4

Bringing up
Children on
Your Own

In the early months of my separation, I didn't handle my
children very well. I had so much pain and confusion of
my own that I didn't pay enough attention to how sad my
children were—I really wasn't aware of their feelings.

My son, Nicky, was nine when his father moved out.
One day he started crying and screaming—he was sitting at
the top of the stairs—and I walked up the stairs, took him
by the shoulders, and shook him. I told him that he'd better
"shape up," that he couldn't manipulate me this way, and
that he had better accept the fact that his father and I were
divorcing.

Looking back on that incident, I think I acted cruelly
and inconsiderately, and, in fact, I still feel guilty about it. I
should have tried to talk to Nicky—to allow him to express
his feelings . . . his sadness that his father was gone . . .
his anger at me. After all, here was this poor little boy
who'd seen a lot of fighting . . . who'd seen the father he
adored pack his suitcase and move out of his home. He
didn't understand what was going on, and he was miser-

able. If I could have put myself into his head—if I could have empathized with his feelings—I would have been able to see how absurd it was to expect this little boy to "shape up." But I had been raised with a "stiff upper lip" approach to life, and I was "handling" my children the way my parents had handled me.

When you're first separated, your children usually seem like just another burden. This is the time you hear women who have custody of their children saying, "These damn kids are a drag," and "Why don't they leave me alone." In the beginning, you are frightened and overwhelmed, and you can hardly think of anyone but yourself.

But as time goes on, life gets easier. And if you can run through the obstacle course every single parent must face (e.g., the maze of sexual, economic, and emotional problems that at times can seem so overwhelming), I promise you that your children can give you enormous satisfaction.

What stops you from enjoying your role as a single mother? Basically, five things:

FIVE ROADBLOCKS TO BEING A HAPPY SINGLE MOTHER

1. *The poisonous pattern of guilt*

All divorced parents probably feel some measure of "failing" their children by breaking the marital bond. I know I felt this way. However, guilt can undermine everything you do. You take Susie for dance lessons, but then you feel guilty because you've deprived her of the Girl Scouts. You take Johnny to a friend's house, but then you feel guilty because he doesn't have a father with whom to toss around a football every evening. You keep doing more and more and more, and nothing is ever enough!

This guilt will deprive you of any comfort, satisfaction, or pleasure you can derive from your family. And children can play on your guilt. Just let one child sit in a corner looking glum, and you're ready to do anything he asks.

Moreover, your guilt can give a child the feeling that there is something wrong with his life—that he's entitled, like a child who's ill, to be made up to.

Instead of feeling guilty, try to take the attitude that you did the best you could in your marriage and that you're doing the best you can now. What more can we ask of ourselves!

Moreover, don't communicate your guilt (if you have it) to your children. Instead, take the positive approach that this new, single life-style has advantages of its own. Because, of course, it does. Now that you're a single parent you won't have to argue with their father over how to raise the children. When I was married, I'd have knots in my stomach over how Andy would react to some decision I'd made or something the children had done. Now that I'm a single parent, I don't have those knots in my stomach any more.

The single state can also have advantages for your children. If your household was a rigid one while you were married, there is an opportunity now for more flexibility. The child won't have to adhere to Dad's demands (the ones that you don't agree with), like putting all his toys away at night. Andy didn't like animals and so the children weren't allowed to have any. Now that he's not living with us, we have a dog, Dusty, and two cats, Elizabeth and Franklin, and an aquarium with big Oscars. For children whose fathers didn't allow them to go on trips, sleep overnight at a friend's home, or stay up late, the gaining of privileges can be a boon. I would point out some of these advantages when your kids are giving you a hard time.

2. *Depriving yourself in order to give the children more*

Divorced mothers are the biggest patsies in the world. They will take their last penny to buy a child an expensive stereo set and will chauffeur the children around continuously. They will even give up their bedrooms and sleep on the living room couch in order to give their children private bedrooms if they want them. (This happens many times when, because of a divorce, a woman has to move to a smaller home or apartment, or when the children get older and demand separate bedrooms.) Many women, because they feel so guilty about their divorces, will even allow their children to be sarcastic and nasty.

This is ridiculous. We are just as entitled to enjoy life as our children are.

How to know if you're a patsy? Look to your feelings and to your bills! Keep a diary for about two weeks and in it jot down all the things you've done for your children. Ask yourself, "How many times did I do something for myself? For my children? Were my children's demands realistic? Was I upset? Do I feel deprived? Resentful?" (If you bury your resentment, you may become depressed.) Ask yourself, "Who gets it all? How long has it been since I've treated myself? Had a new dress? A night out on the town?"

Once you can evaluate your situation, you can begin to change it.

I have to add that sometimes, of course, we do have to give our children what they need, and since money can only be stretched so far, we have to sacrifice. When my son, Nicky, was in therapy and Christina was seeing a diet doctor on a regular basis, I didn't buy any new clothes for about a year. I had to make do with the clothes I had. However, eventually Nicky finished with therapy (he's now doing well in his second year of high school) and Christina finished losing the fifty pounds she wanted to lose. (I'm very proud of her!) Then it was time for Mom to allocate some of the budget to be nice to herself.

Often, however, your deprivation may be motivated by guilt rather than by the real needs of your children. Christina's room is the smallest of our three bedrooms, and she's always wanted a bigger bedroom. I felt that I had deprived her of the room she would have had if Andy and I had stayed together, because before we separated we had been talking of moving into a bigger house. So at one time I had entertained the idea of taking out a loan in order to enlarge her bedroom. The estimate came to some four thousand dollars—which was more than I could afford. However, I still felt it was my duty to provide a larger room for her. Yet, when I began talking to her about it, it occurred to me that the size of the room was not so important—what she was really saying was that she wanted a prettier room.

One day she took time off from school and we went looking for paper to put on her walls. We had a lovely day. She picked out a pattern that she liked, and a week later we began to decorate her bedroom. She was happy as a clam. What she needed from me that time was not a larger room but more care and attention. My feeling that I was depriving her of a large bedroom came from my own guilt. I had the resources to give what she needed here—the attention, the working together on a project, and the time.

I sometimes think it's better to lean on the side of doing more for yourself than doing more for your children, for you can feel pretty grim if you haven't allowed yourself time and pleasure. And your children will be resentful about feeling guilty for all you've sacrificed for them. One clue: if you keep giving and giving to your children and their behavior toward you becomes more and more unpleasant, they may be signaling that they don't feel worthy of everything that's being put in their laps.

3. *Trying to be two people—both husband and wife*

Your impulse is a generous one, but since you're only one person, you really can't be two.

Instead, substitute some other relationships to replace the absent father. Substitute uncles, friends, grandparents, and build a new family around them. Remember, there are other people who can give to your child besides you and his father.

Jimmy, an eleven-year-old boy who lives in my neighborhood, visits his father's mountain cabin every summer. He loves to fish, but his dad doesn't. So he found himself a friend, a fifty-nine-year-old man. They talk to each other about rods and reels, baits and lures, they fish together and even call each other during the winter months. The man needed a friend, too, and Jimmy found a substitute for the kind of father he didn't have.

Be on the lookout for substitutes and encourage your kids to develop relationships. You can say, "Grandmother really enjoys your letters," or "Grandpa will help you build this," or "Joe down the block has a stamp collection, too."

Christina and her grandmother, Andy's mother, write long letters to each other, and Christina spends several weeks with her each summer. This relationship is very important to both of them, and I encourage it as much as I can.

Many women have also made it a habit to get together with their children as a group for a nice big Sunday dinner every once in a while. They make a ritual of it, and it's fun for them and their children too.

You can also encourage a spirit of cooperation in your children. Explain that you feel very burdened and ask how they can suggest making the situation more workable. You can tell them, "Before, we both took care of you, but now I need you more than ever to help." If children are approached in this way and feel they are needed, they will pitch in.

You can make a set of workable rules—decide who'll do the dishes, the grocery shopping, the folding of the clean clothes. Explain that if they help you do these chores, you'll have more time to do fun things with them. And you will, for you won't feel as tired all the time.

Eleanor, a working mother, used to spend all day Saturday cooking and cleaning. "By the time four o'clock on Saturday afternoon came," she says, "I was ready to blow my top." Eleanor was trying to be a supermother. But then she finally changed her household arrangements. She realized that even little Connie could learn to make a bed, and there was no reason why nine-year-old Tim couldn't do the dishes a few times a week as well as some grocery shopping after school.

"For a treat, because the kids were being so helpful, we'd all go to a movie on Saturday afternoons—and that was a lot of fun. We all began to look forward to the day," she says.

If your children haven't been used to responsibility, a new cooperative arrangement may not work the first time you suggest it, but eventually they'll see the benefits to them—a happier mommy and more fun times for them.

As a matter of fact, children of divorced parents usually become much more self-sufficient than children of two-parent homes. And this is a big advantage to them when they grow up. They learn to cook and clean and make money and take care of themselves, and all these things build up their feelings of adequacy and self-esteem. Your single status, if handled properly, can be a golden opportunity for your children to mature.

I might caution, however, that the oldest child is sometimes given too much responsibility—and is often expected to take over the mother's role of disciplining the younger children. But the younger kids usually end up resenting this, and the eldest child is short-changed. Children who aren't allowed childhoods and who are always expected to be adult and responsible are the people most prone to depression in their adult years.

4. *Feelings of hate toward your husband*

It's detrimental for your children to hear how much you hate their father (if you feel you do). Half of them *is* their father, so they're bound to be confused and think that you hate them too. Then, too, they love their father, and your feelings will make them feel guilty and confused.

Bob, who is 36, had a mother who constantly belittled her husband—she told the children he was a shallow, uneducated man who'd never made anything of himself, that he was lazy, incompetent, and incapable of loving anyone. Bob says today, "What my mother didn't realize was that she was damaging me. Because every young boy looks to his father as a male model and learns about masculinity from his dad. By teaching me to loathe my father, my mother was teaching me to hate myself."

I know it's very difficult to control your anger and bitterness. No doubt you have good cause for your anger. But I've found that no matter how angry you are, it is best not to downgrade your husband to your children. Sure, you can say, "I'm upset with Daddy now," or you can convey your disappointment that the marriage didn't work, but try to hold off from undermining a child's trust and confidence in, and love for, his father. Don't say things like:

—He was no good.
—Your father could never manage money.
—He just was never a businessman.
—He was always sloppy.
—He always chased other women.

Don't try to make him sound like a bad, pitiful, weak, or deficient person.

For no matter what kind of a person your ex-husband

was—even if he was the world's worst—your child wants to love him. If he's not allowed to, he may resent you later for it.

Darla told our group that she hated her husband—who had walked out on her—so much that she told her kids, "You're bastards now." She did everything she could to make sure they had no relationship with him. But the children suffered terribly because they felt so abandoned; one developed a bed-wetting problem; the other became very rebellious and had great difficulty in school.

You might ask, how could a woman who'd been abandoned by her husband *not* act this way? That's a valid question and I'm not advocating sainthood for anyone. Darla had a right to be angry. But any way she could mitigate the damage to her children, the better it would be for them.

In the case of a father who has abandoned his family, you naturally don't want to whitewash the situation. You can be honest about your feelings—in fact, your honesty will help your bewildered children. You can say, "He's abandoned me and I'm hurt and angry. When I married him, I thought he was a different person." If you have an explanation for why he's done this—for example he's had a business failure and it's affected him very badly—explaining this will help the children, too.

You can also say, "He seems to have a sickness right now. Normal men don't do this. Perhaps he can't help himself right now, but it's nothing you did. His behavior indicates he doesn't care about anyone right now—perhaps not even himself." It's important to say this to a child because most children do feel it's their fault and if they'd only behaved better, their father would not have left. My son, Nicky, once told me that's the way he felt when Andy moved out.

If you think your husband may come to his senses one

day and might want to see the children, you can hold out this hope to them. Moreover, you can convey to the children that there are many good people in the world—that all men or all people don't behave like this.

Perhaps the most important thing you can do is to empathize with your child's feelings, e.g., "I feel terrible for you. I'd be terribly hurt if my father had done that to me. In fact, I had a friend who once abandoned me even though I hadn't done anything wrong to her, and I know how awful I felt."

However, try not to cross over that thin line into name-calling or taking your husband apart piece by piece. That won't help your child.

If you've been abandoned, should you let your children see their father if he comes back into the picture? What I would do—barring the fact that the man is dangerous—is to talk with the children. Perhaps they are so angry with him they don't want to see him. If that's the case, I wouldn't force them.

However, if they want to see him—unless he's trying to brainwash the children against you—I'd try to keep my anger out of the way. This is not going to be easy. It's natural that you won't want your children to lay eyes on him and that you'll want to use the children as a weapon against him. This would be any woman's natural first instinct. But if you can keep a sense of perspective and resist that approach, it might be beneficial for your children.

For no matter how much of a bastard he is, chances are your children will want to see him and have the chance to live with him part-time. Think about how many people who have been adopted and who've never known their parents sometimes go to great lengths to find out who their real parents are. They keep searching for the missing parents in order to find their identity.

What if he's dangerous or out to brainwash the children and annihilate you? If that is the case, I would keep him as far away from the kids as possible. But this kind of situation happens very rarely, and those women for whom this is true will have no doubts in their minds about what the man is up to. He usually will have threatened the wife and let her know that he is going to take any measures he can to destroy her. One man, for example, who had kidnapped his children on two occasions, told his wife, "I'm going to bury you." However, this kind of sadistic, vicious behavior is not all that common.

When you're angry, it is tempting to say to a child, "You're just like your father." Helen says she used to say to her youngest son, "Your father was lazy and so are you. I can always see him in you." But she eventually saw that what she was doing was destructive to her child's confidence in himself.

Moreover, a child isn't just like his father—he's a different person. A sensitive youngster may think that you hate not only the father, but him, and that you may divorce him also. "You're just like your father" is a familiar phrase, and let's face it—the child knows what you think of his father, so it's possible that you think that of him too.

You can say to a child, "I think you're being lazy," but make an effort to leave out a connection with his father. Divorce is a good dumping ground—even if you were still married, your son still might be lazy!

5. *Resentment over having kids at all*

We all have it—to some degree or another, especially if we have custody of the children. I've heard many women say, "If I'd known I had to do it alone, I wouldn't have had them." This is a pretty common feeling, so don't feel too guilty about it. What your resentment is really telling you is not that you're a bad mother who doesn't love her children but that you are overwhelmed with too many problems. Your resentment also probably has a lot to do with your feelings about your ex-husband—not only your anger with him but your jealousy over the freedom he has. There you are—stuck with the children, while he may have the time and money to go out, meet women, and generally have a pretty good time.

Since I've experienced these feelings of jealousy and rage, too, and still do from time to time, I can empathize and sympathize.

One night as I was driving to a meeting, I felt I had just left a madhouse. I was scheduled to speak at 8:00 P.M. At 7:00 P.M., I was preparing dinner and thinking about the talk I was about to give while trying to help with homework and hear out the arguments and complaints of my children. In the meantime, all one hundred tiles of the shower had fallen off the night before and the tile man was redoing them. I went up to check on his progress and dab on a bit of makeup before leaving. I asked the tile man a question and he quit on the spot, leaving tile and glue in the middle of the bathroom.

I had to leave for the speaking engagement (to try to impart calm and understanding to others). I sat in my car, feeling pulled and tormented, and all of a sudden, I was in a rage at Andy—for his freedom and relatively simple life. But I've also learned from talking with hundreds of divorced men and women that many times the "freedom" the woman envies is really very painful to the man who has it.

Many men feel lost without the structure of their home and children—they may be more lonely and miserable than many women. Even though you may resent your children, if you didn't have them, you might feel as adrift and lonely as these men. I've also noticed that women who don't have children seem to need to fill up their lives with a lot more busyness than mothers with children at home do.

My children have been my salvation. As they become

older, I get more and more pleasure from them. They have provided me with a needed structure at a difficult period in my life, with companionship and a feeling of family. Most of all, having children has forced me to grow up, to learn to be responsible for others. If I didn't have children, I wouldn't be the same person I am today.

Talk out your feelings with other mothers, but try not to take your resentment out on the kids. Joan reported she used to say to her son, Jeffrey, "You can go live with your father if you don't shape up." But what the child was hearing was not "shape up" but "I don't really want you." And he eventually ran away from home.

NOT ENOUGH MONEY

You may *want* to give your children "everything," but if you don't have the money, you can't. Remember, this is true for a lot of married women too.

Feeling guilty won't help matters any, and knocking yourself out trying to buy all the goodies you think your children need may not be the answer either. Karen reports that she worked at two jobs to provide her daughter with music and dance lessons; yet, when her daughter was older, she told her she'd have much preferred to have had her mother around to talk to. This attitude is pretty common among children.

There are various things you can do if you're in a money bind. You can explain, "We don't have as much money as we did." You can ask your child, "What's really important to you? Let's see if we can work something out."

Perhaps the child can work to earn some money. This kind of cooperative attitude—"let's all cooperate and see what we can do"—is better than taking a "poor us" attitude, or "Let's all be mad at Daddy because we're deprived."

This worked in my own family. Christine wanted a trampoline a few years ago and so she worked for eight months doing babysitting in the neighborhood and doing odd jobs around the house for me. In the beginning, I felt bad about this. I really wished I had the money to buy the trampoline for her. But I began to feel differently when I saw how earning and saving money became terrific achievements for her. She felt marvelous about doing this herself—it made her feel self-sufficient and independent—good feelings to have. When she'd saved $175, she changed her mind and bought a beautiful bicycle instead.

Sometimes, too, children are careless with their possessions—until they have to pay for them themselves.

What is most important for many divorced women to understand, and most difficult to accept, is that one's lifestyle will have to change once you are divorced. This can be a blow to your pride, and you can become furious, but the faster you can accept your situation, the better off you'll be. Moreover, if you pass your feelings on to your children, they will use them to make you feel even more guilty.

A last thought: for young children, there are many nice things you can do together that cost very little money—gather shells on the beach, make candles, paint a room, grow plants from seeds. All of these are fun things to do and will bring your children closer to you.

FATHER'S VISITATION DAYS

These days are important and should be encouraged. It is *in your best interests* to make this day as pleasant as possible for your ex-husband and your children.
Why?
- —because your husband will probably only keep a relationship with your children if he enjoys the day
- —because your kids will resent you later on if they feel you ruined their relationship with their father
- —because, when you have a boyfriend or some new in-

terest, and want your husband to spend more time
with the kids, he'll be there

—because if he has a relationship with the children, he'll
be more likely to send support money

—because, when problems with your children arise, you'll
have an interested party to help you

Not to mention the fact that your kids deserve it—it's
their day. They've probably been hurt to some extent by
the divorce. Let them have this one nice day without anger,
tears, recriminations, and bitterness.

Picking the day that will be his

Choose the day that is best for you. Many women pick
Sundays, but that often leaves you alone on a traditional
family day that you might be happier spending with your
children.

Saturday might be better for you because there's more
for you to do after the children leave with their father.
You can shop, meet a friend for lunch, go to the beach the
movies, any number of things. On the other hand, many
women love a long, leisurely Sunday all to themselves.

Make the pickup as easy as you can on yourself. If you
and your husband aren't speaking, arrange not to be there
when he comes if that will make you more comfortable, or
drop the children off at relatives and have him pick them
up there, or have him give a call before he leaves so you can
have the children waiting outside, ready to hop into his car
when he arrives.

If you are having problems with visitation day and can't
see how you can make changes in your arrangement, talk
to a friend. Sometimes another person can give you a solution you haven't been able to see by yourself.

In the beginning, when I as so angry with Andy, I'd
have him come by and hcnk for the children on Saturday
morning. But now that we're friends again, and we are, he

comes into the house—sometimes he takes the children out to lunch and sometimes the three of them cook lunch together in the kitchen.

The more cooperative your attitude is, the less resentful you'll feel.

Encourage your children to tell their dad what they'd like to do. Maybe Tommy wants to see a baseball game but is too shy to say so. Maybe Marie would like to spend the day at her grandmother's so she can show Daddy how she bakes cookies. Women get upset because their husbands end up taking the children to their girlfriend's or to their mother's, but many men really have no other idea what to do with their children.

The best kind of day for the children will be a natural day—one in which they can talk to Daddy, perhaps watch TV with him, eat with him, argue with him—anything that normally goes on in a regular day. Some fathers feel that they have to "make up" to their kids by entertaining them on a grand scale, but kids often get this message and feel uncomfortable about it. They don't like to feel that they're ripping off their father (having him buy expensive tickets or presents), and they might prefer that their dad just help fix their bicycles or go to buy them a pair of sneakers.

When Nicky was young, he and Andy would spend Saturdays playing with Nicky's go-cart or going on the bicycle trail with his minibike.

In the beginning, I felt I had to tell Andy what the children would like because most children have trouble asserting themselves with their fathers. They may be afraid of him or feel he's a stranger. Then, too, if children are not sure of Daddy's love, they may be afraid to risk alienating his affections by asking for anything.

With young children, I feel you should make suggestions, e.g., "Laura loves to spend the day at her grand-mother's with you." But I've also found that as children get older, it's important for them to fight their own battles.

Your children might not have a marvelous, happy day each time, but it's a good idea to make a rule that it's their *responsibility* to go. If a child can bow out at the last moment, or if he's uncooperative, the father may eventually stop coming around. Then, when you or the children want him there, he won't be. It's also good for your children to develop a sense of responsibility toward adults.

Help your children have a good day. Don't have fights with your husband that day so that your kids leave feeling upset. Save the fights for another time. If you can't control your temper, don't be there.

A lot of mothers feel justified to use this day to recount to the man everything he's done wrong. The kids leave crying, everybody has a lousy day, and then the guy takes out his frustration on the kids and stops coming around. Later on, these same women get angry because he's not around. Can you blame him?

Here are some of the many many subtle ways you can sabotage this day:
  —not having the children's clothes ready
  —punishing the child for some "crime" he's done and not letting him go
  —upsetting the child beforehand
  —bringing up facts about the court case while your husband is there
  —bringing up information about his or your family or his personal life that will rattle him or upset the children

Sometimes a woman doesn't realize that she's sabotaging the day—she feels her anger justifies her behavior. However, ask yourself: "Is my behavior in the best interests of the children? In my best interests?" Kids don't need the emotional upheaval and neither do you. You'd be much better off getting them out and then enjoying your day.

Marge said, "I used to have all my fights with Harold when he came for the kids until I became aware of how self-defeating this was. So now I have my 'Tuesday night to sock it out with Harold night.' The other six days, I don't allow myself to get upset."

Lenore suggests, "I try to play tennis the day before Jimmy arrives and also do something nice with my friends the night before. That way I'll be in a good mood."

Some women don't allow their husbands to come into the house. This may be best if you are doing it in a co-operative spirit to avoid a fight, or if you are afraid that once your ex-husband enters your home, he'll start "taking over" again. But if you're doing it to punish the father, it isn't a very good tactic. For one, it makes the visitation day fraught with tension. Everybody is "uptight." I've heard many men say in bitter tones, "I'm not allowed in the house," or "I'm not allowed on the property." These are the men who eventually stop coming around, and who may stop paying, too. If you feel it's difficult and in your best interests not to have your husband in your home, at least try to tell him why, e.g., "I find it painful to have you here."

There are no rules to guide you here—only your own good sense. Some women let their husbands have the run of their homes on visitation days, and while they are usually highly criticized (by both friends and therapists alike), their decision may well be the best one for them.

Karen and Jim had six children and not very much money. Jim couldn't very well take out all six children on the weekend, and going to his one-room apartment didn't seem practical either. So Karen gives him the run of the house—sometimes she goes out, sometimes she stays in her room.

She's been criticized for this—for being self-sacrificing and masochistic, but in her case, she knew that he would show up less and less if she didn't help him.

I am not advising that any woman make herself a doormat. Most women don't have to allow their homes to be used, but in some cases, a woman has to decide what is best for her family and then make a decision she can live with.

Some women prepare food for the entire family on the day that Dad comes around. I couldn't do this with my husband. But some women can, and I respect them for it. I don't think they should be put down. Therapists are always telling these women that they are sending double messages to their husbands and being self-destructive. But the women I've seen are handling their situations well. They do not want to go back with their husbands and their husbands know it. These women have made their own rules.

On the other hand, while you may be comfortable having your husband spend his day at the house in the beginning, after a while things may change. You may resent having your home taken over week in and week out. Or he may develop a relationship with another woman and prefer to take the children to be with her. Your feelings may be hurt. Also, consider that having him around your house so much may keep you emotionally tied to him.

In most cases, it's probably better if the man doesn't stay at your house. But if he lives out of town, or has little money, no relatives, or no imagination at all, this may be your best solution. Your arrangements don't have to last forever. You can say, "Look, this is developing into a pattern. Sometimes this is okay with me and sometimes it's not. Why don't you let me know a few days ahead of time what your plans are and we can talk."

Don't let yourself be taken advantage of. There's no reason for you to play the martyr. On the other hand, it's a myth that any closeness or cooperation between the ex-husband and wife is neurotic. Not only is it not neurotic, but it is always in the best interests of the children. Divorce doesn't mean war!

Give your ex-husband a pat on the back!

If he's coming to see the children every week, you're a lucky woman. Don't be afraid to let him know how much you and the children appreciate this. Men want to be good guys too.

My children wanted to go to the mountains with their father during the summer, and I wanted to go away with some friends alone. I suggested to Andy that he take them. He was reluctant but finally agreed. When they came back, I told him what the kids had said—how much they loved the trip, the things they said about it. Most kids aren't that articulate and the man doesn't get any feedback for all his efforts. Andy was really so pleased and happy that they liked it so much that he now takes them on trips much more readily.

If he's not such a good guy, and he does one nice thing, tell him how much the kids loved it and how much you appreciate it. (Even if the words choke in your throat.) Remember, it's *in your best interests* to do so.

Make visitation day a good day for you!

Planning is the key. Don't sit home feeling lonely and left out. Don't do that to yourself.

Even though you may not be too excited about your plans three or four days before, when that day arrives, you'll be glad you made them.

If you don't plan anything, you can be left feeling that nobody needs you or wants to spend time with you. This can be pretty grim. Laura says, "I remember . . . visitation day used to epitomize my whole life—empty, lonely, nothing. Then I started getting out of the house. I couldn't stand the tears and self-pity any more."

Plan fun things to do. Many Nexus members go to brunch and the movies together on this day . . . and they really enjoy themselves. Shop with a friend. Go to the beach. Take a course that day, get a massage, or take a tennis lesson, even if money is tight; you can afford to do something that will lift your spirits. I've been strapped for money many times, but at times I've still chosen to treat myself rather than pay a bill.

IF HE'S SAYING BAD THINGS ABOUT YOU TO THE CHILDREN

In the beginning of a separation, it's pretty natural that each parent will be hostile to the other. However, if you feel that your ex-husband is making destructive remarks about you and upsetting your child, you will have to take action.

If your child is upset or hostile to you after he's spent time with his father, you can say, "You seem to be upset. Is it something I've done or are you angry about something I don't know about? Can I help in any way?" (This will be better than confronting the child with "What is your father saying about me?") If your child says, "Daddy says you are running around with a lot of men" (men who attack you will usually attack your sexuality), or "Daddy says you've taken all of his money," and you'll know what the problem is.

If your child is old enough (twelve or thirteen), you might help the child say to his father, "I love both you and Mommy and I don't want to hear you talk that way about her." This is perhaps the most powerful way to get the message to the father that he's damaging the child by what he's doing and saying.

You also have the option of telling the father you think he's hurting and upsetting the child by his hostile remarks. Or perhaps a relative you both like could do this for you.

A third option is to have a relative—perhaps your brother or an uncle—talk to the child and allay his fears, e.g., "Your father is going through a rough time right now and he's very angry with your mother because she wants to have a divorce. He doesn't mean some of the things he's saying. I've known your mother for many years and she's a good woman."

If talking to the father doesn't work, and you have no intermediary you can turn to, I would have a child see a minister or counselor. You can say to the child that you're concerned because he seems to be upset and you want to provide some help for him.

P.S. Many women also try to turn kids against the father, and many times they are successful. But as noted earlier, this is damaging to the child and many women later say they are sorry for what they did. Indeed, many times the retaliation of the father is started by what the mother did.

YOUR CHILD'S ATTITUDE

A child's relationship with his or her father is important. If it starts slipping, there's a good chance it will eventually diminish to nothing.

Christina was six at the time Andy and I separated. On certain days she didn't want to go with her father—she wanted to be with her friends. I felt that if we allowed her her choice, we would be controlled by her whim. I said, "You have to go." She had three or four tantrums and that was the end of that.

Today, she is thirteen, and the relationship with her father means a lot to her now. They like and love each other.

If the kids complain they're bored with Daddy, perhaps you or a close relative can explain to the father what the children might prefer. Many youngsters complain, "He

takes me to his apartment and there's nothing to do there."
You can ask, "Would you like to stay here or go to
Grandma's? What *would* you like to do?"

Be forewarned! If you're like the average woman, you'll
be watching to see what he's doing wrong. You will be
looking for indictments. And if you're looking for them,
God knows you'll find them. Practically everything he
does can be criticized: he's fifteen minutes late; he didn't
put a sweater on Junior and he caught a cold . . . the kids
didn't have dinner until eight . . . they were in a bar . . .
they saw his girlfriend.

These petty annoyances are small potatoes compared to
one thing: is he a loving father? If he is, that's what's
important. Ask yourself:

—Does he really care about them?
—Does he visit regularly?
—Does he call on important dates? (Birthdays? Holi-
   days?)
—Does he have a real interest in what you tell him about
   the children?
—Does he pay child support?
—Does he worry about them?

If your answers to these questions are "yes," he is a loving
father in my opinion.

Even if he takes a child into a bar while he has a drink,
that's not so terrible. (If the child has to sit in the bar for
four or five hours a week in and week out, that's something
else.)

Some men are a bad influence—they may drink or beat
the children or be verbally abusive. These men probably
don't deserve to see their children, and they should be
encouraged to get psychological help. But these men do not
comprise the highest percentage of divorced fathers.

It may be hard for you to work out a cooperative arrangement at first, but it's worth many tries. You won't be

sorry you did a few years from now. If you are civil, chances are that he will be civil. Women often have a lot more power and control and influence in these situations than they realize.

Also, let me say that a lot of people who had a hard time cooperating in a marriage have a much easier time after the divorce. The distance makes it easier.

MAKING YOUR LIFE AS EASY AS YOU CAN

Try anything. You can:
—get a mother's helper
—organize a day-care center
—organize a baby-sitting co-operative
—get a housekeeper or a live-in student
—let your husband share more of the responsibility
—live communally or with another woman
—get help from parents or other relatives
—exchange services with other women

As a single mother, you need companionship, support, and help. *You have to stop thinking in terms of being able to do everything by yourself*, especially if you're working outside the home. You need options—choices. There are no rules as to how you should conduct your life. Any kind of help you can get will be an enormous lift for you.

Here are some solutions Nexus members have utilized:

• Fern and Georgia, who have a child apiece, decided to live together. Georgia cooks one night, Fern the other. They both have part-time jobs on different schedules, so someone is always home. If they each were living alone, they couldn't live this way because both children are young. Together they are pretty relaxed working mothers.

• Marsha organized a child-care pool. Each week, seven women would call in to the organizer (each woman took a turn) how many hours she would need baby-sitting time and how many hours she could give. The number of hours a woman gives should equal the number she needs in order for it to work. Each woman had agreed beforehand that she would give at least ten hours a week.

That way, each woman's needs would be covered; as the women equalized their giving and taking, a woman who needed more time than she could give would pay for the extra baby-sitting time she received or get someone privately.

• Lila hired a college girl to work for her in exchange for room and board. Mary Ann asked a high-school girl from a large family to help her out. (High schools and colleges are good sources for young women who may be able to move in.)

• Marion and her husband share joint custody of their children. As a working mother, she couldn't handle the responsibility of full-time custody. With a lot of love, and with two parents who really care about the child, joint custody can work.

Andy and I might have considered joint custody if we had even thought about it. However, at the time, joint custody was not usually considered as an option, which was too bad. I would have liked to have had more help from my husband in raising our children. And I am always appreciative of any help he can give me.

However, since we did not arrange for joint custody, when I went to work, I decided to get a housekeeper. I didn't make the decision easily—in fact, it took me one year to make it. I pictured all kinds of problems occurring. However, I was talking my feelings over with a friend one day and she said, "Look, nothing is forever. If you don't like the arrangements, you can end them." I realized that this was true and so I made my decision to go ahead.

First, I got a job as a saleswoman. After one year of

being home, I was ready to expand my world. Then I put an ad in the newspaper for a live-in housekeeper and interviewed twenty women for the job. The woman I chose, Mrs. Wright, was a wonderful older woman whom the children adored. I gave her Christina's room and Christina moved in with me. The arrangement, much to my surprise, worked out beautifully. She lavished attention on the children and cooked marvelous meals. And she was there for me to talk to when I came home from work, which was pleasant for me. I found that having her there made me feel much less lonely.

Even though I didn't have too much money left over from my salary after I paid her, it was worth it. It needed the experience of a job and having someone to help make me feel like a different person.

It lasted about a year. Then, when I decided to form Nexus and was working on the organization from home, I didn't need her. I had also decided by then that I missed my children and wanted to become more involved with them.

McDonald's and Shaky's Pizza!

Are you addicted to fast foods? Hamburgers on the run? Many divorced mothers and their children are. As Joan said, "The kids love it and I don't have to cook anymore."

I'm all for convenience and comfort for the divorced mother. But not taking the time to sit down to eat with the children once in a while can deprive them (and you) of what could be a lovely experience. If you cooked when you were married and don't cook any more, you may be communicating that "No meal is important unless there's a man here" or "unless Daddy's here."

A pleasant meal together gives the children the feeling that you're still a family. Many children who never get a home-cooked meal feel like divorced orphans. And you'd be surprised how many children resent the fact that their mothers only cook when they have boyfriends coming over.

Meals are important for you too—to get the proper nutrition you need (especially if you're under great stress), to have time to relax with and enjoy your kids, and to treat yourself like an important person.

If you work outside the home, perhaps your kids can help—most children love to cook—or you can have a friend come over and share the cooking. Then it becomes fun! If you don't want to cook during the week, maybe a family meal on Sunday is enough to give you a lift. Cooking, when it's not done compulsively, can be therapeutic.

If your children have been used to eating on the run, they may at first be resentful of being regimented to a family meal. But if you tell them *why* you're doing this— that you enjoy their company and need to see them at dinner once in a while, they'll understand and appreciate it too. One woman set aside Friday and Sunday nights as family nights for her and her five children. A year later, she told a group of newly separated women, "The kids saved my sanity during that first year."

CHILDREN RUINING YOUR LOVE LIFE?

They try. Often they're jealous of your dating or frightened by any implication of a change in their home life.

My son, Nicky, has liked few men I've brought home. And from time to time, he's shown it—especially when he was younger. With one man, he would get in the car and begin to fart. This is one of the most embarrassing things a child can do to a mother! I looked as if I'd brought up a completely uncivilized, boorish child. This was Nicky's way of trying to tell Al to get lost.

When Christina was younger, she'd say to my dates, "Do you know how old my mother is? I know she told you she was thirty-two, but do you know how old she *really* is?"

I never had men for dinner because I never knew how my children would act toward them. I always felt a safer strategy was to get myself out of the house!

Sheryl said, "Whenever I'd be ready to walk out the door with Harold, my two kids would start screaming and fighting. The baby-sitter wouldn't know what to do, and I'd have to go run back in to settle the fight. I could see Harold's mind going click, click, I'm not getting involved with this crazy household."

Older children can pose even more serious problems. Larry, a man I was dating for about a year, had a twenty-year-old daughter who insisted on having dinner with us all the time. She would whine and complain all through dinner. When he told her he had a date to see me, she'd make him feel so guilty that he often ended up cancelling. He allowed her to play on his guilt instead of teaching her to be an adult who had to accept his single life. His daughter was one of the main reasons we stopped seeing each other.

Flora, a forty-three-year-old Nexus member, was going out with Sam, who had a pretty daughter named Belle, who really ran his life. She had replaced her mother as the woman of the house. When Sam began bringing Flora around, Belle felt cheated and acted badly. He had allowed his daughter to get too much control.

Dorothy, a friend, is having a more difficult time—she is in love with a man and wants to marry him, but her oldest daughter is trying to destroy the relationship. She screams at her mother in front of her fiancé, makes insulting remarks, even throws plates. She is sullen, nasty, and negative.

Unless Dorothy asks her daughter to leave home or gets counseling for her, it will be almost impossible for her to bring off the wedding. The point I'm making is that if you allow your children to run your life when they're young, they may only get worse when they're older.

On the other hand, it's helpful to look at your child's feelings and see how you can make her or him feel more comfortable with the men in your life. Children can be resentful and afraid of any intruder into the family constellation. After a divorce, there's usually a lot of juggling for position until they get the rules down pat.

When a child says, "I hate John," try to find out why. He may say, "He always changes the channel when I'm watching Batman" or, "He lies on my sofa." You can fix such small things by asking your male friend to go along with your child's wishes.

Children also resent being told what to do by a man who isn't their father, and I don't blame them. I think the single mother sets the rules of the household and should see that they're enforced.

How Will Not Having a Father Around Affect Your Child?

Divorced mothers have heard over and over again that their children will grow up "abnormally." I do not agree.

I have seen many children actually benefit from divorce. One friend of mine had a son whose bed-wetting continued until the time he was nine years old. As soon as her husband moved out of the house, the bed-wetting stopped.

My daughter Christina said to me recently, "I can't stand to hear fighting. I get knots inside my stomach. I'll do anything to avoid a fight." This is probably a direct result of the anxiety she experienced as a young girl when she heard Andy and me quarreling.

Divorce, of course, can affect children in unforeseeable ways. Children who were well-adjusted before may turn sullen, destructive, resentful, or withdrawn. The poor divorced mother may feel completely overwhelmed. She may wonder why she ever wanted children in the first place. One woman who felt this way told me how she handled her six-year-old daughter who began having tantrums at school.

"I was just going crazy trying to keep up with this and handle my own emotions," she recalls. "Finally, after getting a horrible note from the teachers every single week, I broke under the pressure and screamed at her, at the top of my lungs. 'I didn't want the divorce. I tried to keep it from happening, and I'm the one who asked for you in court. No one else asked for you, and you're mine and I'm going to raise you. You may as well get that through your head, and you and I will get along great.' And we have, ever since."

Women who make it through these crises (and we *can* make it through) do so by drawing on the help of friends, family, church, and counselors—and by trying very hard to make their children feel secure in their new living arrangements.

I feel that any child going through divorce could use some outside help in dealing with his feelings—an adult or older teen-ager to talk to, a minister, a therapist or relative. It is also the responsibility of both parents to provide positive male role-models for the child.

My son, Nicky, went to a male therapist after Andy and I separated, but I believe his problems began before we had decided to break up. He had a problem adjusting to school —and he was pretty antisocial. I think he was an angry child (he and his father had a lot of conflicts) and he didn't know how to express his anger—as many children don't because they fear losing our love if they are hostile.

He was in therapy for a year and a half, and now, at age seventeen, is a much happier person. He likes himself more, and he is interested in school, and now he and Andy are developing a good, rewarding relationship.

Children have problems adjusting to a divorce, but children from happy homes have problems, too. I know many divorced women who are very pleased about how their children turned out. I am one of those women, and I know it can be done.

DATING AND YOUR CHILDREN

Some women who have children at home have a hard time getting started dating. Some feel that the children will think she's immoral if she does, and should only see Mother with one man, the father.

However, you can't stop living because of your children, and it may be that your child resents your dating because *you* feel ashamed of it. Moreover, dating in a child's mind does not necessarily mean sleeping together.

When you feel ready to date, sit down and talk to your child if you feel it will help you become more comfortable about dating. You can say, "I'd like to begin to date and I'm feeling uncomfortable. I expected to be married forever, but it didn't work and I can't stop living. How do you feel about it?"

If the child says, "I hate it," you can say, "I hate it too, but I have no other choice." Or you can say, "I know you are having to accept a lot of changes—and I know it is hard, just like it is for me, but I need friends and to be happy. We'll both get used to me going out."

If the child says, "I want my father back," you have to explain gently that's not possible.

Many children do hate a mother's going out because they are jealous of the time she spends away from them. But you can say that "Mommy has to have her time as you have yours," and you can make a contract to spend certain evenings with them that are family evenings only.

Remember, your children should *not* control your life. They may try to make you feel as guilty as possible, but don't let them. If your first conversation with them fails, or if it only brings out anger, try another talk at a later date.

One woman's two boys, aged fourteen and seventeen, were complaining about her going out with her women friends. ("Where are you? You're out so much!"), and she began to fear they'd really raise the roof if she began dating. "I want them to adjust to our living alone together before I go out," she told me. However, she had been divorced for eight months, and I felt the children were manipulating her, and that it was time for her to take back control.

I told her she would have to begin dating, since she wanted to, and that she should tell her children that men would be coming to the house, and that she expected them to be polite. If they gave her too hard a time, I suggested she punish them or talk to her ex-husband about the problem. (She was on reasonably friendly terms with him.)

I suggested that she think through in advance how much time she wanted to give to dating—for many women are puzzled by the question "How much time is right?" She could decide that three or four nights was right for her (this would include time spent with women friends, and time for her own interests as well), and she could give quality time attention to her children on the remaining nights. If she decided on four nights, but later felt too guilty being out so much, she could cut her nights to three times a week. However, I advised that she should be steadfast in her insistence on her own life, that she should set up a schedule for herself and stick to it.

Many times, adolescents want you to be home, even though *they* have made plans with their friends to go out! Clearly, their resistance doesn't come from real need, but from a desire to retain the status quo.

After observing women and children for several years, it seems to me that older teen-agers give us the most problems. They are truly self-centered human beings and are in the middle of their own life crises, so they have little or no tolerance for change. However, while tact is called for, self-sacrifice is not.

THE FATHER GETS CUSTODY

Although the number is still relatively small, more women than ever before are giving custody of their children to the father.

There is also a movement afoot by men who are angry about the fact that the courts almost always award custody to the mother. This movement for the rights of the divorced father is growing. One spokesperson, who complained he only saw his son for a few hours each Saturday, said, "In divorce, the role of the father is changed from parent to playmate."

Clearly, divorced fathers have rights and I think we should respect them.

DAY CARE

Many women, especially divorced women, poor women, and working mothers, need quality, low-cost, government-subsidized day care for their children. Unfortunately, the issue of day care has become a political football, with male politicians pompously declaring that day care will destroy the American family—neglecting to perceive that there are many of us who comprise single-head families who badly need day-care centers.

Many divorced women who work are forced to leave their children with neighbors or baby-sitters, when their children would probably be better off in an environment where they could play and learn with others. Several studies prove that well-managed day-care centers have the needs of the children at heart and have been very good for children.

Dr. Edward Sigler, a Yale professor of child development, states, "I've spoken to hundreds of women across the country whose lives have been blighted because they are unable to find satisfactory day care. Almost 50 percent of all mothers work, yet so far they haven't exerted pressure on the government. I am convinced it has to do with the nature of women in America. They're *supposed* to be put upon. Farmers and the aerospace industry fight for their interests and get billions of dollars worth of subsidies. The government helps them but doesn't help mothers. We've so conditioned women to get the short end of the stick that they think it's the plight of women to suffer, and they don't expect any action."

I believe that, as divorced women, we should join the fight to get our needs and the needs of our children met.

THE WORKING MOTHER

The majority of divorced women with young children have to work. They have no choice. Unfortunately, many mothers feel guilty about working and leaving their children for a large part of each day. I think this guilt springs from what we've heard from male doctors all our lives— that the only good mother is a full-time mother.

This is nonsense. New studies show that working mothers do not short-change their children.

Moreover, women need to develop a strong sense of self-esteem. Some women get some self-esteem from their roles as mothers, others get part of it from working. It is a woman's right to define her own needs, and I am frankly tired of so-called experts (usually male) telling us what we should be doing and feeling.

I have seen many working mothers who are good, loving, caring, excellent mothers. They try to give their children quality time, a sense of being loved and of being valuable little people. Those are things I think are important.

One woman in Nexus told us the story of how her family worked out an arrangement when she and her husband separated. Olga decided to go back to school to complete her degree and talked it over with her children. The kids, Ted and Elsie, were eight and ten, and they volunteered to start dinner every night. She also lets them stay up later than their usual bedtime once in a while, so she can spend more time with them.

A working divorced mother must relax her "married" standards. You simply cannot keep a "House Beautiful" home, work, and take care of children too. The house should go. This takes a little talking to yourself, but it can be done. I would suggest making a list of the essential jobs every week. Assign some to those children old enough to help. Try not to get too upset when they forget. Don't waste your nervous energy on things like that—save it for the necessary times.

One woman I know had seven children and felt that she had to do everything herself—have all seven children looking bandbox clean all the time and have her house sparkling too. She did all that—and had three strokes before the age of thirty-six too!

There are women who must work whose children are too small to help, and it is a frantic existence. I can only say—the children will grow up, and in the meantime, if you can try to relax when you get home from work, have a glass of wine, perhaps, and sit down and give some time to yourself and to them, maybe you'll get through this period a little more easily. If you can live with another woman or provide living space for a young girl in return for her helping you out, your life will be much less frantic than it now is.

5

Loneliness

The loneliness of the divorced woman is a loneliness different from any other kind.

I was sometimes lonely during my marriage, but even if I couldn't talk to my husband, he and I always went out together on Saturday night! There was much more of a structure to my life—I didn't have to worry about meeting men and making new single friends. I didn't have the feelings of loneliness I have now.

The loneliness of the divorced woman is so acute because she has to rebuild her entire life. She has to face living alone. She has to face having her married friends desert her. She has to learn to meet new people—both men and women—in addition to coping with money and children problems. It takes time to get all this worked out. After seven years of being single, I still have lonely days, bad days. I haven't found any magic cure to take away my loneliness. But I have learned that *I* have control over my loneliness—that I can do things to make myself feel better on days when I'm sick and tired of being alone.

One of the best things I ever did to overcome my initial loneliness was to form Nexus. Through meeting other divorced women, I found that I wasn't alone in my feelings—that other women were frightened, angry, and confused too. I learned to reach out to women, and they reached out to me. These women became my family—I loved and trusted them. And through sharing our worries as well as our triumphs, I felt less alone.

In the beginning of any separation or divorce, the loneliness may be coupled with a feeling of being overwhelmed with problems to face and decisions to make. I've heard many women say during this time, "I've never felt so alone in my life." And because you *are* bleeding, you may not feel up to seeing people.

This is a time, however, to reach out for support and help—from family and friends and anyone else who can give it to you.

This is especially true if you feel panicked and frightened of being alone. You can't concentrate; you feel restless, you don't seem to enjoy a hobby you might have enjoyed before, and you have a desperate need to communicate with other people. My best advice during this difficult time is to give in to your feelings. Don't be ashamed of feeling the way you do, and don't browbeat yourself to pull yourself together or "shape up." Just accept the stage you're in. You need people around you.

Ask yourself who can help you. Can your mother or sister stay with you for a while? Can you get a college student to move in to help you take care of the children and provide you with some company at the same time?

In retrospect, I would have had a much easier time of it if I'd had someone there all along—even if it were a high-school girl who came in for two hours after school each day.

I think I was typical in the respect that, once my husband moved out, I wasn't ready to accept the fact that I could change my life-style. I felt I should be able to run my life just as I always had. This was a big stumbling block in overcoming the isolation I felt.

All women who feel alone and isolated could consider sharing living quarters with another woman or hiring some inexpensive help who can become part of the household. Often, women are reluctant or afraid to do this; as Gertrude said, "Well, you have to find the right person. You don't want to become involved with the wrong one." However, this insistence on finding the one and only "right person" keeps us locked in our isolation. It might be better to find someone fairly reasonable and give that person a chance. That involvement—just the simple fact of having another person to come home to—will do more for you than anything else to overcome the lonely feeling of living all by yourself.

Most of us have been admonished to "handle our problems ourselves"—"be extremely careful about who you take into your home," and "keep a stiff upper lip." All of this advice seems to help perpetuate our isolation, because all these well-meaning clichés make us overly cautious and careful, when the real big bugaboo here—the real problem—is the need to get involved with others, not to worry about how to get unencumbered. I say throw away some of the caution and fear.

Lean on people during this time. I remember one especially lonely weekend when Andy took the children, and I spent two days shuffling around in my pink bathrobe feeling miserable. I vowed I'd never allow myself to go through such a weekend again.

So the next time he took the children, I planned for it. I called up my friend, Joyce, who is divorced and has two children, and asked her if I could spend the weekend at her house. I told her I needed some company and wondered if she did too. She thought it was an excellent idea, and so I packed my suitcase and went.

We had a lovely time. I brought some wine and a little plant for her, and she installed me in her den where I slept on the couch. We cooked together and relaxed together. The weekend was just what I needed—I felt as if I'd had a little vacation.

Most of us have friends or relatives like Joyce to whom we can reach out for support during crisis periods in our lives. What stops us often is a false sense of pride—a feeling of not wanting to "impose on" others. Yet, other people are usually delighted to be needed—and they need company too. Joyce often said that that weekend was one of the most relaxing and pleasant she'd ever spent.

Or, ask a friend or relative to come and stay with you for a while. You can say, "I'm having a rough time right now. I'm pretty shaky. I need your company and I wonder if you would like to come over for a few days. We can cook and talk and go to the movies."

I emphasize reaching out because lonely people often wait for other people to contact them. That's what I used to do and that's what I've seen a lot of other lonely people do too. How many Sundays I spent waiting for the phone to ring! It didn't occur to me then that I could control my loneliness—that I could call others—who also might be sitting at home.

One Monday, after I'd spent a depressing Sunday alone, I told everybody I talked to what a terrible lonely day I'd had the day before. I described my feelings in detail. Practically everyone I talked to said, "Why didn't you call me? I was miserable too." So I wrote all their names down on a large sheet of paper and promised myself that the next time I was lonely, I would call them. I call this my Lonely List.

Often, when you're lonely, you can't think of whom to

call. You also think that everyone you call will be busy. Moreover, if people know they're on your list (you can say, jokingly, when you're in a good mood, "Would you like to be on my Lonely List?"), it makes it easier to call.

It's often difficult to reveal yourself when you're feeling bad. You may feel you don't want to "burden" people with your depression, but if you've prepared the ground, you won't be as reluctant to give a call.

I remember one Saturday when I hadn't planned anything and wanted to see someone. I picked up the phone and called a friend who had just been separated and told him I was feeling a little lonely.

He invited me to drive over and spend the afternoon. When I got there, he told me how glad he was that I'd called because he'd been feeling lonely, too. He had played tennis with a friend that morning and he had a bridge game scheduled for that evening, but even with all this activity, he was lonely because he didn't have his afternoon "peopled up"!

(This kind of panicked feeling usually comes in the beginning of any separation. Later on, you don't have the need always to be with someone.)

I've also learned not to be afraid to share my feelings—to let people know where I'm at. If you say to someone, "Sundays are an awful day for me," he or she may say, "They are for me, too," or "Why don't you call me next Sunday?"

I remember telling one lovely woman I'd met a few times how difficult some weekends were for me, since I wasn't dating anyone I liked at the time. The next morning, she called me and we went out together for coffee. By opening up to her, I gave her the confidence to contact me.

Shortly after, I told another woman I'd just met that I felt bad because I had bumped into Al, an old lover, that morning. Alice stopped dead in her tracks and looked at me for a minute, smiled, and said, "Cathy! I'm so glad you said that to me. You've never shared any of your feelings with me. I feel much closer to you now."

I thought about what she said—she had given me a clue to how other people were seeing me. I was holding myself apart from others and that's why I felt so isolated.

If you've been hurt by someone—man or woman—it can be difficult to open up. You may feel you never want to be vulnerable again. But this kind of attitude always communicates itself to other people—and it turns them off. Most people are not going to be willing to spend time breaking down your defenses.

One of the loneliest times in my life was after my closest female friend abandoned me after I took a job. She felt threatened, I think, by my involvement, and she began to stop calling me. I felt so bereaved that I closed myself off from people. Every other person I met seemed uninteresting. I had a hard time responding to anyone who held out a hand of friendship.

But I tried to learn from that experience with Alice to find the courage to reach out. And I've found that every time I've tried, my openness has had a liberating effect on me.

Sometimes, when you're lonely and depressed, you choose to remain isolated because you're feeling so low you don't think you have anything to give to others. However, while you may not be the life of the party at these times, you probably are more prone to listening—which can be a plus. Think of how many times you wished someone would really listen to what you had to say.

Another reason for our loneliness is that we tend to reject any friendships that don't seem totally correct for us.

When I married, I used to label some people "throw-away people"—people who didn't measure up to my standards. Because I was busy, I resented people who weren't close friends who intruded on my time. I didn't have time for a fifteen-minute phone call from a person I'd just met—my life was very organized and structured and I liked it that way.

However, after I was single, I found that I couldn't operate like that anymore. I had to open myself up to new people in order to overcome the isolation I felt. I, who used to be frustrated if someone couldn't relate to me in my totality, began to accept people and appreciate them for the times when we could relate.

I've learned that one can have degrees of friendship—there are 10 percent friendships, 30 percent friendships, 50 percent friendships, and rarely, 100 percent friendships. For example, I have a divorced woman friend whom I consider a 10 percent friend. I can't take her personality all the time. We have no rapport in terms of our values or interests. Yet she lives close by, and once in a while, perhaps once a month, we enjoy each other's company. She has a good sense of humor, she's refreshing, and she has some value as a friend.

In the past, I'd have discarded the friendship because she isn't totally on my wavelength. But I've grown up a little now, and I believe that we shouldn't so easily throw people away, not when they can provide us with some measure of human warmth and comfort.

A person that you could like a little can be seen as a 10 percent friend—someone you can spend a nice afternoon or evening with once in a while. In contrast, a 50 percent person would be someone in whom you can trust and confide.

Many of us who are lonely are very critical of other people. But I've learned to temper this in myself because I don't think you find that many people with whom you can have total rapport. In order to survive as a single, you have

to open yourself up to life—to different degrees of friendship. I've gone on brief vacations with women who were
not my best friends, simply because they were interested
and able to vacation when I was. And I've always had an
enjoyable time. There are other people with whom I only
play tennis—other than that, I don't see them socially. This
kind of approach to friendship—a healthy, selfish one in
my opinion—works for many single women.

You can begin to establish those kinds of friendships by
taking small steps. Promise yourself to make a phone call or
two once a week to someone you've just met. In the beginning, you can limit it to a ten-minute chat or you can make
plans to see that person again—to go to a movie or have a
cup of coffee in the middle of a busy Saturday afternoon.
Learning to reach out to see people is like learning to stop
smoking—it takes time and effort to break old habits and to
cultivate new ones.

When you open up to different kinds of personalities,
you'll be surprised at the unexpected benefits you'll derive.
You know what you'll receive from your perfect friend
with whom you have total rapport. But you can't know
beforehand what you'll receive from someone who is very
different from you.

As an example, I have a friend who is completely sports-
minded (quite the opposite from me) who wanted my
friendship and had the courage to start me off playing
tennis. In the beginning I was terrible, but she would get
out there and hit balls with me. I did it because she nagged
me at first, but it was wonderful for me and I learned to
play tennis!

Many of us who are lonely get into ruts. But in order to
overcome loneliness, you have to force yourself to act in
your own best interests. You can't wait for things to happen—you have to make them happen.

I have a male friend in his fifties who lives alone in a city apartment. Every night after work, he goes home, watches TV and goes to bed. He is bored and miserable, as you would expect. He believes that if he only had a woman in his life he would be happy.

However, how is he to find this woman? In order to meet her and in order to meet others as well, he is going to have to put himself in the right environment—to make himself available to other people.

What is holding him back is a combination of things—depression, inertia, and fear—but more than that is his pride. I think he is afraid of exposing himself or feeling foolish.

I suggested that he attend a weekly rap session at a local church, but since he doesn't know whom he'll meet, he refuses to go. Now I am trying to get him to take a course or two at a local university. But even though I make the suggestion, he's the one who has to get out and act.

The point is to interrelate with other people. Once you force yourself, your depression will diminish. Even if you have only the slightest interest in something, act on it.

During one particularly lonely period about a year ago, I joined a dream workshop group. I had always been interested in dreams and I found the series of speakers fascinating. Since I was seeing the same people week after week, I made some new friendships there and now two of us are taking another course together involving the occult.

Seven years ago, when I was separated from Andy, there were very few places where one could go to meet other singles—except singles bars. But today there are many more places. In addition to socials, rap groups, and special-interest clubs open to the public, there is group therapy for divorced men and women. Colleges are offering special programs for the divorced person. The increasingly large single population is changing the old established ways of meeting people.

If you're not sure what possibilities there are, you can ask other people what they'd suggest for you. Or put a little ad in your local paper saying something like "singles group forming to play tennis" or "singles book discussion group forming." People will respond. . . . you're not the only person who wants company.

I've found that some women don't like to spend money (for example, for baby-sitters) unless they are going out with a man. "It's not a good investment," one woman told me. These are usually younger women who feel they have limited time to meet another man, and they direct their energies to this end. However, older women and more experienced singles know how erroneous such thinking is, for women can provide you with love, support, and companionship. I never had many close women friends when I was married. All my socializing was done with my husband, with other couples. But as an experienced single, I've worked with women, traveled with women, confided in them, and supported them, and my life has been so much richer for these experiences.

Women who concentrate solely on finding a man to ease their loneliness may find this to be a very frustrating pursuit. Ellen, a divorcée in her thirties, has two young children, and she's home with them all day. Five nights a week, she hires a baby-sitter and goes to a singles bar. But she has become more and more depressed and says, "I don't like myself lately. I'm grouchy with the children, and I'm not too happy with the men I've been meeting."

All Ellen has now is her children and the bar scene. She might be much better off with a part-time job, where she'd meet people, and with reaching out to other women. Being single doesn't have to mean isolation. Some single people are the busiest people I know—and the happiest.

At first, if I didn't have a date on Saturday night (and I often didn't and still don't), I wouldn't call anyone because

I felt so ashamed. Now I've learned that I can enjoy my Saturday evenings even without a date. I've become much less dependent on men for my satisfaction and comfort. I still would prefer to have a loving relationship with a man, but I'm not devastated without it. I feel that, as a grown-up person, I have to exercise control over my life and to make it as nice as I can. So that's what I try to do.

In fact, because I keep busy during the day, I find it's the greatest luxury to spend Saturday night with a glass of wine and a good book, or watching a movie on TV with my children. And many single women feel the same way I do. Time alone, the freedom to do anything you want to do, is one of the big bonuses of the single life.

If I'm in the mood for company, I'll invite a friend to dinner. We'll cook together and chat and have a cozy evening.

This is especially important for the woman who doesn't have children or whose children have left home. If it's painful to spend the weekend evenings alone, make plans ahead of time.

For the woman who has young children at home and who can't afford baby-sitting money, I still feel it is important—and possible—to plan pleasant weekend evenings. Spend an hour or so chatting with a friend on the phone after the children are in bed. Or, visit a friend for dinner, children in tow, or have your friend visit you with her children. It may be a little hard to do this with children, but the inconvenience is well worth the companionship. Many single women still retain a lot of married standards or "shoulds" which keep them from adjusting to the single life. Some of these might be: "Don't take the children out too late," or "Don't drive after dark." But these "Never walk down a street alone" standards don't necessarily apply to your life as a single anymore. *Now that you're single, you have to adjust your life to your needs.* And you'll often find that your children will be delighted by a chance to visit and participate—they'll see it as a real treat.

Reaching out to others is beneficial even if you're involved with a man. Don't drop your single friends and divorce yourself from the activities you used to participate in. You may feel you've escaped the single life-style now that you're coupled up. However, as a preventive measure against loneliness, it's a good idea to keep contact with single friends and organizations, because you are still single. And if the relationship doesn't work out, it will be harder for you to pick up the pieces if you've dropped all contact with the single world.

Elva started dating a man, and eventually he moved in with her. He wanted her to stop attending Nexus meetings. He was to be her whole life. He came home at the same time she did, so she stopped calling her friends because he became angry when she was on the phone. This went on for about a year. They planned to marry. One day, he walked out. Elva turned around to call her friends, but they responded coolly because they had been hurt when she dropped them for her boyfriend.

Friendship takes giving of yourself. Many formerly marrieds don't give because they feel too deprived—you have less money, you're alone, you're angry and needy. However, the more you give to people, the less bitter and lonely you'll feel.

One of the happiest single women I know is constantly giving to others. She always has people around—she cooks for them, gives advice on their lives, helps them decorate their homes, clothes-shops with them. She hasn't had a close relationship with a man this past year, and yet she has been happy, surrounded by people who thrive on her gaiety and generosity.

Another friend of mine, Carla, who leads a very busy life, once said to me, "You know, I've realized that unless I take time out of my schedule to call my friends and give to them and ask how they're doing, no one calls me. They know I'm busy and so they're afraid to intrude."

Carla's statement rings a bell with me. I've learned that I have to devote time to my friends just as I devote time to my painting and my group work. When a friend calls and I am in a rush, I am extra careful to call back.

Part of accepting one's singleness is learning to be alone. In the beginning, it's so hard that it's pointless to try and overcome it. But after a while, you learn not to panic when you feel lonely but to ride with the feeling.

A few years ago, I wouldn't have been able to concentrate on my painting; I would have been too distracted by my own panic at being alone. Yet I find that as time goes by, the panic goes away. While every single has to deal with some degree of loneliness, it becomes tolerable. Today, for instance, if I am faced with a whole weekend with no plans, I know that by Sunday I will be feeling quite miserable—so I will take a clue from my feelings and call a friend or go alone to a museum for a Sunday afternoon and interrupt my weekend with something fun and lively. Years ago, I would have suffered through my loneliness, immobilized.

6

Dating the Second Time Around

My indoctrination into the singles scene was pretty awful. An old acquaintance who'd heard Andy and I had separated invited me to a party at a private discotheque in New York City. I took the train in from the suburbs—I remember I was wearing a very proper silk dress which looked decidedly matronly among the slinky harem outfits most of the women were wearing. The minute I walked into the party, I felt like a country bumpkin, and I never stopped feeling that way all evening.

It was a sophisticated crowd—there were earls and counts and jet-setters in abundance. No one spoke to me for quite a while, but finally a short, bald man asked me to dance. We hadn't danced together for more than a minute when he said, "I'd like to fuck you." I couldn't believe that I'd heard him correctly. I was both amazed and repelled at the same time.

Later, I danced with another man, who, after kissing me, told me he had his private plane waiting outside, and that he would fly me home. "No thanks," I said. "I'll take the train."

And that's exactly what I did—right then. I fled that party feeling I would never make it in the glamorous, callous, sophisticated singles world—that there was no place for me there and that I'd probably do myself a favor if I became a recluse.

I had no perspective on the fact that this was just one party—and not necessarily indicative of the way all single people conduct themselves. Many women's first experiences are just as frightening—because at the beginning, especially if you've been married for a while—almost anything new will look strange.

However, as I relaxed in my singleness, I learned that I could establish a social life that would be comfortable for me. I learned how to handle myself in the singles world, and I believe that every woman who wants to, can.

Anything worthwhile takes practice. When you learn the ropes, it will be worth it, for men are fascinating. The new you will surprise and excite you.

I remember trying to figure out how gracefully to get rid of a man at the door. I described to a friend what I was doing and she helped me analyze it. We discovered that I was racing up to the front door—as though I were anxious to get in there with him! (I really was anxious to leave him at the door.) So we spent the rest of the afternoon practicing walking until we got the right saunter down pat, to give a date the idea that this was the end of the evening. Every time after that, by the time I reached the door, my date had the message.

Dating doesn't come naturally if you haven't done it for a while. It isn't as easy as dating in high school, when everybody was single and available, and nobody had had a bad relationship and bitter feelings to cope with. However, if I learned to do it, you can too.

After my first disastrous party, I was gun-shy of the dating scene. Luckily for me, a friend introduced me to Jay, a perennial bachelor, whom I latched on to for dear life. Since I felt I would never make it in the dating scene, I wanted to find one man, stick with him, and marry him. Since Jay was entertaining and charming, I breathed a sigh of relief. But he told me months later he couldn't marry me because his mother didn't approve of divorced women, and I was thrust back again into the singles world I had come to fear and despise.

One evening, a woman friend took me to a singles place she frequented. We had dinner there, and after dinner, several men came over and began to chat. I had an opportunity then to see how people operated in a place like this. Since I had a friend with me, the experience wasn't as frightening as my first party, and I was relieved to find that the men were polite.

Another night my friend and I appeared at the same place and a man I met, whom I found very attractive, asked me to play tennis with him the next day. I woke up excited and happy; then, as the agreed-on time came and went, I realized he wasn't coming. I was crushed. I kept going over and over what had happened. Had I done something wrong? Said something wrong? Again, I was gun-shy for the rest of the summer. I played tennis as much as I could, but I didn't have a date.

As I look back on this incident today, I see how desperate I was to find a man to heal everything and to make me feel good again. Yet, in retrospect, basing my good feelings about myself on something as chancy as meeting someone once, under those conditions, seems so silly and unrealistic. I still had a long way to go in getting my feet on solid ground.

Perhaps that's why I was so susceptible to Al, who was

introduced to me by a friend and with whom I fell madly in love.

He was married, although I did not know that in the beginning. He was a restaurant owner and his hours were very flexible. He seemed to be around all the time—Saturday nights, Sunday afternoons, dinner hours. I had no reason to believe he was married, and I also, at this time, had had very little experience in the singles world.

He was the most attractive man I'd ever met in my life, about ten years older than I was. One of his most endearing qualities was his interest in me. He would actually *listen* to what I had to say. If you've ever been married to a man who didn't listen, you'll know why Al was so important to me. My husband and I would have fleeting conversations while he was running out the door, going to the den, or to read his newspaper. He was always running away from me. But Al actually sat still and communicated. He loved to hear me talk—to hear my ideas, my worries, my joys.

When our affair was over, I didn't date for ten months after. I wanted no part of men. I was beginning to see I was too dependent upon them and that I had to begin depending on myself.

I began Nexus at that time, and from then on, my dating became less a desperate pursuit and more a way of enjoying myself and other people. One of the best ways I've found to meet men, a way that has been a source of most of my dates over the past years, has been through the parties our organization gives. Even if you are not a member of such a group, you can still follow the method we use. Get together with five or six single women and each invite three or four other singles. They don't have to be people you know well. In the beginning, your list may be small, but as you meet more people through other social activities, it will grow. This is a way to meet people with dignity in a comfortable, homelike setting.

I found that adopting the role of hostess makes you forget your shyness and works toward putting your male guests at ease. Recently, a schoolteacher in her late forties told me, "I was so scared of coming to the party, I almost stayed home. I couldn't imagine what I would talk about with the men who would be there. But when you told me that all the women were responsible for putting the men at ease, I forced myself to put on a smile and go over to them." She found it wasn't as hard as she thought it would be, and that she had a nice time too.

"I HATE THE SINGLES SCENE"

If you've been single for a while, you can hear this refrain again and again—from both women and men. As one woman said, "I can't stand the plastic people and casual sex. Nobody seems honest, and the men don't really want to know you or your problems."

The urban singles scene she is referring to is made up of singles bars and the advertised parties in the papers. Every activity seems to be centered about meeting and keeping a man.

It seems to take over your life. There are the constant phone calls, "Where are you going tonight?" "What happened last night after I left you?" "Did you like that man?" "Did you realize Jessie is going out with Sal—wasn't that Marie's boyfriend?" "Do the married men go there on Wednesday?"

This comprises "the scene," and in it a newly-divorced woman is suddenly catapulted backward in time to her senior year in high school.

Don't allow yourself to be tainted by this "scene" that seems to be permeating your life. It is not your life. It is only one aspect of the single life that you may choose to move in and out of, if you wish—or you can choose to watch from the sidelines, strictly as an observer, while your regular daily routine continues.

In the beginning of a separation, there seems to be the feeling that there is an either/or choice to be made. Either one is happily married, or one is in the "singles scene." This is not the case. There are hundreds of different life-styles, and each woman is free to develop her own. This may include participating in some of the functions or happenings of the singles scene, or it may not. Each woman is in control of what happens to her. Nothing will come in and overtake you—you have *options*.

For example, I've moved in and out of the "singles scene." When I first formed Nexus, I would go with women friends to a bar for a drink after a meeting, but I never visited the bars much more than that, unless I had a date. My life-style now excludes that scene—it's made up of my work with my group, my children, and my painting. I am on the periphery of the scene by choice, and I've learned to meet men other ways.

Some single women are immersed in the bar scene—they know what's doing at every place, and what nights are best for certain places. Other women have never been a part of the scene. For instance, one twenty-eight-year-old member, who works as an office manager, has never ever entered a singles bar. Her social life consists of the skiing, tennis, and riflery clubs she belongs to.

"THERE ARE NO MEN OUT THERE"

I've heard many single women say this, but it's not true. There are many men out there. However, there may not be men abounding who meet one's criteria—e.g., he has to be handsome, have money, be successful, have a sense of humor plus a sparkling intelligence. If we expect a man who's perfect, yes, there are none of them (or few of them) out there.

However, there are men who are pretty decent and

eligible enough. Those women who do best in their relationships pick out one or two of their most important needs, find a man who meets those needs (for instance, a man who's gentle and who loves children), and overlook a lot of other characteristics.

Jane, for instance, is dating a man totally different from what her expectations were. "I always dated jocks—big guys. My husband was a hero. The man I'm seeing now is so completely different from my husband. He is short—and a few years older than I. I met him on a blind date. He was so nice. I have found, in the singles world, that when I have a chance to talk to the men who seem most attractive, they usually turned out to be crude, rude, and vain. I am learning that my feeling that a man must be good-looking, have money, speak well, etc., is a value that comes purely from my own vanity. And it really is hard to get the whole package together. I've done a lot of changing about what comes first, and I am tossing out the looks thing, slowly but surely."

There are bound to be disappointments while you are dating, but I think a lot of our disappointment has to do with unrealistic expectations—with the hope that you'll meet Prince Charming, who will solve all your problems. And while the repetition of disappointment can be disillusioning, you can also become more realistic. We learn to stop romanticizing people and to begin seeing them for what they are. I look upon my disappointment as building blocks in my own growth.

BUILDING A SOCIAL LIFE

Getting out there and finding friends is usually scary. One of the best ways I know is to join a group first.

Many women find it difficult to take that first step—even the telephone call is hard. But after three or four meetings, you will begin to be familiar to the other members—and the barriers will start breaking down.

I can't stress enough the importance of *not* giving up on a group. Even if you feel shy and uncomfortable for four or so meetings, you will eventually be part of it and on your way to making friends.

Some groups you can join:

—an all-woman's group, such as mine
—travel club
—political club
—theater club
—choir
—athletic club
—investment club for buying stocks
—conservation club

All of these are excellent places to meet people. One woman met her second husband at a New Democratic Coalition meeting. Another made a whole new set of friends through getting involved with the theater. Athletic and health clubs are excellent ways to meet people.

Taking a class or two is another tried-and-proven method.

Take evening classes and stick to those that have plenty of discussion, or where your class will be doing something together—baking bread or casting sculpture. Advanced evening business courses are an excellent way to meet men and will also benefit you if you want to advance in your career. Many men go back for accounting or management courses, or courses in finance or portfolio management. Cooking courses, too, are becoming extremely popular with divorced men, who now are learning to fend for themselves. Spend some time leafing through school catalogs, and see what interests you—graphic design? Urban planning? Wildlife preservation? Painting? Italian?

Meet people through your job.

Frequent the company cafeteria or favorite watering spot. One Nexus member told me that there were a few men in her company that she wanted to meet, but she didn't know how to go about it. I suggested she spend one or two days a week eating alone in the company cafeteria, and I told her to pick the same days each week. If any of the men were interested, they would figure out her routine and find a way to talk to her. I've found that many men aren't very good at spontaneous courting. But if they're given a few clues—you usually are in such-and-such a place at such-and-such a time—they can make plans in advance on how they are going to approach you.

Frequent museums, concerts, the ballet, theater, the opera.

Go with a friend or alone. Give yourself an extra half hour before the curtain goes down so you can sit in the lobby. If you're meeting a friend, show up a half hour early anyway.

One of our members, on her way to visit a museum one Saturday, saw an attractive man go to the coffee counter at their local train station. She bought a newspaper, went inside, sat down next to him, and struck up a conversation over a news item. He took her phone number and they began to date.

Another was lunching at a museum cafeteria table where two other people were sitting. When a man she found attractive passed by, she said, "You can sit down here if you like, we have a spot."

I have found museums an excellent way to meet people —I recommend them highly. Besides, I'm genuinely interested in art, so even if I don't meet someone I still have a lovely day.

If you can't handle going alone right now, go with a friend. Men will usually approach two women, although they may not approach a group of four or five.

When you're with a friend, don't stand there looking

grim. I've seen women standing together who looked so uptight that if someone said, "Boo!" they would have jumped out of their skins. Most men would not have the courage to approach a woman under these conditions.

On the other hand, if two women are there laughing and chatting and have an air of congeniality, men will be attracted. They feel they won't be rejected by these happy women.

I met one man that way. Another Nexus leader and I went to have a drink at a restaurant nearby after a particularly interesting meeting. We soon were laughing about some of the funny things that had come up at the meeting. The man standing next to us couldn't help but get involved, and he started laughing, too. I have since learned that he was quite shy, but I would have never known it that night. He felt comfortable joining right in!

Involvement in sports is another excellent way of meeting men.

Most men love sports and spend a large part of their leisure time working out, playing a game, and staying in shape. I suggest:
—play tennis
—play golf
—play backgammon
—join a chess club
—attend football games, stock-car races, the racetrack or hockey games
—play badminton or shuffleboard
—go on a fishing trip
—take scuba-diving lessons
—go horseback riding
—ski

The tennis court has always been one of the easiest places to meet people, and now there are singles tennis clubs you can join. Usually, people are matched as to playing ability. Not only do you meet people, but it's a good way to work off tensions and keep trim.

Golf is another game more women are learning to play. I know a woman who met the man she's living with one lovely Saturday morning when she was practicing her shots and he was, too. If you use your imagination, there are many ways to meet men through sports. You could even begin a singles baseball team!

Other places
- —beach resorts, preferably one that has gambling
- —supermarkets, laundromats, dry cleaners
- —parks
- —bookstores
- —restaurants
- —airports
- —clothing stores
- —doctors' offices
- —church rap groups
- —dating services
- —dances

I think every newly single woman has a fantasy that she's going to find one marvelous place where five hundred eligible men will be packed in together, and she can pick and choose her perfect person out of the group. However, there is no one place where you'll find rows and rows of delicious men—men are any place, just as women are.

I tell women that I expect and look for available men to be wherever I go—at the bank, the grocery store, to get my pictures framed. Once you get the knack of signaling that you're open and friendly, you'll find that you can meet people practically anywhere.

THE SECRET OF MEETING PEOPLE

As women, most of us were brought up to wait for dates to come to us. Years of training have taught us never to go after a man. However, many men are afraid of being rejected, too. In other words, they need a little reassurance just as we do.

If you see a man at a dance who you think is attractive, and you quickly avert your eyes and look down at the floor, how is he to know that you're interested? He can't read your mind, and even though he's attractive, he may not be as confident as you think.

I think we have many misconceptions about the wrongs of "picking up men," flirting with them, letting them know we're available.

Myth 1: It isn't safe . . . you'll meet the Boston Strangler.

Not true. You don't have to go to his apartment or get into his car right away. Meet a few times at a coffee shop or restaurant and find out a little more about him. You can be friendly and yet go slow.

Myth 2: Men don't like to be approached.

Not true. Many men are shy and they need a little encouragement.

Myth 3: He'll think you're hard up.

Not true. He may think you're together and confident. He may be complimented that you want to meet him. I think a woman should take a chance; you can do it in a dignified way.

Myth 4: It's not ladylike.

Not true. I have seen the most ladylike women send signals to a man.

One man told me this story. "When I was on the tennis court one day, I saw this woman two courts over and didn't know how to go over. If only she had come over and asked me the time or something like that, I would have had an opening to talk further."

Being approachable is the key.

You can even seem a little shy. You don't have to act as if you're totally confident. Friendliness and a little shyness can go together. "Formidable" is a word some people hate, and they certainly are not going to warm up to a woman who is striving to be so self-contained or self-sufficient that she needs no one.

Every man I interviewed mentioned one thing right off that attracted him to a woman—she smiled at him. A smile will make you look prettier instantly. Look him directly in the eye, hold it for a second longer than is polite, and smile.

I have learned to be more up-front about meeting men too. Once, after a meeting, I went with two friends for coffee. There was a man at the counter who interested me, so when my friends were ready to leave, I said I was staying. I sat there, and he moved over and I smiled. We chatted for a while and found out a little about each other—it took four years of being single to do that. But that doesn't mean you have to wait so long.

In the beginning I, too, was shy. But today, if I am at a dance or social gathering, I can easily go up to someone and say, "Hi, I'm Cathy," and perhaps add, "Where are you from?" or, "Have you been here before?"

One winter a few women and I went to attend a men's consciousness-raising convention in Philadelphia. As I was walking into a workshop, I introduced myself to a man and he later asked me to join him for breakfast the next morning. When we got to know each other, he told me I was the first person to whom he'd really talked in two months because he had just broken off a relationship and he was still hurting. At the end of the weekend, he told me how glad he was that I'd spoken to him and that our talks had done him some good. We write to each other occasionally now, and I was happy to have made another friend.

If you approach a man this way—as a friend—you'll have fewer fears of being "rejected" than if you approach him as someone you might someday marry. You can initiate a conversation even with someone who seems a little hostile or off-putting at first. Then if he or she really is hostile, walk away.

One woman approached a male friend on a friendly basis a month after his separation, and gently insisted that he come out and meet people. Her warmth charmed him and he ended up dating her.

Another man I know had a similar experience. A woman told him she knew "just the right person" for him and asked if he wanted to be introduced. He replied that he was more interested in her, and would she care to go out. Her genuine consideration opened the door.

SOME GOOD OPENING LINES
Tennis
   —I like your tennis shoes (shorts, shirt, racquet). Where did you buy them?
   —I love your form. Do you happen to know a good teacher nearby?
   —I'm looking for a club to join. Do you know of any tennis clubs for single people?
   —Are there any other courts near here? I live near Chestnut.
Fishing
   —Could you help me with this rod (bait, fish)?
   —I'm new at this and I'd like to know if the boat I take makes any difference?
Golf
   —I see you are alone. Would you care to join our twosome (or me)?
   —Would a five iron be good for this shot?
   —(In the clubhouse) Could you tell me a little about this course? I've never played here before. Is it difficult?

Supermarket
—My package is heavy. Could you lift it for me?
—Pardon me, could you tell me where to find the wild rice?
—I'm new in the neighborhood, could you tell me if there is a cleaner nearby?
—Is this store open on Sundays? I'm new here.
—Have you tried this brand?

Cleaners
—I just moved across the street. Do you know a good laundry near here?

Airport
—I have a two-hour wait. Is there anything interesting to see near here?
—I'm going to Chicago on United flight 221. Are you on that flight, too?
—I have a three-hour wait. Do you know where I could check my hand luggage?
—I have two hours to kill. Is there a good place to eat here?

Museums
—Have you seen the Calder retrospective at the Guggenheim? It is a wonderful show.
—Do you happen to know where the "photo essay" show is?
—I'm just going to lunch. Do you know whether there is a restaurant here? Where is it?
—I notice you have a camera, are you with a newspaper? Are you a photographer?
—(Rapturously) I've seen this show three times. Isn't it beautiful?

Libraries
—Where do you think I could find the art section?
—Does this library have an exhibition room? Would you show me?

—I can't reach this book, would you mind helping me?

Men's Clothing Store

—My brother is about your size. Would you mind trying this on for me?

—I love the jacket you're wearing. My brother would love it, did you get it here?

—I'm buying this vest for my brother and I'd love to see it on someone. Would you mind trying it on?

Politics

—I'd love to know your views on Carter.

—Isn't this exciting? I work here Mondays and Wednesdays. When do you work?

—I'm always so keyed up after a few hours here that I stop for a drink at Charlie's. Care to join me?

Doctors, Lawyers, Dentists

—I need glasses and really was at a loss—until I met you last week at the party.

—I hurt my back and remembered you from the party last week.

—Do you take new patients? Can I come in this afternoon?

—I remembered you from the party and I have a problem. Do you take new clients or could you recommend someone? I was impressed with what you had to say.

Bold and Brazen— Anywhere

—I hope you won't mind, but I couldn't help staring at you . . . you remind me of Burt Reynolds.

—Forgive me, I was staring. I've never seen a man as handsome as you.

—You look so much like my brother-in-law, who is the most handsome man in the world.

—I can't help admiring the way you handle your backhand. It's marvelous.

—You are the most articulate man I've heard in years.

—You just radiate warmth, did you know that?

—I find you so fascinating that I seem to be speechless.

—I rarely have seen a man as sexy as you.

FIRST DATE

First dates can be difficult. One of our members said, "I'd love to give every man I meet a résumé about my life so that I wouldn't have to repeat myself so much."

Dating is a testing situation that doesn't easily produce comfort or relaxation. Even the second or third date isn't too relaxed because the old bugaboo of "are you going to sleep together" is still a question that may not have been resolved.

To help make your date as pleasant as possible, avoid talking about troubles, your divorce, your problems with your children. If he brings them up, you can say, "Maybe we can save that discussion until we get to know each other better. I know we've both had a lot of painful experiences, but when I go out, I like to have a good time."

When you get to know each other, you'll certainly get to know his story and he'll get to know yours. There's plenty of time for that. Personal questions may frighten him, too.

If you're not sure what to talk about, ask him if he likes to fish, play tennis, or ski. Men like to talk about sports, so that's an easy topic. Or you can ask him about his life as a single. How did he find it being a single man and learning how to cook? You can talk about funny things that have happened to you when getting your single life-style together.

Because I wasn't sure what to talk about when I first began dating, I would prepare myself with topics. Corny as it may sound, I still do. I usually have a story or two ready—something interesting that's happened to me recently or I'll talk about a book I've been reading or a play or movie I've seen.

I think work is a good subject too—you can learn a lot from men about business which can help you in your own career. Most men do like to talk about their work, the politics in their offices, how they got where they are.

You can also plan a date in which you don't have to depend on conversation completely. When a man asks you what you like to do, have a suggestion ready. Don't say, "I don't care."

I think that dinner and drinks together for a first date is too long a night. If you're not sure you like him, accept for drinks only. It may be easier to play bridge with friends, or see a show, go dancing, or play tennis together.

First dates can be disconcerting, so take them with a grain of salt. I know many women who will give a man a second, third, and fourth chance before they'll rule him out completely, on the theory that people aren't really themselves on a first date. I never used to do this. If I didn't immediately like a man, that was it, but I've learned that that's not always such a good idea.

I dated a man, Ed, who was awfully sweet and nice—but there were no sparks between us. I really didn't want to encourage him. The next time he phoned me, I turned him down, but I accidentally ran into him some time after that. We had lunch, and he asked me out again. So I said, "Why not?" I really was not dating anyone I was crazy about. He got tickets to the theater and we had a lovely weekend together. I had been in the doldrums and it was a lift to have someone care about making me happy. It was just what the doctor ordered. He wasn't a big love, but I had fun and so did he.

SINGLES BARS

If you go, adopt a watchful attitude and don't trust what you hear. Usually, at any bar, there will be a variety of men, from traveling salesmen, who seem to be very comfortable with the scene, to public persons, to married men.

The repartee is usually superficial—fast, furious, and funny. You can master bar talk if you like, but you don't have to, and you don't have to tolerate much of what is said to you either if you don't like it.

How to do this? I really don't know what a good prescription would be for everyone, but this is what I do. If someone starts off with "smart remarks," I simply say, "I find bar talk so unpleasant . . . I'd rather talk about something else. What do you do for a living . . . ?" Or "I run this organization and I find so much superficial talk that I get sick of it, don't you?" Usually this much gets the story across that I am rather frank and honest and would rather talk on that basis or not at all. Most people respond rather well. If a person takes it as a put-down, you can be sure that he is not capable of any other sort of conversation.

At any bar, you'll hear a continual barrage of sexual allusions. A man may come up and say, "I want to go to bed with you," or variations on that theme. You can say,

—I really don't want to, but if you'd like to dance . . .

—I don't like your remark.

—I don't feel like answering that.

—What's the matter, lose your teddy bear?

Or you can walk away.

I really find most bar talk obnoxious and trivial. You'll be asked, "Do you come here often? How often? Where else do you go? Do you like that place? What kind of music do you like to listen to?" A man may tell you what a marvelous lover he is, or tell you stories about the kind of women he's met.

The banter that goes on is dishonest on both sides.

Many women feel that they have to be polite, even if what the man is saying is crude. This is especially true if the man has bought them a drink. However, you do not have to be polite if he is crude. You can certainly say,

"This conversation is objectionable to me. I don't want to talk to you."

One woman I know went to a bar and was attracted to a younger man. He kept trying to kiss her. She didn't like it, but she had a big smile on her face as she said, "Please stop." The way she expressed, "Please stop" communicated her confusion and ambivalence. She was giving him the message, "I'd really like you to stop; if you don't I'll stay here anyway." What she should have been communicating was, "Stop or I'll walk away."

Many women are fearful of giving any hint of rejection, whether or not the man is worthwhile. Since we have been brought up to please, it is often difficult for a newly separated woman to be downright rude. She holds on to her polite attitude and treats even a crude man with kid gloves.

So many of us have been programmed to believe we need men that we'll put up with anything. But you don't need *any* man that much. Moreover, once you start letting a man get away with this kind of behavior it usually gets worse.

If you want to meet a man at a bar, the key again is eye contact . . . then smile. It may be slightly uncomfortable for you in the beginning, but it works, even for the most ladylike women.

I have a friend who will go over to a man and say something like, "Don't I know you from East Hampton—Janie's house. Your name is Jeff. Remember, we were at that party at Martha's." She gives so many details that the man is convinced he is a double for this man, Jeff.

This friend's philosophy is, you'll never meet the man you like unless you go over to him.

Approaching men may be hard in the beginning, but it's better than standing there looking aloof. If you do that, only the most aggressive men will venture to come over. Most men won't approach you unless you send some signals that you're interested.

I don't know if I could pull off an "Isn't your name, Jeff" routine. But I do smile and act friendly.

I usually can say, "I belong to an organization, Nexus, that has some parties coming up. Would you like to be on our party list? Are you single?" Then they'll usually ask what Nexus is and we can discuss that. This also makes it easier for a man to say, "Now that you have my number, can I have yours?"

Then too, there's always, "Do you have a match?" or "Do you know where the restroom is? I've never been here before."

I know another woman who often says, "You know, I've been looking at you all evening and you're the nicest-looking man here. I wanted to meet you." This may be difficult for those shy souls among us, but it does work for some women.

Don't take any rejection personally. What I've learned is what every woman has to learn: I'm not attractive to every man I meet. I'm attractive to some and not to others and I don't have to please everyone.

If you expect too much from a singles bar, you're bound to be disappointed. I have never felt demeaned by the bar scene because I really don't take it seriously as a source for dates.

Those women whom I see most disappointed in singles bars are those who view the bars as their *only* source for meeting men. The bars become their only hope, and that's why they feel so desperate while they're there. Each silly male chauvinist they meet is a bitter, disappointing blow. A woman in this position would be much better off finding other ways to meet men.

One last thought: if you're not sure about a man (who he really is and what he really does), but you like him, you can give him your phone number but not your address. When he calls, you can say, "May I have your phone number. I'll call you back in a little while." Any legitimate man (who's not married or who works where he said he did) will certainly give you his number.

P.S. If you hate singles bars, don't go.

FOR THE NON-BAR-GOING PERSON

There are people, of course, who will never frequent the bar scene, such as the woman who said, "I'm pretty old-fashioned. I go to church on Sundays and I don't drink. I'm not one of those fly-by-nighters. I'd just like a little companionship."

For that person many churches and temples are forming what are known as "rap groups." I hear about new ones each month. Usually an announcement is placed in the newspaper or on the radio, and people respond on a given day of every week. Men and women of all ages come. A topic is prearranged and the moderator guides the group through a discussion; coffee and cake is served afterward. It is a nice way to meet both men and women. Many churches, too, are sponsoring "singles weekends," so keep your eyes and ears open.

MULTIPLE RELATIONSHIPS

In the beginning of my singleness, it never occurred to me that I could see more than one man at a time. Like most formerly married women, I still had my old married, monogamous values, and the idea of dating two or three men at once made me feel guilty and confused.

However, once you are single for a while, that attitude changes because the singles world is one in which multiple relationships are often the rule rather than the exception. By a multiple relationship I mean that a person is having a full sexual-social relationship with more than one man at a time. (Not just having a sexual relationship with one and then dating a couple of other men platonically.)

In fact, you will save yourself a lot of grief and disappointment if you assume the men you're dating are dating others too. You will save yourself some guilt if you realize that it's perfectly normal to want to see different men at the same time.

At certain times you may want to see more than one man, although you may not want this to become a pattern at all times. It can be an experiment you're trying and can give you a great feeling of power. A woman may have wondered if she could handle these things the way men can and it's thrilling to be able to know you can. It can be good medicine for the love-addicted woman, who is pining away for one man, to realize she can see several men at once. This is especially true for women who did not have satisfactory sex lives in their marriages. Usually, this juggling lasts for only a brief period, since it's hard to do on a regular basis.

I've found that multiple relationships work best when you are phasing somebody out of your life and bringing somebody new in. Over the long haul, it's usually hard to feel the same way about all three men. What is most common is having a primary "relationship," a new man you're dating, and casual sex with others occasionally. Men do this all the time, and women are beginning to, too.

How do you handle these kinds of relationships? It's best to be honest right in the beginning. You can say, "I like you a lot and I want to see you, but I'm still seeing others." Or, "I really care for you, but I do see others."

Many men get possessive and start using subtle tactics, such as dropping over with the excuse that they were in the neighborhood or telephoning at a late hour like midnight or 2 A.M. just to talk. This is a way of inhibiting you and checking up on you. If you are not ready for a real commitment, you must assert yourself and nip it in the bud.

Tell him that he must telephone earlier because his dropping in or telephoning could be awkward for you both. This will subtly remind him that you are dating others and intend to continue.

You can also say, "I'm not ready for a single commitment." Those who have the best ability to handle these multiple relationships are those who have the least difficulty being honest.

Usually these multiple relationships don't last forever—two or three months. In fact, one of the best reasons for them is that you like both people and can't make up your mind. But relationships don't stand still and will move one way or another. You might as well relax and enjoy the attention while it lasts.

ASSERTING YOURSELF

Learning to assert yourself will make your life as a single woman much, much easier. How much assertiveness training do you need? Take the following quiz and test yourself.

HOW PROGRAMMED TO PLEASE ARE YOU?

1. If he starts to touch you at a bar, would you let him, even if you didn't want him to?
2. If he buys you a drink, do you feel that you owe him the whole evening?
3. Would you feel you had to go to bed with him after he took you to dinner?
4. If he bought you a birthday present, would you feel obligated to repay him in some way (continue to go out, etc.)?
5. If he pays you a compliment, do you feel indebted?
6. If he suggests you come up to his apartment after dinner, do you feel you can't say no?

7. Do you have trouble turning down sexual advances of a man you really like?
8. Are you afraid if you turn him down for a date, he will never call again?
9. Do you feel that you "must" go to bed with a man you are dating? (at any point)
10. Do you engage in sexual practices that are not acceptable to you in order not to hurt his feelings?
11. If a man does a repair job in your house, but you really don't care to continue dating him, would you have trouble saying no the next time he asks?
12. Do you feel frustrated that he doesn't realize that you feel going to bed with him while your kids are in the house is not right, but you are not able to tell him?

Answering "yes" to one to four questions indicates you are pretty assertive, but not yet completely there.

Answering "yes" to four to eight questions shows you have to rethink your position and practice becoming more of your own woman.

Answering "yes" to eight to twelve questions indicates you are very frightened of showing your own feelings because you have been trained to please others. However, you may find that your relationships suffer as a result and that you feel victimized, angry, or depressed a lot of the time.

I've seen some otherwise independent women become terribly submissive once they're involved with a man, and they usually get hurt. This lack of assertiveness stems from too great a willingness to please the other person.

I know when a woman is in love it is difficult to be assertive, but I believe if a woman wants to have an identity of her own, and something of a life besides her man, she must make a life plan and let him know he has to work around it, just as you have to work around his.

Keep the door open to your own interests, single friends,

hobbies. You can still have a marvelous love affair and maintain some independence. The relationship may last longer, in fact.

Many women who are familiar with only one type of marriage, in which they played a subservient and submissive role, will find it hard to learn to be "equal" to men at first. But I was submissive in my marriage and I got over the disease. I believe you can, too.

Here, for example, is a discussion three women had on this subject:

MARTHA—It's amazing the things you'll take when you like someone. This man I started dating was introduced by a friend. I thought he would be considerate, but he would break dates and I would still go out with him. Or, he would call me at the last minute to ask for a date. He did every insulting thing he could and I still took it.

CINDY—I dated one man eight times. I thought he was so attractive, everything that I loved. I cooked every time. He never took me out or spent a penny . . . but I liked him so much that I couldn't see that I was getting the short end of the deal.

Then a funny thing happened. He said to me one day, "Some people cry or laugh when they have an orgasm. You don't do anything." He never gave it a thought that I *didn't* have an orgasm! And I didn't have the gumption to tell him that I never did. I wanted to spare his feelings.

MARTHA—One date of mine said, "I'm in a very embarrassing position. I have no money for dinner." So I offered to lend him twenty-five dollars for dinner. Of course, he never paid me back.

DARYL—Some man I had been dating about a month called collect, saying he had no change. Later he called and we met for dinner and I thought he would naturally offer to pay for the call . . . he didn't. So I got up all my courage and asked him for it . . . He was all apologetic and gave me the money . . . then proceeded to put me in a cab to go home without any money again!

When I was first single, I let Al dictate my every move. If I had a date or a plan with a friend and he suddenly dropped in, I would drop everything and run with him, sometimes even without the amenity of calling someone and canceling our plans. I was at his beck and call.

However, I've changed over the years and I would never do that now. I've also learned to speak up for what I want. One day, a man I was seeing invited me to go to a dinner party at his friends' club. I had met these people a few weeks before. They were nice but all married and rather stuffy and we had completely different life-styles. I really didn't want to spend my whole evening with these people again, so I said, "I'd rather not go to the dinner party, but I'd love to have dinner alone with you." He seemed to be glad that I had said what I'd really wanted. It didn't matter to him.

A few years ago I would have suffered through a boring evening without saying a word, but now I consider my time important, and if I can, I like to spend it with as much pleasure as possible.

Here are some ways you can let him know you have a life of your own, too:

—I must go to a meeting tonight. But I can see you tomorrow or Friday.

—I really would love to stay overnight, but my children expect me at home. I can come up to your apartment until about 2 A.M. Then I'll have to go.

—I know you love to go hiking on your vacation, but I'm not up to it. Why don't we split our time? I'll come to the resort and rest in the lodge and then you can come with me to my friend's beach house.

Yes, some men will resent your attempt at a life that does not include them every moment and will try to sabotage your plans or be critical of lessons you're taking. They may suddenly want to make love when you are about to go out, or make you worry about what they are doing when you are scheduled to leave. Usually, this indicates insecurity on the man's part. You can get angry and tell him off, or you can be very firm about continuing, while at the same time giving him lots of reassurance that you adore him.

About a year ago a man I was seeing had told me he would get my tennis racket strung for me. He kept saying "Nylon is better, I'll get you nylon," and I kept saying, "I want gut." No more would be said, and then he'd bring up the subject a few days later and we'd have the same discussion.

Finally I became angry and said, "I want gut, why do you have to try to persuade me to have nylon when I know what I want?"

"I just want the best thing for you," he said.

"But I really want gut," I said. "I think you just want to prevail."

This is a small incident but rather a typical one: he wanted me to do things his way, and I didn't want to.

I sat down with him and told him I thought our argument had little to do with nylon or gut, but with winning. I said he seemed to do this a lot—with me, with his ex-wife, with his daughter. I didn't put him down, but simply told him how I felt. And he was grateful. He told me, "You're the only woman who ever has talked to me that way. You do make me angry, but I realize you're trying to help." A couple of days later he said, "I've thought about what you've said and I think you're right."

Not all men would react this way, but many of them

will, and I think we owe it to ourselves to get our points of view across. I feel I've won my independence the hard way and I refuse to give it up.

When you feel you are being asked to do something that you don't want to do, ask yourself these questions:

—Do I feel comfortable with his suggestion?

—Is it in tune with what I want?

—Does it compromise my values?

—Will I later feel angry at myself for saying yes?

—Do I feel put down by his suggestion?

If you feel you aren't comfortable with his suggestion, instead of just saying no, or simply going along, tell him how you feel and perhaps make a suggestion of your own, too. You can say, "I've been cooking dinner for us practically every weekend, but I really feel I'd like to go out to dinner once in a while." Or, "I don't feel comfortable having you stay over when the kids are here. What other arrangements can we make?"

In order to assert yourself, you have to ask yourself some questions about what you would like from a relationship. How would you like to be shown affection? Do you need a six-minute hug every once in a while? A lot of cuddling? Try to be as specific as possible about what you need. What do you want now? Would you like to go on a picnic, or go out to dinner on Friday night?

Consistency means knowing what you want that's important to you, and being willing to act on the fact that you are prepared to see a person less if your needs aren't met.

I think every woman knows in her gut when there is a minimal amount of involvement on a man's part. She feels slighted and hurt. What you have to do is ask, "How would I like things rearranged? What suggestions can I make to get the relationship more to my liking?"

SAYING NO

I recently met a woman who had just been separated and attended her first singles event, a Nexus party. Later, she told me she'd been frightened about attending the party, since it was her husband's birthday, too, and so she was feeling particularly shaky. She began talking to a man who was friendly, and at one point in their discussion, he touched her arm. She cringed. She was nervous that he was going to make a pass at her. So she walked away from him three times to make a phone call, but he was always waiting when she got back. She felt obligated to stay with him, but she felt suffocated, too. He told her he'd like to see her for coffee in the next few days, and she laughed in his face. She had no idea of how to handle the situation.

I told her that she did not have to feel obligated to spend that whole evening with this man. She could have said to him, "Please try to understand that this is my first singles party. I'm new at this and I am not feeling too social. I think you're nice, but I'm not ready to go out with anyone yet. If you like, I can take your telephone number and if I'm ready, I'll call you." She could have said this even after she had made the mistake of laughing at him. If she wanted to leave him and mix with others, she could have said, "I would like to socialize and meet other people. I'll see you in a little while." Or, "My friend asked me to meet somebody over there and I'm a little overdue, excuse me." This kind of assertion is taken for granted in the singles world.

In addition, if you don't want to give out your phone number, you can say, "I really don't give out my number to people I've just met. Perhaps we'll see each other here again."

If someone calls you and you don't want to go out, you can say, "I'm very busy and involved right now and I don't have time for dating. But thank you for inviting me."

It's better to be frank about your feelings in the beginning, rather than to have the man keep calling and calling as you make excuse after excuse. I had a very hard time doing this, but it's much kinder in the long run.

DON'T SETTLE FOR CRUMBS

I used to accept crumbs in my relationship with Al, but I have tried very hard since then not to accept crumbs anymore. If you don't know if you're taking crumbs or not, take this little quiz.

—Do you never know when you are going to see him?
—Would you like him to take you out to dinner and he doesn't?
—Are you making all the overtures to him?
—Do you feel funny about calling him?
—Does he call you less than once or twice a week, although you'd like to talk to him more often?
—Are you thinking and fantasizing about the better life some other woman has?
—Do you find you make excuses for him to yourself and to your friends? (For example, he's so busy; he doesn't know how to show his love; he had a rotten childhood; he has to protect his wife; he needs me to come to him because he has trouble showing affection.)
—Do you wish he'd give you a gift for birthdays or holidays but you're afraid to ask for them?

If you've answered "yes" to two or more of these, chances are you are feeling sad, angry, or abused because you are receiving crumbs. Crumbs are:

—He calls you consistently at the last minute to go out.
—He calls you at five on Saturday to ask you out for the night.
—He only takes you out on Tuesday, never on the weekend.
—He only calls when he wants to have sex.

While the long-suffering role is one women have played for quite a long time, I think it's about time we took some responsibility for changing things—by standing up for our rights.

For example, a friend of mine was seeing a man. On her birthday, he showed up without a present, without a bottle of wine, without flowers. A few months before, he'd bought her a bracelet so she felt guilty about complaining. She excused his behavior to me by saying, "He's not mean, he just didn't have any money. After all, he loves me because he bought me a bracelet a while ago."

However, I felt he *was* mean, that he was saying, "I'll give you a present when I want to. The relationship is all on my terms. Don't expect anything from me because you're not going to get it."

Any involved man will know a woman will be hurt if she doesn't receive some token of affection on her birthday. I think he was being sadistic. He punished her, knowing she would accept his terms.

A woman I know has a married friend who calls her about every eight weeks. She runs to meet him wherever he suggests. She is convinced that he loves her. When I was discussing this with her, I gently suggested that perhaps she deserved more than this from a relationship. She said, "But he loves me. The last time I went to meet him, he said to me, 'Drive carefully, I want you to get home safely.' So I know he really cares about me." What could I say? In my opinion, anyone—even a neighbor—would tell you to drive safely. This is a crumb, which she's built up into a case for love.

One way to keep from accepting crumbs is to set some rules for yourself in a relationship—and stick to them. For example:

1. Join a women's group and go to the meeting each week no matter what a man suggests. This applies to dates

with women friends, as well, once they're made. I don't believe in breaking them just because a man calls. This will build up your self-esteem and your sense of dignity and courage. I attend many meetings during the week and one of the men I was dating resented their intrusion on my time. But I never missed a meeting because he wanted to see me. I'd make a date to meet him for a drink or a cup of coffee after the meeting had ended. He occasionally made remarks about "those meetings of yours" but I was committed to them.

2. If you have a date with a man who seems decent, give yourself time to enjoy it. Don't see a man from whom you're getting crumbs that same day.

3. If you work around his schedule, have him also work around yours.

4. Genuinely enjoy what you're doing when you're away from him; don't just fill in time.

5. Try to see other people you have something in common with.

Many men treat women badly because they can get away with it. I really believe that you will be valued by the way in which you perceive yourself. Men will act respectfully toward a woman who demands respect.

GAINING CONTROL

Many times, the agonizing over the breakup is the worst part. A woman will hesitate to end a relationship because she doesn't want to be unkind. Properly labeling what has happened, e.g., he lies, he only comes over every two weeks, his feelings aren't so strong—helps to put things in perspective.

Once you've made the decision to end a destructive relationship, 50 percent of your anxiety will be gone. And that is the absolute truth, even though you may not believe it at the time.

I feel I have learned control. I will not hand over my life to a man. I do this by keeping a continuity in my life made up of other things—my children, my friends, my painting, reading, gardening, and Nexus. If a relationship isn't making me happy and isn't something I can count on, then I'd rather have nothing.

What I learned when I stopped seeing Al was that I could put the brakes on. I don't fantasize over men as much. I've been disappointed and hurt, but I haven't let these feelings inundate me—I always have other things in my life that excite me.

Learning control of my feelings has given me power over my life.

WHY DIDN'T HE CALL?

Of all the questions about dating that come up again and again, perhaps this is the one that causes the most anguish, especially with women who have been separated or divorced only a short time. A man has spent the evening with you and has asked for your number. You've spent the next few days fantasizing about him, but he never calls.

There may be a reasonable explanation for his behavior which has little to do with you. Many men get cold feet the next day, even though they promised to call. Many men take as many numbers as they can. One man said at a recent party, "I'm having a great time. It's early and I already have three numbers." One was mine and he never called. As you can see, his motivation was collecting numbers in order to boost his ego.

A man may have enjoyed the evening, but his life may be too complicated at the moment to become involved. Also, many times asking for a number is an amenity. It can be awkward to say, "So long, nice talking to you." It's easier to say, "Let me have your number, I really enjoyed talking to you."

Often we become enraptured just because *somebody* is interested in us. We forget we may not have liked him once he came around. We may imbue this person with wonderful qualities that aren't really there. Try not to take his not calling so personally or seriously. It happens all the time.

FUTURE TALK

You spend an evening with a man. You don't know him very well. It's February and he says, "In the summer, you can see my boat." He'll ask you what you usually do at Easter and you say, "Well, I usually see my mother on Easter, but you can come, too." You spend a short evening together, but you can go through talking about all of next year.

I call this Future Talk and I've found that it usually doesn't mean anything. Why does a man do it? He may settle you into next Christmas so he can get you in bed tonight. Or it may be at the time he believes what he says. It all seems possible. He may have broken a relationship, but by the time he's supposed to call, he and she are back together. Most women's initial reaction to Future Talk is euphoria, and this tells something interesting about ourselves. Why do so many women respond to this?

I think it's because we want our lives planned out. By talking Future Talk, a man provides a future for a woman, a future she doesn't have for herself. She may feel she's worthwhile because he's so interested. She has something to look forward to, something reliable and steady.

If you realize this, you can begin to ask: "Can I plan a future for myself in case his Future Talk doesn't work out?"

It is really such a relief to hear that something is finally going to be *stable* in our lives and we will have a Saturday night date and someone to go to our cousin's wedding with—that for a few hours or a few days, you forget that you don't yet know who this man *really* is. He is bringing you into his fantasy and playing on the fact that you do fantasize. However, realistic women will know very well that they may *hate* this man in ten days!—let alone next New Year's!

LOYALTY TO WOMEN

At Nexus, the subject of how to be loyal to other women when you are competing with them for men comes up often. The problem is that there are no rules here. People feel caught in a bind because they want to be loyal to friends, but they want a man, too. I think there are ways to handle this.

For example, two women, Joan and Toni, went to a dance together. Joan had dated one of the men there. Instead of dancing with Joan, he danced with Toni. Toni was uncomfortable because Joan was sitting on the sidelines. So, at one point, she excused herself from the gentleman, went to Joan, and said, "I hope you don't mind that Chuck is dancing with me." Joan said, "Oh no, it's okay, I haven't dated him for over a month." But Joan certainly appreciated the courtesy of being consulted.

We can't always control our jealousy and emotions, but we can give courtesy to the other person.

DATE A VARIETY OF MEN

Use your single experience to date as wide a variety of people as you like. A year after our organization began, I dated a man eleven years younger than I—he was twenty-two. It was a crazy, happy time in my life and I'll probably never have one like it again. We rode around on his motorcycle, I began wearing different clothes with him—younger clothes, like cut-off jeans—and it was fun the few months that it lasted.

A friend once said to me, "I've gone out with cowboys, businessmen, doctors, and lawyers. One year I had a hundred and fifty dates with thirty-nine men." And I might add that she is an attractive woman but average-looking. She is forty-one and has two children.

She was making the point that she wasn't very selective about the men she saw in the beginning—she had a destructive marriage, and she needed her self-esteem boosted by having a lot of men take her out. Once she had had her fill of running, however, she began to become more discriminating; she felt her experiences had helped her learn something about herself.

If you feel you are not meeting enough people, you may be sending out negative signals. I know that when I'm feeling blue it's hard to be enthusiastic and interested in others. You might ask yourself: "How am I coming across? Do I seem bored? Angry? Uninterested?"

We often overlook how important our own attitudes can be. Anytime that I have been particularly open and friendly, I've found that most people usually responded with friendliness, too.

Some single women, on the other hand, who have established their independence the hard way and who don't want to be in the position of being vulnerable or hurt by a man again, put up all kinds of barriers to keep men away. One Nexus member, upon meeting any new man, would immediately tell him about her five children. "Usually, when a man hears I have five children, he backs off," she boasted.

In Nexus, we've named this kind of behavior "getting men to cross over the alligator moat." That is: a woman will tell a man every single negative thing about her situation that she can. In this way she is staving off possible disappointment, but she is also hurting her chances of a possible relationship.

She lets a man know all the negatives first and if he is still interested after that, then she has the assurance that he won't leave her. In reality, this doesn't provide any real insurance, but it does pose quite a challenge. A man taken with challenges may be quite interested. However, for a more sensitive man, this tack might be too tough.

If you find yourself reeling off all your liabilities—stop and think. Does he really need to know all that? Can't you just have a nice evening together and let things develop naturally?

Whether the primary bond in a new love affair is sexual, emotional, or intellectual, the relationship in the beginning can be marvelously therapeutic for a woman. And often, it's the small things that mean the most to us, that help us to heal. I remember one woman telling me how she glowed when the man she was seeing said to her, "Gee, this is a terrific cup of coffee." This may seem like an insignificant thing, but to a woman who's lived with a critical husband and whose self-esteem has been ground into dust, that kind of compliment has significance. That a man will provide you with recognition, appreciation, and affection can help you to feel happier and have a much more positive attitude about your life.

For the feminists among us, this may not be where you want all your good feelings about yourself to come from— from men. But a woman who has been through a difficult marriage is pretty shellshocked and in need of repair. Therefore, if one man, even any man, can help repair some of the damage one man has done, I believe it's beneficial. I believe the same is true for those women who, since their divorces, have looked to other women for emotional and sexual sustenance. Human warmth and intimacy can always help us get a more solid and improved perspective on the world and on ourselves.

As long as a relationship has some positive qualities to it, it can have far-reaching benefits. A woman who was married to a boring husband may have forgotten how bright she is or how much she loves and needs intellectual stimulation. A woman who had a nonloving husband may have had her own emotional growth stunted and can learn to get in touch with her own capacity to give, nurture, and love. This knowledge about oneself, surprising and satisfying, can be a milestone in one's personal growth.

MEN AS FRIENDS

I believe in having men friends. I try to keep friendly with a man even if we've dated and then stopped—I never close the door. I can say, "I don't love you, but I still want to remain friends," and that seems to work. I still invite them to parties and ask them for help and I'm happy to hear from them when they call.

I always wanted to have men friends and I let them know they are valuable to me. A good male friend can become as close as a family member.

I have developed a philosophy for living successfully as a single and that is: I don't discard anyone. Too many women discard men because they are looking for Mr. Right. I don't. For example, Jay stopped seeing me because his mother didn't want him seeing a divorced woman. Many women would have been so upset that they would never have spoken to him again. But Jay and I are friends today.

I also think that for those times when you don't have a man in your life, an old boyfriend or comforting male friend is marvelous. To have several men around who you care about, when you don't have one man you adore, is a nice feeling.

COMPLIMENTS

I once said to a man, "Women eat up ego-building compliments." He touched my arm and said, "Men need them, too, and we rarely get them." Then we discussed this with a third man who said, "I had a woman who was so nice to me on our first date that I sent her flowers the next day."

I've found that men do need compliments as much as we do. They're insecure, too, and that's what makes them act so silly sometimes. My motto: two compliments per date! For example, "That's a nice jacket. It looks well on you," or "You really are fun to be with."

LETTING HIM KNOW YOU WANT HIM

The most successful single women I've met are the ones who have learned to be aggressive toward men. We've been taught that we should conceal our desires, but a man likes to know that you find him attractive. Even if he isn't turned on by you, he is happy and flattered by the fact that you let him now.

Being a little bold is excruciatingly difficult for many women in the beginning, but you can learn if you want to.

A friend of mine met a man one evening and saw him the next day for coffee. She was very attracted to him. After coffee, he said to her, "Let's go to my apartment and have a drink, etc." She said, "I'd love to see your apartment one day, but I'm not sure about the etcetera right now, so I'd prefer to wait."

He said he'd call her and he never did.

Because she liked him and wanted to see him again, she wrote him a little light note which said in effect, "Just thinking about you." He called her immediately and he asked her what she wanted to do. She said, "I'd like to go to dinner with you."

Later he told her he'd felt rejected when she hadn't wanted to go to his apartment. But her note pleased him, so he called. Here she was thinking he didn't like her, when *he* was afraid she didn't like him. Later on she was honest about the fact that she was ready to sleep with him. I think it's good to remember that even if you're nervous, chances are the man is even more nervous about being rejected.

True sexual equality means that you are able to seduce, too. You can say to him, "Let's forget this party and just sit here and hold hands," or "I love being with you." One friend used to say to men she liked, "Let's go to my apartment for a little cuddle." This certainly was more direct than saying, "Would you like to come back to my apartment for a sandwich?"

I see more and more women calling men, asking them for their phone numbers, inviting them on dates. Some men will give women their business cards—these are the ones who love women to call them. If you feel comfortable doing this, it's perfectly okay. An easy way to ask is to say, "Some friends are having a party soon. If you let me know your number, I'll call you," or "A friend gave me theater tickets for Wednesday evening. Since you said you liked the theater so much, I thought you'd like to go."

Learning to relax in your singleness takes time. If you are new to the single world, look upon what you do and say as practice. It will take you time to get to know your way around. If you are sensitive and still hurting from your marriage, don't try the bar scene. Join a group or two instead.

Eventually, you will settle into a regular social pattern. You won't expect everything to be rosy all the time, and you won't expect to find Prince Charming around every corner. You will become much more realistic about dating and about men.

I've had a lot of fun dating—much more than when I was dating as a teen-ager. There are many times when I've laughed and laughed over some of the funny, silly things that have happened to me as a single woman. Once I was able to put my social life into perspective and not to fret when I wasn't deliriously happy and in love, I was able to enjoy it.

7

Man Shopping

THE MARRIED MAN

My experience with Al was typical of the kind of relationship single women often have with married men. We rarely went out and yet he provided me with a lot of comfort. I'd heard, as you probably have, that single women date married men because they don't want to become involved in a committed relationship. But this explanation is too pat. I, for instance, was very attracted to Al before I found out he was married. And from seeing so many divorced women become involved with married men, I've come to a different set of conclusions.

I think the married man—who comes from a fairly secure home environment—is an easy transition for us. He's a married animal and we're accustomed to having this kind of man around. He's a husbandlike person, appealing because he's so familiar. He's relaxed, not trying to be the sexiest man in town. (Single men are more nervous and insecure.) He has nothing to lose because he's got his safety in marriage. Married men are also very available.

A friend of mine, Tina, a forty-three-year-old redhead with one son, met John about a year after she divorced. She hadn't dated much and she was frightened of the singles scene. She met John in a parking lot: she dropped a bag of groceries she was carrying, and he helped pick them up.

"I really needed a nice man to talk to and there he was," she says. "I was having problems with my eight-year-old, and he'd take Jerry out on the lawn and throw a football around.

"Eventually, I wanted him to leave his wife and he couldn't do it. I don't see him now—I don't know how his life is going. But I still think of him sometimes. He was a good man."

Tina had not chosen a married man solely by accident. Because John was a father himself, he was able to relate to her son. He became a kind of substitute husband. He was used to living in a household with children and so he understood the day-to-day problems that come up.

A married man is unlikely to have more than one mistress. There aren't that many hours in a day. Besides, every new woman is a set of new problems for him. He has to explain that he's married, that he can't take her out on Saturday nights, etc.

I've often discussed the morality of dating married men. As in my own case, many women would never have considered "stealing" another woman's husband before they were divorced. But they find they do see married men, not out of a desire to take away someone's husband, but because this man is interested and they're needy. It's that basic and simple.

One woman I knew, who was devoutly religious, condemned other women harshly for seeing married men. However, a year after she separated from her husband, a married man pursued her and she was attracted enough— and lonely enough—to begin seeing him.

A married man is usually willing to commit himself to seeing you once or twice a week. He'll call a lot. You'll have more control than you might with a single man who may have a series of multiple relationships—and therefore more stability.

If his needs are being met, he is liable to go along with what you want most of the time. If you want a semblance of family life, for example, the married man will take your kids on outings. He'll do that much more than a single man will.

If you want to go dancing one night a week, he'll do that for you if he can; if you want to have long intimate discussions, he'll do that, too. Al knew I needed talk and sex and so that's what he gave me.

On the other hand, the more you become involved, the more dissatisfied you are going to be. You may want him to leave his wife. Even if you don't think you'll feel this way, be forewarned that you may after awhile. And the percentage of married men who do leave their wives is very small.

Many times this relationship is exciting *because* it is illicit and limited.

Marlene, who's thirty-seven, began seeing Jack, a handsome married man with quite a bit of money, after an attempted reconciliation with her husband failed. While she is very attached to him, she's savvy enough to know their relationship wouldn't work if she were living with him. "He had a cutting tongue," she says, "but I don't see him often enough for it to bother me. But he'd probably make any woman's life miserable if she were living with him.

"He doesn't demand much of me—he comes to the house once or twice a week and we make love and talk and it's exciting. I don't think I would feel the same way if I were seeing him day in and day out."

Sometimes even this kind of insight isn't enough to allow

us to avoid pain. I know that I did not want to marry Al and yet I was devastated when our affair was over.

Having a relationship with a married man also prevents you from relating to eligible men. Even if you say, "I'm going out with other men, too," it's almost impossible to be emotionally available if your emotions are tied up with someone else.

Most divorced women do see married men at some time in their singleness. That's just the way it is, and the comfort, affection, and support that a man provides can help a woman through difficult periods. For an older woman, who might not have many men her own age available to her (remember, men die earlier than women), this kind of relationship can provide needed solace. Yet I think those of us who can make the effort to meet single men should try.

Since Al, I have met several attractive married men who seemed interested in seeing me. But I don't want that kind of a relationship now—I want a man who can be there for me. Sure, I've been tempted to settle for a married man during some painful, lonely periods, but I always do a lot of talking to myself during these times. I say, "No, Cathy, this isn't going to be good for you." This kind of talking has worked for me so far.

THE JUST-SEPARATED MAN

If he and his wife have just split up, he's still licking his wounds. Because he's just come into the single world, he's scared and lonely and frightened.

And that's why the just-separated man—a man who's been out of his marriage less than a year—is not a good bet. In fact, I won't date any man who hasn't been living apart from his wife for at least a year. These men are in too much emotional turmoil—they may go back with their wives, or decide to go through a period where they see a different woman every night of the week.

One story that haunts me, because her pain and confusion were so intense, is Lisa's. Her husband had been having affairs during most of their marriage. She had entered the single scene with a lot of fear, and for a while had gone through an all-work, no-play period in order to finish her degree in education. She met Harvey at a friend's home. He'd been separated two and a half months. Within four weeks, he had moved out of his hotel room and into Lisa's apartment.

"I had a feeling that he should get his own place first," she says today. "But I didn't want another woman to find him. This man was special. One night, he even broke down and cried because he was feeling so miserable about his children, only seeing them on Saturdays.

"And then things began to change; I think he became attracted to a new woman in his office. He told me that he wanted to get his own place, that he'd moved in with me too soon. He felt he'd never enjoyed his freedom. I was really hurt. And that was the end."

The just-separated man is too newly separated to know what he wants. Even men who swear they will never ever go back to their wives do! Moreover, some men who don't feel very attractive when they get out of a marriage find, after they've been in the single world a while, that they are attractive to women. They may want to experience a lot of women and perhaps prove they can see several women at once.

Because this man is so mixed up, you can't really fault his unpredictability. His actions may have nothing to do with you personally, and you should remember this. The newly separated man just isn't rational. He's too torn with guilts, needs, and conflicts. He doesn't know where he's at.

Because his need is so great, he may snatch at the first nice, available woman he meets. He zeroes in on the woman who's a good listener, the woman who's understanding, the woman who can play the mommy role and hold his hand while he cries over his wife. I don't mean to put down his need or to negate the value of being an understanding, loving woman. What I'm saying is that while this man may not *mean* to harm you, he may end up doing so. Don't be surprised if he promises a good deal and doesn't deliver. Don't be surprised if he seems loving one day and hostile the next. Don't be surprised if he seems to have little regard for other people's feelings.

The just-separated man is simply in a difficult period in his life. You may want him as a friend and that's fine, but try not to fall in love with him. This is really a very good piece of advice!

I met a very attractive man at a restaurant one Saturday evening; I was spending the evening with a woman friend. Since our table wasn't ready, we sat in the lobby, where John was sitting alone. We started to talk and he later joined us for an after-dinner coffee.

I liked him, but he talked about his marriage a lot and that bothered me. I felt he was confused about his marriage and I didn't want to be the instrument to help him get out of it.

Instead of becoming lovers, we became friends. And my instinct was right. He did go back with his wife. They stayed together for a year; then they divorced.

Now, he sees a lot of women and is candid about the fact that moving from one to the other is good for his ego. It will probably be a year or two before he's ready, if he ever is, to make a commitment to another woman.

THE PERENNIAL BACHELOR

The perennial bachelor is the man who's over thirty-five and has never been married. My first love, Jay, was a perennial bachelor and, like most men of this kind, delightful. The perennial bachelor will wine and dine you. You'll picnic by the ocean. Go for boat rides in the moonlight. Meet his friends (most of whom are bachelors too), and party it up together. If you came from a marriage that wasn't much fun, this relationship can be a marvelous change of pace.

I had one of the best times of my life with Jay; he had a sense of style and was marvelously entertaining. From the moment he closed the car door after me, he would regale me with dramatically acted-out stories of his clients, judges, and opposing attorneys. He knew of the most unusual restaurants and all the maître d's. I felt I was in good hands.

Men who are bachelors are nice company as long as you don't fall in love with them, for while they may like excitement and glamour, they may not want to participate in your real life. They don't want to be bothered with the nitty-gritty of taking your son to the dentist or holding your hand while your mother is in the hospital, or helping you to get your dog to the veterinarian to be spayed. They want life on the surface, and they've arranged their lives so that they get what they want. For example, although Jay was very sweet, he would never dream of rearranging his schedule for me. I once needed to be picked up at the train station and taken to the doctor, but he could not see his way clear to change his tennis date. That's just the way he was and a lot of confirmed bachelors are like this. While they *seem* to be interested in women, their interest is not too deep. For many of these men, women are to be wined and dined and seduced, but not people to be taken seriously.

I know an IBM executive, a confirmed bachelor in my opinion, who is witty and clever and can tell story after story. He knows how women like to be treated, and he accommodates them. But he won't take a woman to visit his relatives, and he won't even talk about his childhood. His real interest in life is business; women are just a sideline.

Many bachelors do the things that matter to them with their male friends—like vacationing together, racing cars. They may enjoy the high of an intense love affair, but it probably won't be long-term.

The perennial bachelor is finally unable to share. This is the crux of the matter. Because he cannot share, he is unable to be married, doesn't want to be married or *need* to be married.

He may say, "I just haven't met the right girl yet. When I do, I'll settle down." But perhaps he's fooling himself most of all. And this is not to judge him because, as long as he doesn't promise what he can't deliver, he's not hurting anyone, and can be the most charming of companions. Just don't take him seriously.

THE PUBLIC PERSON

If he's been divorced, it's been for over five years. The length of time he's been divorced is a clue to whom you're dealing with.

The public person, like the perennial bachelor, can be great fun. He's only dangerous when you don't realize what he's about. That is, like the perennial bachelor, he's unable to have a loving, close relationship with a woman.

How can you spot a public person? Here are three clues:

—He's very much a part of the social scene. He's at *all* the parties, *all* the openings, *all* the bars. The public person can't be alone—and so he peoples up his life.

—He's very attractive—dashing. He wears vogueish, up-to-the-minute clothes. But he looks younger than his age warrants.

—He usually has a wonderful repartee. He can be funny and charming. He has perfected bar talk (the superficial talk that goes on at singles bars), but he throws in a few honest lines too. Because he does, it's often hard to recognize him. He makes it seem as if he's not a plastic person. But basically, that's what he is.

The confusing thing about a man like this is that he is involved in trying to please women and he pretty much knows what women want to hear. Men like this get clues as to what they should be. For instance, most women like honesty, so such men talk "honestly" about themselves. If they've done some self-examination and lived through a few crises in their lives, they'll be able to reveal something about themselves, enough to convey that here is a nice, honest, feeling guy. However, he has closed off a lot of feelings from himself, and at a certain point, he simply withdraws.

The basic clue to what this man is all about is that he's out all the time, at different places, with different people. He probably knows every bartender in town by name. He has few real friends, many casual acquaintances. That's why I call him the public person.

Common sense will tell you that a man couldn't meet hundreds and hundreds of women without meeting one special woman. And most normal people could not spend night after night with relative strangers—it would be too draining. So what happens, whether intentionally or not, is that the public person develops a line, a repartee, to sound as if he's revealing who he is. But basically, deep down, he is playing a role. His real energy goes into maintaining his image.

If you can accept that about him and see him occasionally, fine. If you think he's going to change into a man who will have an intimate, honest, personal relationship with you, you're heading for a disappointment.

How does the public person become that way? It's hard to say. It seems as if somewhere way back he decided that marriage (or an intimate relationship) was "for the birds" and he was never going to get involved.

He may, underneath all the ego-massage he receives, be a very lonely man. But he probably won't recognize that, or if he does, he won't be able to do anything about it.

I know a man who dates a different woman every night of the week. He says he is bored and unhappy, but he doesn't know how to get off the treadmill. He's become addicted to his way of life. If he stopped and spent a night alone, or spent two nights with the same woman, he'd probably become extremely anxious.

The public person may come on very strong for a while. He may put all his energy into making you fall in love with him. One clue to this variety of the public person is that he's been married—two or more times. He may think he wants a real relationship, which is why he has tried marriage. But he doesn't feel comfortable in an intimate relationship and will spend his life in serial relationships.

I've never been attracted to a public person—his slick talk usually arouses great suspicion in me. But I've noticed some women, especially those who haven't had much experience in dating, can really fall for him. Don't say I didn't warn you.

THE REAL MAN

He's been divorced or widowed between one and five years. He doesn't have a line and doesn't try to hook you right away. He may not be the sweep-you-off-your-feet type of man, but he has a lot of good qualities. He's honest, considerate, self-motivated, and appreciative of women. He may look a little more settled than some of the other single men you'll meet; he doesn't wear shirts open to his navel and no love beads hang around his neck. He seems to have good self-esteem and he's ready to marry. This is the kind of man I'm looking for now. I've become disenchanted with the dashing seductive-sadistic types of men I've dated.

Two men I've seen recently are what I consider prime real-men types. One is an engineer who's been divorced for three years. He dresses conservatively—not too flashily—and he has two grown children. He's had a love affair and is over the active-bleeding stage. Now he says he is interested in "getting on with his life." He's proud of his house and talks about his children and his work. He is not trying to impress me all the time and is willing to let me see the real him. He has decided what he wants in a future mate—a woman who can be more of a partner to him. Although I am not attracted enough to marry him, I feel he is more of a real man than many others I've dated.

Another man I know, a photographer, is also in this category. He is well dressed but doesn't let his singleness dictate how he dresses. He has been divorced almost two years and has learned a lot about himself. He feels that he was too tied to his business and will guard against that in a future relationship. He likes to do things with the children. He loves family things. He isn't afraid to talk about what he does in business or what he hopes for his life for the future.

8

Sex and the Formerly Married Woman

Sex is the most talked about topic in the singles world, and this is probably very healthy. When we were married, most of us did not discuss sex—what went on between husband and wife was strictly private, and if you had fears, problems, or unmet needs, you kept them to yourself.

In the singles world, however, sex is not a taboo subject, and most people want to learn as much as they can. As one of our members, who had not had a good sex life with her husband, said, "I always thought I was frigid. My husband used to tell me I was. But after hearing many of you talk about your sexual experiences since your divorces, I am wondering if I can have a better sex life too. Maybe I really am capable of enjoying sex."

One of the reasons I was excited about being single was that I was eager to learn about my own sexuality. I think Andy and I could have had a good sex life, but like many married couples, we got into a marital routine which inhibited spontaneous lovemaking. We would never allow ourselves to spend a nice leisurely Saturday morning in bed—

we always had chores to do, errands to run. I had read a lot about multiple orgasms, but I was confused about what they were. Yet I never discussed this with Andy; I was afraid he would think I was depraved.

When I became single, however, I made a conscious decision that I would let all the barriers down and learn.

I started to practice with Jay and that's the way I looked at it—as practice. Jay was actually more prudish than my husband had been, but I didn't let that bother me. I was determined to be uninhibited, and I was assertive about what I liked. I had never been able to be that way with my husband because I feared his disapproval, but as a single woman I had nothing to lose.

Jay was a little taken aback by my exuberance, but I think he also liked it. My experience in the singles world has been that men respond to women who are uninhibited. They like to know that you like their bodies and that you enjoy them.

My experience with Al as a lover was a very lucky one for me. He taught me much about myself.

He was a connoisseur of women. He believed women had a larger capacity for sex than men did, that women desired sex more and enjoyed sex more. Since I'd never had a satisfactory sex life with my husband (he seemed always to be running away from intimacy, too), what I wanted most of all was to know that I could function sexually. I learned that I could be multi-orgasmic, that I could rejoice in my sexuality, that I was sexually adequate. I felt so grateful to him that our relationship dominated my life a little too much at the time. But I had wanted this part of me to be released for so long and he was the person who did it. I guess it was natural to fall head-over-heels in love.

There is a basic difference between a married sex life and a single one. I see it this way. In a marriage, there is an air of propriety, of what "should be" with a husband. There is also the daily living with the same person. Sex can become dull in marriage and lose its flavor.

In single life, however, there is no accumulation of many years to dull the spirit. Sex can be exciting and it usually is. A person with a new partner or several new partners usually develops some creative ideas.

One friend went shopping with her boyfriend to a sex store and they bought each other sex toys—a special vibrator, some flavored foam, and unusual cut-out underwear. Another found her boyfriend loved to read to her from pornographic books. A third woman discovered she was a bit of an exhibitionist. Her boyfriend brought over a camera and took pictures of her in the nude.

My friend Jane, who never had a tender sex experience with her husband, has a lover who treats her like a goddess. She was never felt so adored in her life.

Although single sex can be adventurous and unpredictable, many people have the mistaken idea that the single life is brim full of sex. The "gay divorcée" is a stereotype that fits in with the supposed swinging life-style. Like other myths about single people, this one dies hard. There are very few gay divorcées around. Most divorced women, moreover, resent that label. As one teacher said to me, "Do what you can to tell people that single women do not spend every night of the week making love. That bothers me. My married next-door neighbor probably makes love much more frequently and regularly than I do and I resent being thought of only in terms of my sexuality. I'm a whole person with many different interests."

Many members have often asked me, "What do you think about my desire for having several men?" or "for having an affair with a younger man?" or "trying out some kinky fantasy?" And I always say, "If you think you can handle it, try it." Being single is a time for us to experiment, to test out fantasies.

This doesn't mean that you should go to bed with every Tom, Dick, and Harry just because there is a new code of sexual morality. That kind of thinking may be in men's best interests, but it's certainly not in women's. But if you want to try something, you shouldn't let your old married, conservative values dictate to you either.

Many women hover on the brink of trying something and decide not to, for fear of being forever committed to a sexual style. Not true! When you try something once, it isn't forever. You can always stop. If you do jump in with both feet, you will be able to evaluate your own feelings afterward and begin to know what you can and can't handle and what feels good.

If you can imagine yourself doing something and it excites you, like going to bed with two different men in a given week (a very common fantasy for many women), fine. But if a fantasy produces an inordinate amount of guilt, my advice would be to postpone it.

It can be difficult to step out of a married role. You may deny you have sexual needs, or feel guilty for having them. Most women I've talked to also fear being "promiscuous." I remember one woman saying to me, "Oh, my God, I've counted up the men I've slept with and the number is eight. What's happening to me?"

The fear of "sinking so low"—dropping all your standards and values—is very real and frightening. I would like to be able to help women to see realistically what usually happens.

A marriage breaks up and a woman is thrust out into the world. Her regular sex life has come to an end. At some point she will want to have affection and sex again. She begins to date. Now she has to deal with the realities of having a single sex life. With whom? Where? How soon? How many men? How often?

How many and where are the two questions that are the hardest for women to cope with, because so much in our upbringing tells us that having sex with anyone other than our husband is wrong. However, only a very small number of women never have sex after divorcing.

Who will a woman sleep with? Usually, the first man who attracts her physically. It could take a few weeks to over a year for this special chemistry to happen.

Then she must decide where. I've known women who absolutely refuse to make love in their own homes, usually because there are children around. Then there is the woman who regularly brings home a date and sleeps with him in her own bed and has breakfast with the kids the next morning.

My advice on this is that a mother must remember that she has very, very impressionable lives in her charge and some of her sexual practices, if carried on too openly, could have a disturbing effect on the child. I may be more conservative here than some younger women. In the final analysis, however, do what is comfortable for you. You can have your lover arrange a place for your time together, either at his apartment or, if he has his children, somewhere else. Most men will understand your attitude.

The other touchy question is, how many men is too many? This is such a variable situation that numbers no longer count. If you are a normal sexual woman and want and need sex and do not have a regular lover, your number of men may be much higher than the woman who has a regular boyfriend. The main thing to remember is not to force yourself in any direction.

If you are single for a while, however, you have to expect that you will be experimenting with sex quite a bit and that, in fact, this is one of the benefits of the single world.

I don't think that the number of men you sleep with has anything to do with promiscuity. Feeling guilty about our sexual needs is outmoded and outdated.

Most divorced women go through a Running Stage in which the choice of sexual partners may be pretty indiscriminate. But this stage doesn't last forever, and we usually learn about ourselves.

Many women have said that they were feeling so bad after the end of their marriages that having many partners was something they needed, to build up their egos, to make them know, just for themselves, that they were desirable, feminine, and sexually exciting.

Many men don't put down a woman for having "one-night stands," but some men still do. I don't believe in "one-night stands" for myself, but I don't think them morally wrong; if a woman wants to go to bed with a man, she has the same option to choose as he does. However, now that I am well out of the Running Stage, I cannot comfortably consider a sexual relationship until I know something about the man. That's what I find works best for me.

One week, during the early part of my separation, I was seeing two men and had the feeling I wanted to see two more. But I found out that this just wasn't me. I had to have several drinks before I could relax, and I had too much guilt afterward. It was such a struggle that I just said to myself, "Why bother?" I realized I could not handle sleeping with several men at one time, and so I set some limitations for myself.

At that time too, I didn't want to think I was going "premeditatively" after sex, and so, when I wasn't seeing anyone special, I didn't use contraceptives. However, if I then did have a sexual encounter, I wasn't prepared. Now,

I look back on that period and marvel at my naiveté.

I have met divorced women even today who become pregnant because they haven't prepared themselves. There is no excuse for this.

Unless you are involved in a long-term relationship, there are going to be times when you want sex and have no partner on hand. I think you are going to have to evaluate your needs here. Most divorced women do sleep with men they are not in love with, but they choose people whom they like and feel comfortable with—people they care about and have good feelings for.

I think if it's a choice between feeling irritated and deprived or having sex with someone you know pretty well but aren't crazy about, I'd opt for the latter. You are bound to feel 100 percent better the next day.

As a single woman, I have gone through months at a time when I have been celibate, and I've found that this is the norm for most formerly married women. During those times I have simply tried to comfort myself as best I could. But it's terribly difficult, and I have found I'm moody and irritable during those times. It's a feeling of being deprived not only of sex, but of warmth and affection, too.

Some women who are celibate for months don't feel that deprived. Others simply masturbate; others turn to other women and find this life-style suits them better.

After being in the singles world for seven years, I have found this method works for me: I hold on to old boyfriends. It's like going to bed with an old friend, and it's often a nice thing to do.

What you learn once you've been in the singles world for a while is that all of the old sexual rules you had adhered to during your marriage no longer apply. Sex becomes the fulfillment of relatedness rather than the duty of the marriage partner. At the same time, the climate of sexual freedom makes it imperative that each unmarried person set self-accepting limits. Within the context of this new freedom, a woman is free to explore her sexuality and to assert her needs.

I have learned to say what I need and not to be ashamed of my preferences. I am proud of my sensuality. I like feeling that I own my own body and that I can handle getting my sexual needs met.

The single life offers a multiplicity of options to women and men. You can indulge in group sex, heterosexual or homosexual relationships, casual sex, a monogamous affair, or celibacy. Each woman has to create a life-style that suits her best. We should trust ourselves, in the end, to do what is best for ourselves.

IMPOTENCE

Most women who have been divorced a while have had at least one experience with a man who's been impotent. If this happens to you, try not to be disturbed about it. Some women have said to me, "I felt so inadequate. I couldn't turn him on." But this problem probably has very little to do with you. It's his problem. The best you can do is to be compassionate. Sometimes, impotence can be temporary, and you can wait it out.

SAYING NO

A lot of newly divorced women feel obligated to have sex with men if they take the women out for dinner or buy them a drink. Don't be trapped into that. You are not obligated to go to bed with anyone, no matter what he says or does.

Many men will accept a statement such as, "I'd rather not go back to your apartment because that really puts us both in an awkward position. I'm not ready for that. I would rather wait."

I have always found it much better to refuse to go to a man's apartment, rather than go there and then have to fight off his advances all evening. If a man tries to persuade you to come up, you can simply say, "Please don't pressure me. I need to wait and I hope you can respect that."

You don't have to defend yourself, or give a more detailed explanation. You have a right to feel the way you feel.

Many a date has been ruined by a woman's anxiety over what to say if and when he makes a pass. It's often best to be direct as soon in the evening as possible; you can say, "I'm really interested in you, but I like to get to know a person a little better before I go to bed with them. That doesn't mean it will happen, but I'm not ready yet."

Very determined men often won't take a first no as the final no. They may try to make you feel guilty by saying:
—Are you frigid?
—I thought you were a sexy lady.
—I thought you were a liberated woman.
—It's amazing how you let your intellect control your emotion.

But don't pay attention to these remarks. Sleep with a man when you're ready and not before. You do not have to feel obligated or guilty and if a man is rude or crude, you do not have to be polite.

I remember one time a man I'd dated about three times insisted that we go to his apartment. I said I'd rather not, but he insisted.

We got to his apartment; he proceeded to light a fire and make us drinks. Then he turned the lights down and snuggled next to me. I said to him, "You know, Joe, I told you I wasn't comfortable coming here. Now I'd like to talk to you and finish my drink and then I'd like to go home."

He took me home and the next day he called to apologize for "making an ass of myself." I agreed he had.

YOUR SAFETY

Make some rules for yourself and stick with them. If I meet a man at a party, I will have a drink with him if he asks, but I always meet him at a public place and go in my own car. I will never get into a man's car or go to his apartment until I know quite a bit about him. I don't give out my address or phone number indiscriminately either.

THE NEXUS SEX QUESTIONNAIRE

Since the biggest question that many of us have is "What's normal?" we sent out 300 questionnaires to Nexus members and other formerly married women to find out how they were handling their sex lives. Their answers are fascinating and show the wide divergence of attitudes among divorced women.

Question #1: Did you have a satisfying sex life with your husband?

    50%—Yes

    50%—No

The 50-50 response here corroborates my own rough tally made in discussions with divorced women.

Question #2: Did your sex life have anything to do with your breaking up?

    48%—No

    52%—Yes

Here are some women's comments:

• Everything. . . . I did not love him.

• My husband had sexual difficulties with me. He blamed the problem on me, but he would never try to seek professional help or even try to communicate with me deeply to try to work this out. There were resentments and hostilities on both sides that manifested themselves as sexual problems. He tried to work this out by having affairs.

• Sex was fine, but *very, very* infrequent. It was a major cause of our breakup.

• In comparing me to his girlfriend, he claimed I was not vocal enough (sighs, screams, etc.).

• I think there was no giving on my part, which caused Jim to stray.

• It brought me much dissatisfaction along with a hundred other reasons for breaking up! He had many hang-ups about his body. He felt I was oversexed.

• Sex was the biggest thing we had in common and when I became turned off to our relationship in general, I also became turned-off sex-wise.

Question #3: Do you feel your ex-husband was a good lover?

　　50%—Yes
　　50%—No

• The mechanics were all right, but there grew to be too much antagonism between us. The necessary feelings of really caring were lost and that made the sex get worse and worse.

• I did, but now that I've tried others, he's not so hot.

• No, my husband was a slam-bam type, and he usually fell asleep right afterward.

• Not really.

• All the years he told me what a good lover he was and at that time I had no means of comparison, but in retrospect, I would say average.

• Not really. He was not inventive enough—you need a person with imagination.

• He had a lot of passion—we had it toward each other, but I wasn't sure what I needed, and I could never tell him what I liked.

Question #4: Have you ever had an orgasm with your husband? With another man?

　　80%—Yes
　　20%—No

Among the 80 percent who said yes, 40 percent were

with their husbands first.

• Yes, not with my husband . . . but a man I fancied myself in love with . . . not through intercourse actually, but when he kissed me . . . it was a very sensuous kiss.

• When my husband learned to touch the right spots, I got an orgasm. I think he finally learned from another woman. If we had had more caring, talking, and real communication, we could have reached this point earlier. We were both at fault here.

• Have had many, but only *after* my divorce and with a lover who is extremely knowledgeable, kind, and fun.

• About twenty years ago with my husband through oral sex and not again for many, many years.

• I invariably had orgasms during sex. I would have orgasms during petting sessions even before I indulged in intercourse.

• After four years of marriage with my husband. We were away on vacation and making love on the beach and it finally happened.

• Yes, with my husband, but the orgasm became increasingly better with another man, reason being the other man was quite relaxed about sex. We had known each other for a while and developed a good relationship.

• I have had many orgasms with my ex-husband, but none since. I've yet to meet a man who really satisfies me in bed although I do find sex very enjoyable. However, I must explain that my sexual life has been very sparse since my breakup. My experience is very small.

• I had been having sex with men for about five years—enjoying it, but no orgasms. I met and began dating a very physically oriented professional man who was extremely adept at sex, and the first time we had relations, during oral sex, I was overcome with panting and other physical sensations which I had not previously experienced.

• I was married but I had my first orgasm in the car with

my lover—who was my music teacher.

• I've had many orgasms, the first was when I was twenty-eight, after reading a sex book. I masturbated—it was like finding a new toy.

Question #5: How would you describe having an orgasm? What imagery comes to mind?

• I felt like I melted right into him.

• It's a delicious letting-go feeling.

• My hair roots tingle and my skin feels tight. Afterwards I feel like I've just taken a tranquilizer.

• Chills throughout one's body. A feeling that's almost too pleasantly painful to bear.

• Exquisite throbbing feeling—body seems to be out of control—hard to describe.

• A muscle spasm in the legs and vagina. I describe it as a warm, satisfying, long body sigh.

• I react physically as well as mentally. I lose awareness of everything or anyone around. The moments before orgasm (I'm so excited, I can't spell or write), my entire body tenses and I become almost rigid.

• It's sort of like my whole body opening and saying "thanks."

• Exhilarating high spiral going higher and higher. Like leaving the world and being completely suspended.

• When I think of having an orgasm, a very warm, rushing, full feeling comes to mind.

• There are often body tremors and often waves of heat and often "shock waves (sensations traveling through my body internally, usually from the lower end up and out through my extremities)." These are sometimes in combination and sometimes occur separately. Often, afterward, there is a feeling of exhaustion. Sometimes I have cried with joy.

• Tingling sensation erupting all over my body.

• Falling down a long, black tunnel.

• I get a colorful image, either purple or orange fluid shapes, moving in and out of each other.

Question #6: Do you have fantasies while making love?
            70%—No
            30%—Yes

• Yes, I think of someone I went out with last year. That turns me on every time. Also, I have one lover who likes me to dress up like a hooker. Actually, he had the fantasies.

• I only fantasize during masturbation. My favorite is many men stimulating and making love to me at the same time.

• I used to have many fantasies. The one that stands out in my mind is lying in a field with my lover and having him make love to me.

• Think about sexual episodes, pornographic films or books I have read.

• When I was married, I fantasized being with other men.

• Oh yes, they are so great. I dream of two men and one woman "doing me"—me the center of attention.

• Of sorts. More like thoughts that my partner is very proficient sexually—or truly loves me—or a combination of the two. Sometimes, during masturbation, I think about approval and encouragement from him.

*Question #7: What do you like men to do for you in love-
            making? What turns you on?*

• I first get turned on when a man looks at me in a certain way.

• Oral sex or slow, long foreplay and lovemaking.

• I like to be treated like a queen for the moment any-way. Afterwards, it doesn't matter.

• Stroke me, kiss me, stay with me as long as possible during and after orgasm. I like to be told something endear-ing after orgasm. The sound of the man's voice during lovemaking turns me on. Dancing can turn me on.

• Intense touching, massaging make me feel I'm adored and beautiful.

• I enjoy being made *love* to—not an exercise in expertise. I'm turned on very easily if I like the man. I think a man's enjoyment turns me on. I like to perform fellatio.

• Oral intercourse or manual stimulation is very important to arouse me. I prefer finishing with vaginal intercourse.

• Take their time. Lots of touching of the face.

• Speak, while he makes love, about his feelings. Be creative and try new ways. I don't like to know exactly what he's going to do next like a robot. Kiss me everywhere.

• Stroke me all over my body, be very tender and loving. Kiss me gently during lovemaking, etc.

• I have to first be turned on to a person and then anything he does turns me on sexually.

• I like cunnilingus. I like him to start very tenderly, sometimes touching my face—other times I like him to tell me his favorite fantasies.

• Oral sex; massages of all parts of my body; toe-sucking; anal intercourse, particularly combined with cliteral manipulation; kissing; declarations of approval of my responses, but *definitely not* obviously rehearsed and repeated statements of any kind. Some men seem to feel and others have expressed that such statements are expected and appreciated.

Question #8: Do you have to like or trust a man in order to have an orgasm?

    75%—Yes

    25%—No

Question #9: Do you have orgasms during intercourse?

    50%—Yes

    50%—No

• I have it during intercourse as long as the man manipulates me manually after. No slam-bam, thank-you-ma'am.

• I like the feeling of a man inside me, but I like his touching me, too. I need both.

• Yes, providing I have had several orgasms before we start to have intercourse.

• No, but I like the feeling anyway.

• Most of the time. The longer the relationship and the more quality to the relationship, the more orgasm.

Question #10: How important is orgasm to you?

> 80%—Important
> 20%—Not important

• It's the best part, but just being intimate and feeling close is a good feeling too.

• It's quite important, but a good, tender lover who knows what he's doing and makes you feel important will take the place when orgasm is not possible.

• Now that I've had them, I want them all the time, but cannot achieve them all the time.

• Not important at all times. It is important if I haven't had sex in a while.

• Very important. If I do not reach orgasm, I do not mind as long as I reach it in another way.

• Not as important as really being wanted and loved by the person you are with. But I love to come.

• I feel very satisfied and sexually fulfilled and the more quality, the better. But I've had intercourse without an orgasm and felt sexually fulfilled.

• I really need to have several to be satisfied.

Question #11: Do you masturbate? Do you have a vibrator? How do you feel about masturbation?

> 85%—Yes, do masturbate
> 15%—No

60%—Own vibrator
40%—No

• My ex-husband took the vibrator with him, then it blew up. Masturbation isn't bad, but why bother when there are so many guys around? There is always someone available.

• I have a vibrator and masturbate with it only for fun. Since I have discovered it, I feel it is useful because when you are not relating with a man, it keeps you sexually alive.

• I use a vibrator together with my lover. Do not masturbate.

• A vibrator is great when needed.

• I do not own a vibrator, but I have used one and find it very exciting. I masturbate. I love it. I have only discovered this luxury a few years ago and sometimes will masturbate a few times a week.

• Yes, yes. Sometimes good especially if I'm having a relationship; otherwise, it's a lovely feeling.

• Yes, especially after being involved with a man for a while. I have a vibrator. Masturbation is a healthy, normal occurrence.

• I tried masturbation without success. I intend to try a vibrator next.

• I do when I have the feeling and there is no man around.

• I used to masturbate occasionally when I was married. I don't, now that I'm single. I don't own a vibrator.

• I think it is fun. I like it when I have a lover. I love to masturbate with him watching, but I don't like it when I have no lover.

Question #12: If you have no sex for a month or longer, do you begin to feel deprived or irritated?

60%—Yes
40%—No

- I feel a longing at certain times, not constantly.
- Yes, uptight would be a pretty good word.
- No, because sex is just not a physical outlet to me. Without an emotional involvement, I just don't miss sex.
- I have conditioned myself to go for long periods without sex. Yes, when I do think about it, I feel extremely deprived of that thing which is part of my existence, but I keep myself very busy and try not to think about it.
- No, I just masturbate a lot.
- Definitely!
- Yes, I find I need the whole touching, affection, sex thing altogether, and I get crabby unless I have it.
- I've never been without sex for a month.

Question #13: Describe the best lover you ever had.

- He was the man I was in love with . . . the fact that I loved him made him the best lover I ever had.
- Never really had what I would call a very good lover.
- Physically, he wasn't the best (not a technician), but he really turned me on. It was my feelings for him that made it so good.
- His technique is good. He uses a variety of positions and he can maintain an erection for a long period of time and is ready for lovemaking again in not too long a period of time. He tries very hard to please you and bring you to orgasm.
- I've only had one—my current lover. Fabulous! Devoted, monogamous, affectionate, adoring, jealous, sexy, perceptive, keen sense of what I need.
- He is and was very tender, very anxious to please me and enjoy sex along with him. A "joy of sex" is a good phrase. He is also fun to be with all the time and charming and intelligent. He enjoys having *me* enjoy. It's a mutual giving.
- The best lover I had was the one that found sex as

marvelous as I do and who spends time planning new sexual experiences.

• The best lover I ever had and have is a black man, ten years my junior. He is very loving and sensitive and has no sex hang-ups at all.

• The best lover I ever had made me feel like I was his love goddess. He courted me verbally as well as physically. I was also very free to do the same. He was gentle. He didn't fall asleep soon afterwards. We basked in our bodies afterwards and it made looking forward to the next encounter beautiful.

• Very sweet, loving individual. I held him in very high esteem—had a really good feeling about him—trusted him and respected him.

• He was gentle, with great endurance. His aim was to please me above himself.

• He was a man with no inhibitions and expected really to make a woman happy. He could make love for hours and hours and he put me first and had a technique that made me have many orgasms.

• He would call in the afternoon and tell me what he wanted me to dress in and I would get dressed up and when he arrived, he went wild. It was all those hours of fantasizing.

Question #14: If you really care for a man, how important is it that he is a good lover? How important to you is sex in a relationship?

• If I really care for a man, he automatically becomes a good lover for me. Sex is very important in a relationship for me.

• If I care deeply for a man, he need not be a great lover. That would be a bonus.

• Not important, as long as he is trainable and most are. Sex is *very* important, but it can be improved if two people really want it to be.

• It's very important because if you care for a man, satisfying lovemaking makes the relationship more complete.

• Good sex is important. It is the dressing on the salad.

• Sex is very important in my relationship. I would not continue a relationship even if I care for somebody if he were not a good lover.

• Important, important. Sex is very important to me in a relationship, because I happen to love to love.

• He doesn't have to be a good lover in the beginning. I don't see why I couldn't teach him techniques or tell him what I like. Sex is important to my relationships because it's a way of coming closer and being intimate with one person.

• A good lover is one who would recognize my needs and pleasures and be sensitive to my feelings. In my next relationship, I would like a good and satisfying sex life.

• Quite important. If we care for each other, we talk and make the sex better, finding out what each other likes and needs.

• Definitely—this must function well as anything else.

• Sex is very important to me in a relationship—but there has to be a lot more in the way of common interests.

• It is very important. I feel I must have it. If I don't have sexual feelings, I have no desire to be involved. It is the bottom line.

• Very, but if he isn't, I can help it along.

Question #15: Can you express your sexual needs to men?
                65%—Yes
                35%—No

• I have always been very inhibited about expressing my sexual needs to a man. I think I'm devastated by the idea of some kind of rejection.

• Yes, after a while in a relationship. Not at the beginning though.

• Only recently. Women's groups, raps, and CR have taught me to communicate with the man. I'm still not too outspoken. I either tell him or guide his hands and penis to satisfy me. Before becoming single and learning how to communicate without embarrassment, I had problems.

• Have never had trouble with words.

• I can only express my needs to a man who asks me to tell him what I enjoy. And that is the only kind of man I will continue to see.

• I can express my needs, but with some difficulty. I find verbalizing more difficult than moving his hand to show him what I mean.

• After I feel comfortable with a man, I can express my needs to him—if he's aware of me, he'll know soon enough.

• I talk about it quite directly. When they do something I like, I tell them it really feels good. If it's something I don't like particularly, I don't respond.

• I had problems when I was married, but now I can express my desire by telling my partner or I can express it nonverbally.

Question #16: Is it hard to find men to sleep with? How do you feel about casual sex?

            70%—Yes, hard to find men to sleep with
            30%—No
            40%—Yes, casual sex, okay
            60%—No

• It is very easy to find men to sleep with. I do not enjoy casual sex, therefore, I do not participate.

• There are men I could sleep with, but physically I don't want to sleep with just any man. I am not attracted to most of the eligible men I meet.

• It is easy to find men to sleep with, but I find it hard because I'm really picky. I have to be involved, one way or another first. I don't like casual sex.

• Men that I would care for in a complete way are hard

to find. Any old kind of guy is easy to find, and casual sex is okay if you like the guy.

• I personally cannot have casual sex. Just cannot melt into that with someone not very "special" to me.

• I feel casual sex is fine if casual means a casual relationship that I know will lead nowhere, i.e., marriage. If you mean sex for sex's sake with one and all, then I don't like casual sex.

• If I dig someone I've just met, I would have sex with him.

• I don't look for men to sleep with. I sleep very well alone. Casual sex leaves me feeling empty, like a disposable cup.

• Casual sex is out of the question. I tried it once and got so frightened that I ran like hell. I'm talking about a pickup at a bar—to me that is casual. I have to feel something and know the man a little while. This is very difficult for me, as most men I meet I only see two or three times and then I am usually turned off by their advances.

• No, I am not interested in casual sex.

• I don't get turned on to a man easily. Therefore, casual sex with me is completely out.

• Not hard to find men, but I don't like casual sex—so I do without it if I have no men I like.

• It isn't hard. I let a man know I want sex, if I like him—either by the way I dress or I just say it!

Question #17: What have you learned about sex since you've been single?

• I think the most important thing I've learned is that it's necessary to tell your lover what you want; I still can't really do it, but I'm trying.

• I've learned a lot. Every man is different and you really don't know what a man is like until you've slept with him. That's when you learn if he's selfish, giving, outgoing, uptight, or whatever!

• That I enjoy it immensely and found out how much I missed it when my marriage was sexless.

• Everything.

• There seems to be a lot of it. It can be lots of fun with the right partner.

• I have been more relaxed and more experimental in sex than when I was married.

• How to be free to express what I feel.

• Men are not that free sexually. They are more hung up about their bodies than I am or was.

• The biggest revelation is the openness among women and even discussing sexual problems. I would like to know really how to masturbate or use a vibrator instead of the hit-and-miss things I do now for relief.

• I've learned I can have good sex with more than one person and that each person can teach me something about myself.

• It's important in a relationship.

• Sex had always been good—married or single. I don't think I could learn anything more than I already know.

• I've learned that I am very sensual and very sexual and that I like to have a gentle sort of lover sometimes and a rough one sometimes and that I can be the initiator of sex and I like that a lot.

• A lot of fun can be had and I think I'm more sexual than a lot of the men I meet.

The wide range of response to our questionnaire shows how different we all are. As single women we have to make our own rules for our sexual behavior.

9

How to Get Into the Job World and Move Up

Women who can find work they like have a much better adjustment to divorce. Work can bring you money and a sense of achievement and independence.

Yet one of the hardest things for a newly divorced woman to cope with is *having* to find a job and having no self-esteem and very little experience in the working world. It can be a very bitter pill to be told to go out and get a job in order to "get your feet wet," and find yourself being offered dead-end, low-paying positions.

One forty-seven-year-old woman who had spent her time in the home raising her children, and was forced to go back to work as a secretary after her husband left her, said, "I had to swallow my pride. I felt like I really had come down in the world." Yet she was able to persevere and to learn enough about her boss's job in a hotel to eventually take over more responsibility and move up as an administrator in the banquet office.

SOME FIRSTHAND REPORTS
Geri

Geri, another organization member, created her own job. It began when she went to work as a secretary for the manager of the creative packaging department of a large corporation.

"My boss was very, very difficult," she says. "Even though I couldn't pass the secretarial skills qualifications (I wasn't fast enough), he wanted a person with an art background.

"I worked myself up to my present position because the president's secretary wanted someone to help her catalog the company art collection. I continued in my regular secretarial job and did the art cataloging on weekends and at night.

"However, the work load became too heavy to do on overtime, so they asked me to write a proposal of what I thought needed to be done to the collection. So I wrote a job description and got the job.

"I was still on a secretarial pay scale. By the time a year had passed, I was managing a huge collection of art. So I called a friend in personnel and she suggested I write a new job description and she would see that it got to the correct people for consideration to upgrade the job.

"After this, they made a decision about what I was to be paid, and I was promoted to a managerial level. Now I am making a nice salary in a job that I created called Curator of Collections. In corporations there is a tremendous amount of leeway or flexibility to move around and use your own abilities and talents. You must look around and make yourself useful."

Darlene

Darlene is twenty-seven years old and has one child, eight years old. She has been divorced seven years. She worked at two jobs when her husband first left, one as a book-keeper in a fish company. "They told me I would like it or hate it, but if I learned to love it, it would never be out of my blood," she says today. She found the business fascinating. Fish were being shipped from all over the world. "Fish has more personality than meat," she says. "One day I ran into a friend who was opening a fish-fry place, so I helped and learned to cut fish. I started going to the Fulton Fish Market with him. The first time I went there, I fell in love with it. When everybody is sleeping, the place is so alive and bustling.

"It is a lot of heavy work, but I did it. The fish come in 125-pound boxes, which I had to lift. I did all the cutting of the fish. I really developed muscles. I started to work at 3 A.M., would open the store at seven and work until seven at night. I got tired, but I really loved it.

"When I originally started in the business, I had a lot of trouble from the men. Their general attitude was "Why don't you go home and knit?" or "Why don't you go find a husband?" They just couldn't take me seriously in the fish business. Later on, though, when they realized I took my job seriously, they developed respect for me."

Kitty and Claudia

Kitty is fifty, Claudia is forty-three. They met in a women's group, and started a business together—a clothing boutique.

CLAUDIA: When we started, we decided to use the space in Kitty's house because we knew we couldn't afford to rent a place. We mailed cards to anyone we could think of—and about seventy-five came to the opening. A friend in the business had told us where we could buy clothes at a discount.

KITTY: We had cheese and wine and plants all over. It was really one of the most exciting things that has ever happened to me.

CLAUDIA: And we truly set it up by ourselves, without any help.

KITTY: We turned the merchandise over very quickly.

We were not taking any salaries, we paid for my phone bill, a little rent, and a little electricity.

CLAUDIA: It was strictly work and no money at the beginning. It was primarily a feeling of wanting to do something for ourselves and stand our our own two feet because we were all victims of being so dependent on our men. This was something we felt would make us feel like whole persons.

KITTY: I've never worked before in my whole life. I just didn't even know how to go about it. This boutique gave me something to do, something for myself. It made me want to get up in the morning. For a year after my separation, I felt I was vegetating, talking to myself: "Shall I go back to school? Shall I get my degree?" I put all that aside for a while. This was therapy for me, the best therapy I've ever had.

KITTY: It was a monumental thing to do and a worthwhile experience. I would advise anyone who has a dream to go ahead and try it.

Janet

"I got involved with making jewelry when I was nineteen years old. I was working at a secretarial job at the time. Then I got married and sort of dropped it.

"But about six years ago, I heard of a teacher teaching jewelry-making and smithing—the art of making big pieces, silver bowls, and trays. I began to take a class and wear my own pieces. As I wore my jewelry, my friends started to ask me to copy some of them, so I did. I started working with gold, too.

"I am really doing better financially than I expected. It is a nice thing for a woman to do at home. I have my studio set up in the basement and I feel very good about it."

If you are looking for a job, here are some tips from co-author, Victoria Pellegrino, who directs Victoria Associates, and runs career counseling workshops for women.

CAREER ADVICE FROM VICTORIA ASSOCIATES

The first thing to do is to look for a career goal. Work for someone you would like to become, and/or invest in training. If you're not sure what you want to do, talk to as many people as you can to get job information. You can also look through the *Dictionary of Occupational Titles* in the library.

Sit down with a pencil and paper and analyze your strengths. What are you good at? What skills can you transfer to the job world? Are you good with money? Detail work? Organizing? Selling? Can your cooking, gardening, or sewing talents be utilized? Do you know enough about your husband's business to venture into that field yourself? Would you prefer a job working outdoors? Are you strong? Are you creative? In what areas? Would you like to work with children? Older people? Animals? Are you good at fund-raising? Writing? Do mechanical things fascinate you?

Do an inventory of your own skills so that you can come up with a goal that is meaningful to you. Most people are successful doing the things they like best. Remember that. Don't settle for less than you can do. Keep investing in yourself and building your potential.

Once you have a goal, you can take steps that are in your best interests. If you need additional help, find a career counseling service through your local YWCA or university. Make contacts in your field of interest to find out what jobs are available. Update your résumé and spend time on putting it together.

Résumé Tips

Many women hate their résumés because they know their résumés don't represent them. Too many unimaginatively list dates and duties. *Your résumé should paint an integrated picture of you as an achiever.*

Rule 1. List achievements; do not simply list responsibilities.

For example:

Before: Assistant to Personnel Director. Responsible for interviewing candidates for management positions.

After: Assistant to Personnel Director. Set up a new system of interviewing which cut interview time in half. Decreased number of irrelevant interviews by devising pre-interview forms.

Rule 2. Show cause and effect. Present your skills in the language of the work world.

Before: I made crafts for the local hospital and fair.

After: I made crafts which netted the Society for Retarded Children $700 in a two-day sale. I increased the sales volume of the local children's hospital gift shop by $3,000 a year.

Before: Clerk: Medical coding, insurance forms, preparation of hospital records for investigation.

After: Medical Records Department: Supervised medical coding of all in-house cases for hospital with an annual census of approximately 4,000, processed all outpatient insurance claims for an average of 700 E.R. cases per month; designed a system of record keeping for special services subject to periodic state inspection.

Here are some common résumé traps:

• Don't list names of people with whom you have collaborated. It's better to list what you did by yourself.

• Don't list names of others unless they're famous enough to make you look impressive.

• Don't say what your husband did. It looks as if you don't feel your achievements are strong enough without his name and position.

• Don't say you were "involved in" such and such a project. Say what you contributed.

• Use dates only when they're good for you.

• Use words like: designed, coordinated, initiated, produced, supervised, made major contribution in, recruited, hired, arranged. Words that show you are an active, energetic person.

• Show what you did: what the problem was and what you did to turn the situation around. For example: "The school had never made any money on this particular dance; however, I brought in $2,000 in profits as chairman of the dance."

• Use the word "I" or "we." It's better to say "I sold 300 tickets" or "We sold 300 tickets" rather than "300 tickets were sold."

• Be as specific as possible. For example, say: "I selected graphics" rather than "I worked with artists."

Or, instead of saying, "I initiated, conceptualized, and researched a new product packaging that is currently in use," say, "I designed the first attractive box for tapes for use on home shelves."

Instead of saying, "I initiated program developments for the college," say, "I initiated six new programs for the college."

Here are two résumés—one was done first chronologically, then a Victoria Associates staff person redid the résumé in a functional style. Look over the two résumés and see which one you think is the strongest.

EXHIBIT A
"Before" Chronological Résumé

JOB OBJECTIVES

Researcher

EMPLOYMENT

1971–Present   Free-lance writer and active
                        in organizing and operating

a cooperative day-care center

ARTICLES

"The Home," *Woman Power*, Peter Workman Press, 1973
"Affairs," *Pageant Magazine*, August, 1972
"Legal Rights," *Pageant Magazine*, 1971
"Interview with Germaine Greer," *Pageant Magazine*, 1971
"Woman's Yellow Pages," *San Francisco Chronicle*, April 11, 1971

RELATED EMPLOYMENT

Research Asst.

Controversy, Holt, Rinehart and Winston, 1969 A college freshmen reader organized around such controversial themes as: sexism, racism, and political and aesthetic theories

Research Asst.

Point of Departure, Dell Publishing Co., 1967
An anthology of short stories centered around the theme of adolescence.

Editorial Asst.

Robert S. Cold, *A Jazz Lexicon*, Alfred A. Knopf, 1969 A dictionary of jazz slang and musical terminology

OTHER EMPLOYMENT

Actress in various Off-Broadway productions and summer and winter stock companies from late 50s to mid-60s

Grinberg Film Libraries, Inc.
630 9th Avenue, N.Y.C.

Film Images, Inc.
Rosalind Rossoff
c/o Bimberg
357 W. 55th Street., N.Y.C.

Film Library, Museum of Modern Art
Margareta Ackermark
21 W. 53rd Street, N.Y.C.

"After" Functional Résumé

Job Objective: RESEARCHER

Research

Selected essays, both classical and modern on provocative and relevant subjects such as the mass media, racism, sexism, political and aesthetic theories for a college freshman reader. Published by Holt, Rinehart and Winston, 1969.

Selected short stories on the theme of adolescence for an anthology. Published by Dell, 1967. To date, it has sold close to 200,000 copies and has been adopted as part of the curriculum in numerous high schools throughout the country.

Assisted a jazz expert with his research for a dictionary of jazz slang. It was published by Knopf, 1969.

Writing

As a free-lance writer, I proposed, researched, and wrote articles on *Infidelity*, *An Interview with Germaine Greer*, and *Legal Rights* (all for *Pageant Magazine*); *The Home* (The New York Woman's Directory); and *Woman's Yellow Pages* for the *San Francisco Chronicle*.

Film

Coordinated in the circulation department of the Museum of Modern Art Film Library.

Assisted in all phases of distribution of 16mm films on art and art history, mainly circulated to film societies and colleges and schools.

Cataloged ABC-TV news footage at Grinberg Film Library.

An actress in several educational films as well as Off-Broadway and summer and winter stock companies. Also appeared in a number of Children's Theatre productions.

Interviewing:

During the course of my free-lance writing, I have interviewed feminist writer Germaine Greer, civil rights attorney Ephraim London, psychiatrist Dr. John Schimel, as well as women in architecture, civil engineering, and blue-collar jobs such as carpentry, bricklaying, and house painting.

Communications

Guest lecturer on the theater at New Jersey State College and before the Association of University Women of New Jersey. I

have also been interviewed
on local radio stations:
WBAI
WNEW
BBC

Other Job Experience

Worked as parent/teacher with day-care center for almost four years: Village Day-Care Center Cooperative.

Education

Texas Christian University, Fort Worth, Texas. Radio/Drama Goodman Theatre of Art Institute of Chicago.

The second functional resumé has more punch and is more directed. The first, in comparison, seems to have too many unrelated loose ends.

The second functional résumé also shows accomplishments rather than simply duties and responsibilities. Dates in this case were left out because the woman seeking employment is forty-four and has been unemployed for some time. By leaving out dates she gives herself more of a chance to be selected for an interview, and that's the purpose of a résumé—to get your foot in the door. After that, you can take it from there.

Job Interview Tips

Prepare yourself for your job interview. Instead of thinking about the negatives in your background, concentrate on your strengths.

Write down the functions of the job you're applying for, and next to each, write down two or three things you've done which relate to each function. If the job calls for organizing ability, what have you organized? If the job calls for sales ability, what have you sold? You can even bring in your volunteer experience—you haven't sold real estate before, but you have sold community fund drive tickets. Once you know beforehand how your experience relates to the functions of the job you're seeking, you'll feel much better and more prepared and confident.

You have to sell yourself on a job interview. If you are overly polite or modest, an interviewer may fail to notice what you have to offer. Have some well-thought-out stories ready which show up your skills, e.g., "I convinced six organizations to back our community efforts to improve Lawrence Park. I can really convince people to do things, which is why I know I am a good salesperson."

Be prepared to be asked difficult questions and work on your answers beforehand with a friend. If you haven't worked for a while, emphasize your commitment to work now.

Divorced women with growing children especially have problems, because an employer may be worried about child-care arrangements. You must reassure him by saying something like, "I've arranged to have a housekeeper take care of my children and I'm able to devote my full time and energy to the job. I realize I've had a problem with young children, but I've come up with a satisfactory solution which works for many women." You must show that you have things firmly under control or you will probably not be hired.

As you work, you must continuously take the initiative for advancement. Don't wait to be noticed; make things happen, solve problems, define *yourself* through your own activities.

Many women who are returning to the work force for the first time lack confidence in themselves. But you have to take your best bet and jump in and move on from there.

Again, the most important thing to settle on is a goal—a direction, so that you can earn a decent wage. You will meet obstacles as you move toward your goal. There is still great job discrimination against women, and the fight for equal rights has yet to be won. But remember this: freedom is in the striving. You are not alone. Many, many women are in this struggle with you.

10

How to Stretch Your Dollar

Divorce makes us poorer. Each and every one of us has to deal with that bitter reality.

Some people still believe that women who are divorced live lives of ease as a result of alimony. What a myth that is! Alimony is awarded in about 14 percent of divorce cases, and that percentage is shrinking fast. One out of twenty of the 2.8 million divorced women receive alimony today. Many women are entitled to alimony but are not receiving it. In a recent study of alimony payments in Indiana, nine out of ten men were in arrears in their alimony payments. Moreover, only 44 percent of all divorced women receive child support, and only 47 percent of those collecting such support are getting it on a regular basis.

The nonpayment of child support has been an important factor in the increase of families living in poverty. Today, one-third of the families living in poverty are headed by women, and there has been an increase of 33 percent of female-headed families living in poverty in the last decade. Many of these poverty families are the ex-wives and children of affluent fathers, according to a Rand Corporation report. The report verified that "children of many physicians, attorneys, and other $25,000 to $30,000-a-year men are on Aid for Families with Dependent Children."

Surprisingly enough, many of us did not realize there would be much less money after a divorce. People concentrate on the emotional aspect of divorce and because of the stress and shock, forget the financial aspect until it is hitting them square in the face. One study showed that almost half of all divorced people find their poor financial situation after divorce totally unexpected!

While men have less money, too, after a divorce, statistics show that it is women who still bear the brunt of loss of income. According to one study in the 1968–1972 period, women who were divorced, widowed, or separated showed a family income drop of 16.5 percent, while comparable men experienced an income rise of 10.4 percent during the same period. Intact families meanwhile had an increase of 35.5 percent.

The reasons why women suffer more financially after divorce are complex. Obviously, most men earn far more than women and their incomes increase with seniority. A woman who has not earned a paycheck in years, or who is in a low-paying, low-level job, is bound to have a more difficult time supporting herself. Then, too, courts do not award financial settlements that allow women to live in the same life-style as before. Over and over, you hear women say, "I can barely scrape by with money for my kids, and my husband has remarried and bought a new house and a new car." Many women, too, who want to work find they can't because they have young children and there are no affordable day-care centers available. Because the credit rating was probably in her husband's name and because of discrimination, a woman may also find herself unable to get a loan if she needs one.

I know that I had to cut down on my spending after my divorce. I am careful about what I spend on clothes, whereas when I was married, I would have thought nothing of spending money on a shopping spree or a trip to the beauty parlor. It was a tough adjustment to have so much less money and really not to know how to get more. Suddenly I had to put myself on a budget in order to make ends meet.

One problem we have is insisting on living the way we lived before we were divorced. We want to live in the same house, shop at the same stores, have the same little luxuries we have been used to. And because we're experiencing enough emotional deprivation after divorce, the financial deprivation makes us that much more angry.

From my experience, those women who have the toughest time adjusting to divorce are those who refuse to live any differently from the way they did during marriage, and who feel a tremendous loss of pride as a result of their change in financial status. Those women who have adjusted best are those who are able to change their way of living to a more compatible life-style.

Arline, thirty-five, took this route. "I realized I couldn't keep my house in the section where I lived, so I decided to sell it. I began looking at a house that would bring me an income. I had to look in a neighborhood where two-family housing is allowed. I found a nice house, with much less upkeep and grounds. I rent the top floor and that pays my mortgage. It was difficult to 'come down' but I felt wonderful having the security of that money paying for my mortgage . . . smart, too, that I could decide how to make my assets work for me."

Another woman I know owned a lovely house on a good-sized piece of property. Her husband had abandoned her and she was determined to keep her house. It was a matter of pride. She sacrificed and worked, but rarely had food in the refrigerator or decent clothes for her daughter. However, she did keep her house.

Other women I know have coped with less money by adding kitchen facilities and a bathroom to an upstairs area or den, so that it could be rented out to college students or a couple, to bring more income into the family. This makes sense and many women can do it.

Women should make it their business to learn as *much* about money as they can. A consciousness-raising event occurred at the women's art gallery I belong to. We had to fill out tax forms and nobody wanted to do it. Nobody knew how. The decision was almost made to hire an accountant—or to ask a husband or boyfriend.

But then we said, "Hey, wait a minute. Aren't we independent women? We should know how to do these things." So we decided to struggle through.

FINANCIAL TIPS

I think that all women should learn about money—how to get a mortgage, get credit, how to save and invest. There is still great discrimination about money and credit, but we can help ourselves by learning as much as we can, and then fighting for our rights. Women need economic consciousness-raising very badly.

Because all divorced women are so concerned about money, we usually have a financial speaker attend some of our meetings every year. One evening last year, we had Barbara Dank, a financial and money management counselor in the New York area, talk to a group of about two hundred. Here are some of the highlights of her talk:

Budgeting Yourself

She suggests that every woman do an inventory of her entire financial picture. Buy an inexpensive calculator and sit down and figure out what your yearly expenses are. Know what it costs you in interest for your mortgage and loans; what your yearly phone and electric bill costs are. After doing this, you can determine what you need each week to support your life-style.

Miss Dank also suggests that you calculate future costs you are likely to encounter, e.g., college, vacations, or moving expenses. Start planning for the future, she emphasized.

Social Security Benefits

A woman is eligible for her social security benefits at age sixty-two if she has worked forty quarters in her life. A quarter is a period of three consecutive months, e.g., January, February, and March.

A woman is also eligible for the social security benefits of her husband if she had been married twenty years or over (even if she gets a divorce).

Ms. Dank advised all women to call their local Social Security office and ask that information on their status be sent to them. Each person can get a complete computer "printout" analysis of her present social security status by calling her local office.

If a woman lies to her employer about her age, this will not affect her social security benefits, says Ms. Dank. The government won't tattle on her to her employer. When she is ready and eligible to collect, all she needs to do is present legal proof of age and begin collecting.

Practical Suggestion for Liquid Cash

If a woman finds herself in the position of needing liquid cash and has no money, Ms. Dank suggested that she carefully look around her house for furniture, jewelry, and silver, sell those possessions she doesn't need, put some of the money in the bank, and start collecting interest on that money. You could also have a garage sale to earn cash.

Passbook Loans

Pass book loans are the cheapest way to pay off your car.

You end up paying only 2 percent interest on your loan, since your money is earning interest while it is in the bank.

How much money should I spend on an apartment or house?

A rule of thumb is to say that 30 percent of your income should go toward housing. The rest should be divided up for other expenses.

All these suggestions are good ones. Obviously, there are only limited ways you can stretch a dollar. But you can evaluate your money situation and then make some financial decisions. I've found that many women are afraid to think about their situations, and consequently there is no financial planning at all. But it would be better for most of us to set up a budget and stick to it—this would lessen a lot of anxieties over money.

You also may be able to make some of your skills pay off. One woman I know, who loved to sew, began an alterations business in her home. She was then able to deduct part of her apartment rent when taxes were due. Two other organization members began a paper-hanging service!

I know it can be aggravating and infuriating to have to scrimp and save. But if you can look at some of your struggles as a challenge, you won't make yourself so unhappy. It *can* be challenging to handle your own money without having to account to anyone.

As a last tip, leave aside some pin money just for treats for yourself. This needn't be a large sum of money, but even a few dollars a week spent on pampering yourself will make you less grim.

Many divorced women take a tough "I have to tighten my belt" approach. But don't pull the belt too tight. Don't spend every last cent on your children either. Budget some money for yourself—it's important for your well-being.

YOUR HOME

After a divorce, the home is the first to show wear-and-tear. Because there's less money, the repairs don't get done. Because a woman is not so interested in playing the homemaker any more, there's a tendency to let houses or apartments go.

I have found, however, that letting my house go downhill really depresses me. My environment is important to me.

I changed my bedroom after my divorce, but I didn't spend a lot of money. I got a great big mirror from the Salvation Army for eight dollars and hung it over my bed. My mother-in-law crocheted me a black lacy tablecloth and I put it over an old table, and bought a 1920 wicker lamp for two dollars at a garage sale. I got some big pillows and put some hats on the wall and plants around, and had a lovely bedroom that makes me feel happy every time I enter it.

When I need something done around the house, I try to do it myself. I stapled fabric to Christina's bedroom walls myself. If I need wallpapering done, I'd have a friend or two help me.

I am certainly not the concerned housekeeper I was before my divorce—I used to read *House and Garden* magazine, and now I never do. That's pretty typical, I think, of the way most divorced women feel. But I do like to keep some comfort. My motto for my house: Presentable Plus Plants. Plants cover a multitude of sins.

I always keep a lot of candles around, too. When I can, I try to have one room painted a year. This keeps the house somewhat presentable.

CLOTHES

After a divorce, many women feel they have to make themselves over in order to attract a man. Sometimes, getting a new image can be a great lift, and when you're ready for it, I say, why not? If you're not sure of your shopping sense, bring along a friend who can help you.

Be careful, however. Some women deliberately buy sexy-looking clothes, but they have a tendency to look cheap. Moreover, one or two nice outfits will look better than four or five cheap ones.

I would opt for looking classy and chic rather than blatantly sexy. You don't need piled-on eyelashes, long earrings, or tight sweaters to look sexy.

I like clothes, but I don't think they're that important. I think people notice if we're happy, rather than what we have on. Haven't you ever worn a dress once or twice and then had someone say to you, "Is that new?"

I don't think we should be so uptight about what we look like. Looks are important for self-esteem, but other aspects of our lives are just as important, so let's concentrate on those, too.

11

Tips and Asides

- FINDING A THERAPIST
- DEALING WITH RELATIVES
- DEALING WITH YOUR MOTHER-IN-LAW
- DEALING WITH HIS NEW WIFE
- WHEN MECHANICAL THINGS GO WRONG
- MOVING
- HOLIDAYS
- ENTERTAINING
- TRAVELING AS A SINGLE WOMAN

FINDING A THERAPIST

I have been to a therapist two times in my life, while I was married, and while Andy and I were separating. Then I felt I wanted to be on my own and test what I had learned. I would not hesitate to return to therapy if I felt the need again.

Seeing a therapist can be very helpful during this stressful time. However, choose a therapist carefully. I believe that the best therapists for divorced people are those who have been divorced or separated themselves. They seem able to empathize much more than a therapist who is safe and secure in his or her marriage.

Many therapists who have not been divorced cannot understand some of the extreme stages divorced people go through. Some therapists, too, have a textbook attitude toward divorce. They feel that once you are divorced, the marital relationship is over, and they look with suspicion upon those of us who continue to have contact with our ex-husbands. However, contact with one's ex-husband is *normal*, fantasies about the ex-husband are normal. The relationship isn't black or white. Some women have close, affectionate relationships with their ex-husbands; some cannot speak to each other without screaming. There are no "shoulds" or "should nots" for this postmarital relationship.

I think, too, that almost everything we say as divorced people is viewed with suspicion by many therapists who haven't been divorced. They start from the premise that there is something wrong with you, or you would be able to find a healthy man to relate to. They also can be very antagonistic toward the idea of your seeing a married man, viewing it as a deep need to keep away from a more committed relationship, rather than seeing that a married man is often just an instant man to cling to at a lonely and vulnerable period in your life.

Occasionally, too, I've heard stories about therapists who were blinded by unconscious prejudice against women. Here, for instance, is a story told to me by a Nexus member:

"I felt my children were undergoing a trauma, so I went to family counseling, even though my income was very small. We had a very nice lady, a very kind woman, the children related well to her, even though they didn't want to go—they minded everything at this time because their father was moving out of the house and had tried to poison the children's minds against me. I had just filed for divorce. The children were totally upset. We would go to therapy twice a week. Sometimes I would go alone. The therapist was convinced that my husband's main concern was that he wanted the kids to come through the divorce the right way. She kept saying to me, 'Oh, you know, you have good cooperation from Mr. Smith because he really is trying.' I used to say, 'What he tells you is one thing and what he does is another.' What he was doing was really horrible. He kept taking the kids on weekends and after the weekend, they would be completely out of hand and incorrigible. My daughter would come back and say all the things that my ex-husband had said to her, like 'Because of you, our lives are being ruined,' and, 'Daddy really loves you, he really wants you, you are the miserable, horrible one.' They kept pointing the finger at me. I would say, 'Daddy is upset now and is hurting you by telling you these things.' I tried to explain why I wanted the divorce, but I didn't think they could understand very well because they were so young, and I really didn't want to point out his faults. I thought they would find them out as they became older. He really went about destroying their minds and I believe that they always will be scarred.

"My ex-husband was not living in the house for nine months . . . and we went to court to get the divorce and we had a jury (requested by my husband) and the divorce was denied! My nerves were completely shattered. I said, 'You know I am absolutely fearful of what is going to happen now. He is going to move back into the house, and now that he feels as though I have destroyed him, he is going to destroy me.' And the therapist said to me, 'Oh, I think you are overreacting to this, you are just nervous, he would never, ever come back into the house because he knows what this could do to the children.' I said, 'You are absolutely wrong.' Then, I knew that she never did believe in me and she had been fooled by him. She thought I was a hysterical divorcée.

"That very night he moved back in. He proceeded to destroy all of us. He was despicable. He would come in in the middle of the night and start making dinner and drop butter and eggs on the floor and leave the mess all over the house. He made as much noise as he could.

"Roland was a good con artist and he made the therapist believe he was telling the truth. He also is a fighter and can never let anyone get the better of him. The therapist later said to me, 'I really thought you were acting out of emotion and I really didn't believe that he would do all that,' but I had lost all confidence in her by then."

Irene's story, while an unusual one, does point up what I've seen many times. The divorced woman, especially the woman who is economically dependent on her husband, allows her feelings to show—her anger, her fear, and "society" (therapists, doctors, lawyers) looks at her as neurotic, hysterical, and in the wrong. The man, who has a responsible job and has been used to winning all his life, is able to hold his emotions in check and convince people that he is a good guy and that his wife is the hysterical one.

If you get the feeling that your therapist (or lawyer) is not taking you seriously, find another.

Studies show, too, that a startling percentage of therapists take advantage of their female patients. In 1973, a survey in the *American Journal of Psychiatry* showed that 13 percent of the psychiatrists questioned had indulged in erotic practices with their patients and 20 percent thought that such contacts might occasionally be beneficial to the patient.

Dr. William Masters, the respected sex therapist, and co-author, with his wife, of the book, *The Pleasure Bond*, has blasted these "patient rapes" and called them a "disgrace to the profession." I couldn't agree more.

As a patient, you often are lonely and susceptible to any show of love. Built into the patient-therapist relationship is trust and some intimacy, and a doctor can exploit this. So beware!

Make sure that you carefully check out the credentials of any therapist you find. Studies are revealing that fraudulent sex, marriage, and divorce counselors abound, because these counselors do not have to be licensed. If you are seeking help, check out credentials. Be sure you like and respect her or him, feel good about the way you are being treated, and that your therapist believes that women are whole people who can achieve the same autonomy that men can.

While I believe therapy can be most beneficial at some times for some people, I do not look upon it as the only answer. Therapy can be expensive, and I've found many times that I can rely on myself and work out my own problems through the ways I've suggested throughout this book.

DEALING WITH RELATIVES

Your relatives may be a big help to you, but if they're not, it probably isn't because they don't want to be. Unless a family member has been through a divorce, he or she may not be able to relate to your pain. Moreover, they, too, may have had an emotional investment in your marriage and may be hurt and bewildered by your breakup.

Because they want you to "fix things up," they may suggest silly things like, "Why don't you two have another baby?" or, "All you two need is some time alone, why not take a three-week vacation?" They mean well, but remarks of this kind aren't too helpful.

Don't feel that you have to keep up a smiling front if you're hurting. You can say, "It's a difficult time for me right now—I'm just not feeling well." Don't feel you have to explain to your family all the details of why you're splitting up. Some things are private.

One woman told me, "My mother-in-law kept saying, 'How can you do this to me?' To her! What about what *I* was going through?" All you can answer to this kind of complaint is, "I know it's hard for you, too." Try not to let your family cause you to feel guilty. It's your life!

Some of your relatives may want to maintain their relationships with your ex-husband. If your brother and your husband were fishing companions for the past fifteen years, neither one is going to want to give that up. Remember this has nothing to do with how your brother feels about you. Time has a way of working some of these things out. Usually in the end, blood is thicker than water.

DEALING WITH YOUR MOTHER-IN-LAW

This is an area of great confusion for many divorced women, one fraught with complex emotions.

In the beginning, you may be delighted and grateful if his family doesn't reject you. But it is difficult to remain involved with your in-laws, because seeing them will only serve to remind you of your past married life, and may make you feel your loss and "failure" even more acutely.

Moreover, at some time in the future, you will probably want to pull out of any close in-law relationship. Charlotte, a thirty-eight-year-old art therapist, divorced, and her ex-husband remarried. She and her mother-in-law liked each other and continued to see each other once a week. At first, Charlotte was delighted with this closeness. But later, when she was involved with a new man, she felt hemmed in. "I feel his mother is still snooping into my life, and I want more privacy now," she says. "But I feel guilty, too, because she has been so nice to me." If Charlotte had known her feelings would change (and it's predictable that they would), she wouldn't have established as close a relationship in the beginning.

In addition, if you are close to your ex-husband's family, you may hear more about his exploits ("Did you know Harry has a new girlfriend?" "Did you hear about Harry's raise?") than you would like.

On the other hand, it's nice for your children to have a relationship with their grandparents. And grandparents usually don't want to be cut off completely either. Many divorced women make it a point to have their children visit grandparents on holidays and birthdays, and I think this is an excellent idea.

My best advice here is: try to maintain a balance that you feel comfortable with. Ask yourself: "Why do I want to continue the relationship? Do I really like my mother-in-law? Is it for the children? Am I doing it in order to keep in touch with my husband?" Once you are clear about the positives and pitfalls, as well as your own feelings, you can initiate the kind of relationship you want to have

DEALING WITH HIS NEW WIFE

This isn't easy. You probably feel jealous and angry, not necessarily nice feelings, but very human ones! The adjustment to a new wife takes time, even if you're glad you're divorced, or you wanted the divorce.

What can you do to make your adjustment easier? As a general rule, especially if you have children, you're better off to establish a distant but cordial relationship, especially if you're still dependent on your ex-husband financially, and/or you want your children to have a good relationship with him. However, situations arise that send all good intentions out the window.

Situation A:

What do you do if his new wife calls you to discuss him? This is more common than you might think.

It's probably better not to become deeply involved. She's really asking you to collude with her, and this could hurt you. She might also tell you things you'd be better off not hearing.

On the other hand, many women tend to fantasize that the husband's second marriage is without problems. By talking with the second wife, one can find out that things may *not* be so rosy.

Andy's new wife, Françoise, called me and I resented it at first—but my curiosity got the best of me. I found out that they were having difficulties, and she was, in fact, quite unhappy.

You can be nasty, or simply tell her you don't want to talk. But this may not be your best decision. If you're not sure how you want to handle this relationship, say you're busy and call back. Then think it over carefully. Are you capable of talking to her without upsetting yourself? Will it enhance or hurt your relationship with your children? With your ex-husband? *Why* are you talking to her?

At one time, the children were upset about some of the things Françoise said, e.g., Andy was working so hard he might die. She also asked them about me and pumped them for information.

I tried to explain to the children how to deal with her. I told them she was immature and that they could say, "I'd rather not discuss that." Most kids think they have to answer anything. I suggested another alternative, saying to their dad, "I'd rather be with you right now, she's asking me a lot of questions." Of course I told them they could always say they didn't know.

When she called me to discuss Andy, she told me how good she was to the children and how much she loved them. I told her I was happy about that, but that what she'd been saying to them was destructive. She stopped, and I was glad I'd spoken to her.

Situation B:

Your alimony check was due two weeks ago and you are frantic. His new wife always sends the checks. Should you call her? You've called him and can't reach him.

Call and be nice. It's hard to do this because she's in the top-dog position and your tendency might be to be nasty. But take the attitude that it's a business call and that you're just inquiring about the check. Have they sent it? Or perhaps it's been lost in the mail? If she is nasty, you can call him or drop him a note.

Don't start fighting. If they don't want to send a check, your nastiness can give them the excuse they've been waiting for—"Why should we send her anything? She's a bitch who's making our lives miserable." Appeal in terms of the children, and how they need the support.

WHEN MECHANICAL THINGS GO WRONG

What to do when the TV blows a fuse and you feel like blowing yours? Or when the basement floods and you feel like crying? Or the car breaks down in the middle of the parkway? You will feel most overwhelmed by these problems during the first year of your separation because your level of tension is so high. You may cry because a toilet breaks down, or because it's just snowed heavily and you can't get your car out of the driveway. A friend told me, "Once my basement flooded soon after he'd moved out. I remember thinking, 'I wouldn't be in this house and worried about this damn water on the floor if it weren't for him.' Every time something went wrong in the house I used to sit down with a yellow pad and write down all the things I was furious at him for. I was obsessive about it.

And I would go over and over that list in my mind—it was a broken record in my head."

What can you do this time? Before you push the panic button, sit down in a quiet place. Have a cup of tea. Think. If the crisis can wait, deal with it when you are calmer, perhaps tomorrow. If it can't, and you don't know what to do, call a neighbor or friend, even if you feel slightly silly. People will understand, and usually are willing to help.

Secondly, when you have a few minutes (hopefully you won't be in a crisis all the time!), make a list of service people. Have this list handy by your telephone. If you don't have someone to fix your washer or car, get a recommendation from a friend.

When you're feeling up to it, get to know how to handle some of the repairs yourself. You can buy a book or have a friend give you a lesson or two. Or get a group of women together and take a course.

Men, by the way, have flare-ups of rage too, but usually over different things. A man living alone for the first time who finds he has no clean shirts in his drawer before a morning business meeting can feel just as upset and angry. Or he may fly into a rage when he has to cook his first meal or go to the laundromat for the first time. Or when he's caring for the kids and one of them gets sick. (He may just bring the child back to Mother when that happens!) Many men won't cry when they feel helpless—they may just throw a pan or two. But the underlying feeling of helplessness is still there.

MOVING

I recently read a question in a magazine addressed to a so-called divorce expert. The question was: I am thinking about moving now that I'm divorced. Do you think it's a good idea? The answer was: go ahead and move if you can afford to move.

I question whether this is good advice.

I think the first thing you should ask yourself is: "How many other changes have I had recently?" We know now that divorce is one of the most stressful periods you can go through. Moving is another. Therefore, if you are overwhelmed with financial problems, problems with your children, and are looking for a job, I wouldn't take on the stress of moving, too. Consider your emotions first, if you possibly can.

Some people see moving as a break with the past and an opportunity for starting over completely. This is true and, at the right time, can be very beneficial. But during a tense time, it can be too much. For even though painful memories are associated with your old place, there's also some comfort and familiarity there, too. If you move too quickly, you may feel quite isolated—not only is your husband gone, but so are your neighbors, your butcher, the newspaper boy—all the people who gave you some sense of rootedness. A move at the right time can be a lift. But in the beginning, it may not be the most positive thing you can do for yourself.

Plan your move carefully. Find a pleasant place to rent at first. Or perhaps you should stay with relatives for a short time to collect yourself. If you have a friend or roommate you can share space with, that can make things much, much easier.

I might add, too, that some women help their husbands move out. Obviously this will only work in cases where both parties are not too embittered. Most men have a difficult time finding and decorating a place, because they don't have any experience in this. I know a woman who helped her husband make the transition by choosing furniture for him. They had an amicable divorce and are friends to this day.

HOLIDAYS

Andy takes the children on Easter, Thanksgiving, the Fourth of July, and Labor Day, and these holidays are still pretty sad for me because I miss the children. Christmas, too, has been hard because, when I was married, this was a big family holiday—Andy's mother would make a ten-course traditional Italian meal and we would all exchange gifts. Now, Andy comes by on Christmas for a few hours to see the children, and this serves as a reminder of the past. It's easy to get very nostalgic around holiday time, and this is why loneliness and depression are so high during these periods—especially for divorced people.

One thing that helps me is to be realistic about what past holidays were really like. In my mind, I may romanticize them, but when I try to look at the facts plainly and squarely, I see a different story. For example, a picture comes to mind . . . ten years ago . . . it was Christmas . . . Andy then was having his first affair. He was grumbling about putting up the tree, I was suspicious, and we just weren't happy together.

What I do around holiday time now is to plan well and to make sure I have people around me. I put out the news that I am hoping to be invited somewhere, and I've found that if people know this, they usually will come through for you.

I also have a party each Christmas Eve for all my single friends. They stop in for punch and bring a little ornament for the tree or something for the children . . . these people have become my family now. I have candles everywhere and music playing. Christina always has a new long dress, and we really have a lot of fun. The kids sometimes go caroling; one year it snowed and they went sledding.

If you are depressed around the holidays, break out of the patterns that depress you. Invite people that you like to your house. If you can't stand spending New Year's Eve watching television, make plans with a friend. I've had plenty of New Year's Eves when I haven't had a date. One New Year's Eve, I made plans to spend the evening with a woman friend. At the last minute, her car broke down and she couldn't come over, and I didn't have a baby-sitter for my children. So we each poured ourselves a drink, after the children were settled, and talked on the phone right through midnight. Then we hung up and went to sleep, and that's how we welcomed in the New Year! This certainly wasn't one of the most wonderful memories in my life, but the time did pass pleasantly, and the most important thing was that neither she nor I felt completely alone.

I can't emphasize enough: make plans for the holidays. Involve yourself with people. Even a quiet night with a good friend can be a boon to your spirits. As time passes, when you feel more up to it, you can plan festivities with friends and learn to enjoy the holidays as a single person.

ENTERTAINING

Did you enjoy entertaining while you were married? If you did, don't give it up!

Unfortunately, many divorced women do. Carol said she didn't have people over because "my home doesn't feel like a home now." Jane said she was "frightened to have people over without my husband being there. Who's going to pour the drinks and play host?" Marlene said she stopped entertaining because "I don't have the money I used to have and my house is getting shabby. I'm ashamed to have people in."

All three women learned to open their homes to others once they'd realized they were depriving themselves of something that had once been a source of great pleasure to them.

The women in Nexus have thrown many, many parties. Here are some things that we've learned to keep in mind:

• Single entertaining is different from married entertaining. When you were married, you may have felt that you had to prepare gourmet dishes and put out your sterling silver. But these standards don't necessarily have to apply to your life as a single.

• Don't worry if your house doesn't look the way it looked when you were married. That's true for most divorcées' homes because there's less money. Certainly, my home needs a lot of work. I would love to have the place wallpapered and new carpets put down, but I can't, so I don't worry about these things. I still have people over, because I want my home to feel like a home. What I do is put the lights low, and have candles and fresh flowers everywhere.

• You don't have to entertain elaborately. If you're short on time, have some friends help you cook. I always do.

• The less formal the party is, the better. The most successful parties we've had have been when we've invited an accordionist, someone who'll teach the latest dance steps, or a woman who'll read palms. This gives people something to talk about, and it breaks the ice. I once had a wine-tasting party and hired a guitar player for the evening. It was a lovely party and didn't cost very much money.

• People love to be crowded in together, so don't worry that your house or apartment is too small. Serve food buffet style. You can ask a few women to play hostess, too, so that all your guests are taken care of.

The big question is whom are you going to invite? If you don't know anyone, you should join an organization or two where you can make some friends. But if you think long enough, you may come up with the names of four single people you know, and that's plenty. Invite all four and have them each invite four single people *they* know. You can try to keep the number of men and women equal, although it's perfectly okay to have a few more women than men, or vice versa. Don't invite only married friends, or your party may end up depressing you. You can also ask male friends to bring some new men with them.

You may not feel up to entertaining right in the beginning of your singleness, but once you've been single for a year or two, you should make the effort to entertain. Having a party *always* cheers me up.

TRAVELING AS A SINGLE WOMAN

Andy and I traveled together during our marriage, but our trips were not always fun. Andy was really more comfortable on his own turf and traveled only to please me. We went to Europe together one summer, but he didn't like being in places where he couldn't speak the language. He was upset at not sleeping in his own bed, he complained about minor things, and, all in all, he was cranky and couldn't wait to get home.

I, on the other hand, love to travel and to have adventures. The first three years after my separation, I didn't do much traveling because I had little money and young children to care for. But after that, I did put aside money to take some trips, and I've found that I have much more fun traveling as a single than I did when I was married. I've talked with many divorced women who have felt the same way.

The first thing to decide is where you want to go. Is there some place you're dying to see? That's where you should go. If you're not sure, spend some hours leafing through travel folders and guides. Talk to travel agents. You may not be able to afford a trip to Europe or to a Caribbean island, but there is probably some place close by where you could spend a few nice days. It's very much worth saving your money, because the feeling of independence you'll derive will be well worth the effort.

My friend Jean and I thought we needed to treat ourselves, and being single wasn't going to stop us. We chose a short trip—a tour and charter flight—to Rome, Florence, and Venice.

I was so excited. I took travel books out of the library—that was fun in itself. I had seven months in which to save money.

I made plans with my ex-mother-in-law to take care of Christina and Nick. Andy was to pick them up toward the end of my stay and bring them back home.

Jean and I arrived in Rome early in the morning, dropped our luggage off at the hotel, and went out to explore the city. The ruins . . . the Colosseum . . . were wonderful. The Roman men were the most gorgeous I had ever seen—we were constantly turning our heads to stare at them again and again . . . just like men do to women.

Jean and I had agreed we would divide some of the jobs that are part and parcel of traveling. We kept a "community purse," for instance, and every day we put a certain number of lire in the purse to pay for our meals, taxis, and museum fees. Jean handled the money, and I was responsible for getting us from one place to another.

We decided from day to day what we would see and where we would go for dinner. We had guidebooks with us and we also asked questions of people in the hotel. I don't suggest asking a taxi driver where to eat; he may suggest someplace "nice" for his pocketbook and his taste, but you may very well hate it.

One night we chose a darling Neapolitan restaurant in the old section of Rome called Mea Pateca. There were long tables covered with gay cotton cloth, and diners rubbed elbows with their neighbors. It was a gregarious, noisy place with colored lights strung above the candle-lit outdoor tables. Strolling guitar players sang lively songs and the food was good, too. Soon a good-looking Italian man sat down next to us. By the end of the meal, we were friends. He invited us to join him for an after-dinner drink . . . we went down some winding alleyways in old Rome, finally coming to a door with no markings. We went into a small, dark room where there was a real mixture of people . . . even Cubans singing revolutionary songs. The place was a find—we would have never found it on our own in a hundred years.

On to Florence! It is a magnificent city and to see it is to fall in love with it. We had two interesting experiences here. The tour bus driver had asked Jean out, and we agreed that after dinner she would go out with him—I needed to catch up on a little rest.

About two hours into her date, she burst into the room howling with laughter. He had taken her out in the big touring bus! She couldn't hold the laughter in another moment so she had to come back and tell me.

Another night we went to an Italian discotheque. We met two men there, one of whom invited me to spend the next summer in his villa near Florence. He carefully explained that his mother must be told I was his secretary . . . I agreed, of course!

All over Italy the men make you feel that you were born just for them to admire. They are fun, funny, and outrageous!

We had a marvelous time and never slept over five hours a night. I never once thought of home or my problems. It was a complete cultural change and more fun than any other vacation I had ever had.

Monica tells another story. She decided to treat herself to a trip to Europe three years after her divorce.

"I decided at the very last minute to go. I got on an

illegal charter, it cost $322. I never worried about how I would get from one country to another. I thought, once I'm there, I will be able to make my connections.

"Finally, I was off to Brussels. I met a woman on the plane who was going to Paris, too, so she and I made our train connections together. The next day I went to American Express; for two francs, they will recommend a hotel. I didn't like their choice, so I went walking around the area and came across this darling little hotel that was just exactly what I wanted, a half block from the main boulevard. I loved it and took it right away. It was in the low twenty-dollar range. I showered and got ready to go out and have dinner that evening.

"While I was crossing the boulevard to go to Le Drugstore (a sort of coffee shop), I saw a man who was very attractive to me. Our eyes met. I continued walking across to Le Drugstore and asked for a table. Within a few minutes the man sat down next to me. My heart was palpitating, he was so handsome. He started speaking in French, and when I told him I didn't speak French, he immediately spoke English. He was delightful. He asked me all about my trip. He said, "This isn't really a good place for dinner, why don't we go to another place?" He took me to a lovely restaurant. He was an engineer working for an American firm in Paris.

"After dinner we went to a very tiny Parisian discotheque, and we danced. After a while, he said he wanted to make love to me, and I said, 'You must be crazy, what is this?' But he continued pursuing me and finally later he took me back to his apartment.

"Before opening the door, he announced, 'I am married, you know, I have a wife and daughter.' But I liked him so, he was very warm, kind, and sweet, and he made me think I had known him forever. Later I learned his wife and child were on vacation in Spain and wouldn't return for a couple of weeks. I felt quite awkward in the apartment, but he was a wonderful lover. We spent the night together and the next morning he helped me map out my day of sightseeing by using the public transportation and said he would meet me at five at Le Drugstore. I left him not knowing whether I would see him again.

"I did my sightseeing and had a wonderful day at the Louvre. I carried my little maps, one walking map and one map of the Métro system, always in my hand. They are invaluable. I never took taxis; they are much too expensive. I found the language barrier difficult at times, but everything was very well marked and I did quite well. I also found that I met dozens of people by having my maps in hand. My advice—get those maps.

"After my day of sightseeing at the Louvre and the Eiffel Tower, I hurried home, showered, and went off to meet John. I was hoping he would be there, but I had some fear. As I rounded the corner of the boulevard, I could see him. My heart skipped a beat. Again we had a wonderful evening.

"One day I was in Versailles—I had rented a bike. A man came along and asked to ride with me. He was German. Later, we got into his van and he began looking for a place to stop to have lunch. He found the most adorable little farm, with a beautiful setting, and began to set up lunch. First he took out a small folding table, put a red-checkered cloth on it, and took out two chairs from the van, then wine and croissants. It was absolutely delightful."

As a single, you may be better off staying in less expensive places than you did when you were married. You'll have more adventures, and you'll meet a wider variety of people. In the more expensive hotels, you'll probably only meet businessmen and married couples, anyway.

If you'd like to travel alone, try to get the names of one

or two people in each place in case you get a little lonely. Many women feel that traveling alone is the only way to go. One said, "I don't feel like having anyone with me when I travel because I like to go at my own speed. I don't like having to worry about whether the person I'm with wants to do something else.

"I meet many more people when I'm traveling alone. People are afraid to approach a twosome, but they feel that a single person is more open, more receptive."

If you don't know if you'd like to travel alone, perhaps you can try a weekend trip first. See how comfortable you are. If you decide to travel with a friend, make sure you have spelled out the ground rules in advance. Many women's excursions are ruined because they quarreled with their traveling companions. Don't choose someone who is sloppy or who is always late, if you think these habits will bother you.

Talk out your plans and *feelings* ahead of time. What do you both want from the vacation? To relax? To sightsee? To meet men? Both of you should be frank about why you're going. If you want to rest, and she wants to meet a man, it won't work.

Ask what things she'd like to spend her money on—this will tell you how she likes to spend her days. On a nicer hotel? On great restaurants? Guides? The theater? On gifts, clothes, and souvenirs? If she wants to spend time in great restaurants and you want to eat cheaply and save your money for gifts, problems may arise, unless you can agree on a compromise *before* you go.

Ask if she'd like to have some days alone or does she prefer doing everything together? Again, if you like to be alone, and she doesn't, it may not work. Find out if she feels at home in a foreign country. Will she be too dependent on you?

Discuss what you'll do if certain situations with men

arise. Will each of you be able to bring a man to your hotel room? I've seen this cause a lot of problems on vacations. I know one woman who went with two friends to Puerto Rico. She was asleep in the room when she heard one of the women come in with a man; they proceeded to make love in the next bed. She was embarrassed and upset, but afraid to say anything. She was newly single, and she thought she was expected to be "open" about this kind of behavior.

I know another woman who was locked out of her hotel room one night because her roommate was using it to make love to a man she'd met.

I wouldn't be able to tolerate this, and I would always make this clear to a woman before I go. I once went to a little country inn with a friend for a few days, and she wanted to use the room one afternoon. But I don't like being locked out of my room, and I told her I wasn't comfortable with the idea. Moreover, I would never put her in that situation. I feel that if a man wants to spend time alone with you, he can work out the arrangements.

Keep talking to each other throughout your trip. Don't let your anger or disappointment build up. Assert yourself, e.g., "I don't want to be alone at dinner tonight." If something is bothering you, mention it right away. Of course, you have to be prepared to compromise and to accept some things you don't like.

Jean met a man while we were traveling and he invited her to dinner. She told him she'd love to go, but that she'd like to bring me along. He said fine. After dinner I went back to my room while Jean spent a few more hours with him.

He invited her to spend the next evening with him, and she was confused about what to do. I said, "I don't want to be alone tonight, but if you really want to go with him, I'll accept it. But if you don't care, then let's the two of us go out."

She said, "Oh, I'm so glad you told me how you felt. I've been anxious about the whole situation." She decided she didn't care whether she saw him again, and so she and I went out together, met people, and had a great time.

Traveling as a single can be a great joy. If you're friendly, have a positive attitude, and look like you're having fun, you'll bring home lovely memories.

12

Tying the Knot Twice

Most divorced people can hardly wait to get right back in there pitching—another marriage, I mean. Even though they have been burned, the majority of men and women I've met hope and pray to find Mr. or Mrs. Right and get married again. The American Dream includes husband, wife, house, and car, and no one is complete without them, or so we all think.

A second marriage, however, while it means companionship, can be difficult. Think about how complicated handling all your ex-relatives, your present children, his ex-relatives (children's grandparents, fathers, aunts, uncles), and his present children will be, let alone the relationship between you two.

It takes two very mature people to try to put together a new family from a "leftover" family and make all parties happy—some of the time. A book could be written on the subject.

There seem to be several trouble spots that many people overlook. One is where to live. The remarried people I know insist that the only way to begin a new marriage is to begin on new turf for everyone. Don't try to live in his house because "rooms are larger" and the "mortgage is lower." If children (or wife or husband) must move into someone else's home, they always feel like intruders, while the person who "owns" the space feels a certain superiority.

The other big problem is who disciplines the children, and the showing of favoritism for one's own children. Rules must be talked about before a marriage takes place.

One couple, Howard and Mary Lee, both married for the second time, gave me a list of questions that a couple could discuss before contemplating a second marriage.

This quiz might also give those seriously thinking of remarrying some food for thought.

SOME QUESTIONS THAT MIGHT BE ASKED BEFORE A
SECOND MARRIAGE

1. Do I plan to keep my money (stocks, bonds, bank accounts) for my own use and for my children or will I share it with you and your children?
2. Will I insist that my possessions (furniture, dishes, pictures) furnish the house, or will we use some of mine and some of yours?
3. Where will we live? Your place or mine? What should we consider before deciding? Should we move to "neutral turf"?
4. Will the children be expected to share a room with stepbrothers or stepsisters? Will we give them a say in the matter?
5. How do I feel when you say, "My first wife (husband) did it this way"? Can I accept this kind of thing without resentment?
6. Will I allow pictures and other mementos of your first spouse in the house?

7. Should I get to know your former spouse so that I can get to know you better? Do you appreciate the fact that what you are is partially a result of what he or she was?

8. If you are less satisfying sexually than my former partner, should I tell you? Stew over it? Resign myself to it? How should I handle it?

9. If you are more satisfying, should I tell you?

10. How about your former in-laws? Other relatives and friends? Will we continue to see them?

11. Will I find it hard to love my stepchildren? If I do, how can I prevent it from affecting my treatment of them?

12. I probably love my own children more than my stepchildren. How will this affect our relationship? Will I be able to avoid showing favoritism? Or will I go the other extreme and treat them stricter in order not to show favoritism?

13. Am I the jealous type? Will I resent the time, attention, care, etc., that you give to your children? Will I be angered that you don't show the same attention to mine?

14. When your children treat me as a stepparent instead of a parent, how will I react? Will I be able to accept words and actions that hurt?

15. How will I handle relationships if my kids don't like the person I'm marrying? Or if your kids don't like me?

16. Will we insist on being called Mom and Dad, even if they don't want to?

17. Am I prepared to act contrary to my feelings for the good of the family?

Howard and Mary also indicated that there are stages in a second marriage.

1. *Cloud Nine stage*

Mary says this is like being a sixteen-year-old girl again. She says she never had that 'big wow" attraction to her first husband. This was the first big sexual attraction of her life. Everything was wonderful. "I felt giddy and silly. The world was rosy. This was the BIG romance."

2. *Reality sets in*

Mary says that when Cloud Nine started wearing off, there was realistic coping to be done. She didn't want to "rock the boat," so she kept her complaints and gripes to herself. She really wanted to make it work. In the first two years, she doesn't feel she was communicating.

3. *Realization that work on the marriage needs to be done*

After the two-year period of "keeping the lid on," Howard suggested Marriage Encounter because their neighbors had gone and felt it helped their marriage. So they went, and they say this completely changed their marriage. They learned to communicate.

Today they feel they must always continue to work on this relationship. They will never again take anything for granted. I think they are right. I think a second marriage starts with twenty strikes against it, and that continuing to work at the relationship is the only way it will work.

I attended a wedding recently—both bride and bridegroom had been married before. Amy is proud, dignified, a traditionalist—no justice-of-the-peace wedding for her. They had a 4 P.M. candlelight church ceremony, with all their children as attendants, his sons, her two daughters and three sons. Everyone looked gorgeous, including the guests.

Amy had planned the reception, cooked the food, rearranged the house, and redecorated every room. They had help on hand, and it all went beautifully.

The children, however, were sad and nervous-looking. It was clearly not a happy day for several of them. I believe the children were under pressure to be happy, gay, and polite. As an example, the groom's son caught me in a room where I was making a phone call and said, "This is happy for my dad, but it is too hard for my mother." Shortly after I left the room, I saw him in a near fistfight.

This little incident shows how difficult it is for children to adjust. Many of us fantasize that all the kids will get along great like the Brady Bunch, but I don't know any people like that.

If you are aware of all the problems involved, this can be handled. But many people push their emotions under the rug. As one woman said, "The moment we started to argue, I used to get blinding headaches. I couldn't face my conflict because it reminded me of my broken marriage and I was terrified. Later I had to learn to deal with our problems. Now things are fine."

What these stories point up is that a second marriage is not necessarily the answer to our problems, but simply presents a new set of problems that have to be dealt with!

PART TWO

13

Growth Through Eight Normal Stages

Your growth as a single woman will come in stages. You'll have triumphs and setbacks, good days and bad ones. But overall, I can honestly say that there is hope and a good life awaiting each one of us.

Three years after I began my organization, I realized that there were common emotional patterns in recovery from divorce, and this knowledge made me feel relieved and triumphant.

There is something very comforting about realizing that you are not alone, that the feelings and conflicts you experience are not crazy or neurotic, but are actually perfectly common and understandable reactions to the stress of divorce.

I have found that there are eight stages in recovery from divorce. Naturally, the sequence of stages can vary from person to person, and there will be women who will not experience each stage in its entirety, or who will skip some altogether. I see the stages as a useful guide for taking your emotional temperature as you journey toward the self-discovery and self-fulfillment that is your rightful heritage.

Stage 1
Active Bleeding

Question: Life is full of losses, big and little. Death is the greatest of all. How is our reaction to death different from our feelings about the other losses life brings us?

Kubler-Ross: This reaction happens with any loss, not just death. It happens if you are separated or divorced, or if you lose a boyfriend or girlfriend.

From *Psychology Today*

The period prior to the breakup of my marriage was a terrible hand-wringing, dramatic time for me. I would pace around the house like a caged animal and cry at the drop of a hat. I would try and try to squeeze hope for our marriage out of Andy—only to be constantly disappointed. Finally, after about seven months of this, when we did separate, I felt relief and some euphoria! However, I call this devastating hand-wringing period I went through the Active Bleeding Stage. When I formed my organization, Active Bleeding was the best way I could describe what had happened to me and what happens to practically every woman who goes through a separation or divorce.

I coined the term Active Bleeding, admittedly a dramatic metaphor, after I'd heard what seemed like the hundredth member say, "I'm always bleeding." As one woman graphically explained, "I feel like broken glass is inside me and I'm afraid to bend over. I feel like my insides aren't there any more."

I had a second Active Bleeding Stage a year and a half after my husband and I separated from each other, as I lay in a hospital bed having an operation to remove labial cysts. When I got out of the hospital (I had to return later for a second and third operation), I stayed in my bedroom for three days unable to stop crying. A friend came to cook meals for my children. I was deeply ashamed I wasn't able to take care of them myself.

Lying in bed, staring at the ceiling, I grieved for my marriage. I was finally allowing myself to look at my situation squarely—to see that I was really alone. Any fantasies I'd had about the marvelous single life had vanished, and everything seemed bleak and hopeless. I longed for my marriage; I longed for Andy; I longed to be a whole family again. This longing is part and parcel of the Active Bleeding Stage—a time of grief, crying, and remorse.

The Active Bleeding Stage can manifest itself in a number of ways:

• Geraldine, who has been separated from her husband for four months, is in the supermarket buying food for the week. As she turns from putting some dog food in her shopping cart, she sees a young couple walk by—they are laughing and holding hands. Geraldine feels tears well up in her eyes and tries to choke them back. As she moves up the aisle, however, stopping to pick up chocolate chip cookies for her two children, the tears begin to run down her face. She feels out of control, embarrassed, and most of all, terribly sad.

Geraldine is an Active Bleeder.

• The car won't start; the kids are late for school; the washing machine has broken down the night before. Marie sits sobbing helplessly behind the steering wheel. "Nothing works," she says, 'Everything is breaking down. I just can't cope anymore." Marie manages to get out of the car and arranges to have her neighbor drive her children to school. Then she sits in the living room, cigarette in hand, feeling overwhelmed. How is she going to get the washing machine fixed? The car fixed? Once she had considered herself to be a capable woman who attended PTA meetings, threw dinner parties—a woman who *handled* things. People would come to *her* for advice! Now, since her divorce, she feels incapable of handling anything.

Marie is an Active Bleeder.

• Margaret has walking pneumonia—the latest of a series of illnesses this year. Yet she still tries to keep up with her job, her family, her community activities.

Margaret, too, is an Active Bleeder.

What *is* an Active Bleeder? An Active Bleeder is a woman who hurts. It's that simple. Any woman who is going through a separation or divorce—even if she wanted the divorce—will go through the stage of Active Bleeding. It's normal; it's predictable; it's to be expected. You may not go through Active Bleeding right away, but at some point in your journey from a married to a single woman, you will. It's important that you know this. If you know what to expect—and you know that others have had the same feelings that you have—you may not feel so alone, confused, and devastated when you go through this stage.

Sometimes you can experience Active Bleeding during

the time that the decision to separate is being made, or in the beginning of a separation. Other women initially experience a feeling of euphoria after a separation or divorce. When the euphoria ends (and it inevitably does), the Active Bleeding Stage can begin.

Active Bleeding usually lasts from two to three months to a little over a year. It is *not* a stage that lasts only a week or two. If you can understand and accept that, you will be doing yourself a favor. You will stop blaming yourself, e.g., "I should snap out of this." Active Bleeding is nothing to be ashamed of. It does not mean that you are neurotic. It does not mean that you will always feel this way. (You won't.) *It simply means that you are going through a necessary stage as you move from suffering to health and growth.* Active Bleeding is a time of catharsis: a time for going over the marital relationship and allowing your feelings to surface so that you can heal.

QUIZ: ARE YOU AN ACTIVE BLEEDER?
1. Do you feel on the verge of tears a good deal of the time?
2. Does seeing couples or families make you want to go home and cry?
3. Do Sundays or dinner time make you particularly blue?
4. Do you find yourself getting angry with someone in your family who has a happy marriage?
5. Do you feel like a failure?
6. Do you find yourself thinking, "If only I'd done _____, my marriage would have lasted"?
7. Do you feel ashamed about the breakup?
8. Do you find yourself not wanting to talk to people?
9. Do you relive the marriage in your mind?
10. Do you stay home because you feel you can't face the world?

If you've answered "yes" to three or more questions—particularly if you cry a lot, feel remorseful, and stay home a lot—you are an Active Bleeder.

There are varying degrees of Active Bleeding, from mild to acute. If you are suffering badly, rest. Don't act as if it's business as usual. If you were going to the hospital for major surgery, you would plan to rest—you'd be prepared to watch TV, perhaps read, or do some knitting, and you'd make things as pleasant as you could by bringing along a pretty robe and some comfortable slippers.

Well, divorce is major surgery. Be prepared for a convalescing period. Don't expect to accomplish as much (or more) than you would when you were well. Don't add any new responsibilities (if you possibly can help it) during this stage.

1. What about staying in bed when you're depressed? Is this good for you? Or should you force yourself to keep moving?

The answer depends on your attitude. If you look on this as a time to pamper yourself and to heal, it can be very beneficial. If staying in bed is comforting to you, stay there.

On the other hand, if you stay in bed out of negativism or inertia, you are liable only to make yourself feel worse, especially if your hair needs washing, and you hate yourself every time you look in the mirror.

Remember, too, that when you're in bed, you aren't allowing anything new to come in and mingle with your old, negative thoughts.

If your resting isn't comforting you, take a shower, put on some makeup, and get out of the house.

2. The healthiest thing you can do for yourself now is to talk to people you can trust. Find someone who has time

and who isn't troubled herself. Other divorced or separated women are invaluable to talk to. They can help you see that *they* have lived through this trying time and that you will too. Talking is the best catharsis.

As a group, however, your married friends should be told very little.

Some married persons love only too well the gory details of someone else's divorce. If you and your husband reconcile, you may find yourself angry and humiliated that you confided so much. Moreover, you may find that your married friends love to hear how miserable you are, but won't be quite so willing to listen when you have good times to report. Generally, many people will be glad about your pain, especially if they envied you when you were married.

3. Don't make any drastic changes in your life now. Postpone major decisions—like moving or getting a job—until you aren't feeling so shaky.

4. When you can, treat yourself to things you used to enjoy. Go to films or the ballet. They may not make you feel as good as they once did, so don't shoot for feelings of euphoria. Just feeling fair, just some distraction from the worst of your pain, is enough for now.

5. Don't make elaborate plans. Keep things simple. A day in town. A movie. Dinner with a friend.

6. Make plans on a regular basis. Have a sitter come every Tuesday afternoon or Wednesday evening. Don't wait until the last minute to arrange things. I'm not talking about parties which are liable to depress you more, but quiet evenings with friends, seeing a movie or play, or that sort of thing.

During Active Bleeding, you may not be able to read or concentrate as before. Some artists say that they weren't able to create during this time. Women who had hobbies find they can't be absorbed as they once were. So don't worry about this right now.

7. If there's one small thing that makes you feel good, do it. Pamper yourself as much as you can. Jane went out and bought herself some new slinky underwear. "I felt good after I made that purchase," she said. "For a few hours, I felt like my old self."

What if you're broke? *Find* five or ten dollars somewhere! Treat yourself like a human being. You have a right to be nice to yourself. Try to give yourself a little treat every day if you need it. You will feel ever so much better. Many women have a tendency to be harsh with themselves during this time. They know that money is tight and so they deprive themselves of all they had formerly enjoyed. But that's not helpful.

8. If you don't know what you want to do, make a list of things that make you feel good. You can even divide the list into sections: one-dollar, five-dollar, and ten-dollar treats.

TREATS FOR YOURSELF

For $1
Buy a plant
    a magazine
    some writing paper
Go to the library
Spend an afternoon in a museum
Listen to a concert on the radio
For $5 or under
Buy some fresh flowers
    a bottle of wine
    a new cosmetic
    something for a hobby—like paints or pencils
Make a long-distance call to a friend
Go to a movie

Put a dress in layaway
For $10
Go to the hairdresser
Have dinner with a friend
Buy a book

Be kind to yourself during Active Bleeding. That's the most important thing I can tell you right now.

THE SOCIAL SCENE

Don't throw yourself into going out before you're ready. "I thought I had to meet a man right away," a woman will say. Her friends may tell her, "Don't sit home crying. Go out and meet somebody." However, there is no need to rush out and meet people. You have time.

One friend of mine was devastated when her husband said he didn't love her anymore. "I would get the children off to school," she said, "make a whole pot of coffee for myself, and then sit with my cigarettes. The table was in a corner and I'd push myself into the farthest corner of it. It was as if the table and the two walls were holding me up.

"During this time, I had an operation and part of my hair was shaved off and I had bandages on my head, but I got a wig. And when I got out of the hospital, I felt more desperate than before and decided I couldn't sit in my kitchen any more. I *had* to get out. So I went to a singles party. There were about a hundred and fifty people in that house—it was just like being in a crowded subway station. People walked back and forth. Nobody seemed to be making contact—people were just sizing each other up. And there I was, just out of the hospital, with my head in bandages, and a wig over it all. Now that I look back on it, I can appreciate what a gruesome experience that was."

Dotty had really pushed herself into the social scene before she felt up to it. Better to stay home in front of the television!

Letting Your Anger Out

In all depression, there is anger. In order to get over your depression, you will have to get rid of some of your angry feelings. When I was first separated, I made it a point to play tennis several times a week. I practiced hitting the ball as furiously as I could. It was wonderful. Here are some other suggestions from Nexus members:

1. Mary mounted a punching bag in her bedroom. When she was angry, she used it!

2. Loren got free scraps of lumber from a local lumber yard. She took a hammer and nails and made dents in the wood—distressing it. When she was in a better frame of mind a few months later, she stained some of the nicer pieces of wood and mounted them on her walls.

3. A tape recorder is an excellent investment. Talk your angry feelings into it.

4. Talk to strangers. Sometimes you can gripe to them and they'll listen and tell you their own troubles back. You'll find people who have worse problems than you do.

Dealing with Your Children During Active Bleeding

During Active Bleeding, you may be so concerned with yourself and your own emotions that you'll have little time and energy to give to your children. Try not to berate yourself too much for this. The stage that you are experiencing is so difficult that it's almost humanly impossible for you to give your best attention to your children. Here are some suggestions to make life a little easier.

1. Try to give each child fifteen minutes of concentrated time sometime during the day. Make up for quantity with quality. If you feel too depressed, or you can't talk to your child (or to anyone) without crying, then forego this suggestion until you can handle it.

2. It's best that you don't burden your children too much

with your own worries. (Easier said than done!) Children may resent the burden or may not be able to deal with your pain (in addition to their own). Be careful, too, about what you say. Don't think that just because a child is young, he or she won't understand what you're talking about. Young children listen and absorb and worry just like adults do—even though they may not be verbal about their feelings. And children can distort what they hear. A mother may say, "He's always late with the money. I never have a dime in my pocket." A child hearing this can worry unduly. It may seem that disaster has struck!

3. Be very careful about taking your anger out on your children. When her husband walked out, Joan didn't cry, but she became angry and bitter. She found that she couldn't cope with her children; the smallest infraction of a house rule could send her head spinning. Once, she hit her daughter with a steel brush and the brush stuck in the child's skin. The poor child had to be rushed to the hospital. If you find yourself wanting to hit your children, or if you find yourself screaming at them all the time, you are out of control. (Do you hear yourself saying, "All I do is scream at my kids."?)

Many women think it's okay to vent their emotions—to scream and carry on. It's not. This is extremely harmful to children. They are upset enough about the divorce. In addition, now the mommy they depended on is no longer someone they can count on.

If you find yourself in this situation, it's time to get some therapy—for yourself and perhaps for your child. You can find a therapist through your doctor, friends, a women's center, or a family service agency.

4. If your children are old enough, you can give them some techniques to help them communicate their feelings to you. My son Nicky and I had a prearranged line he

could say when he felt he'd heard enough of my pain and anguish. It was: "Hey, this is one of those times when I can't handle this talk right now, although I appreciate this is really bothering you." When he said this, I would drop the subject. This is a good way of preventing flare-ups of anger.

5. Divorced women sometimes isolate themselves too much. Your children can benefit from having other people to talk to—especially if it's hard for your child to express his anger or frustration to you.

On a day when you're feeling a little up, ask your child if you can provide someone for him to talk to. Try to find a nonjudgmental, sympathetic person—an aunt, older friend, neighbor, or teacher.

You can arrange a meeting by saying, "You know, I've invited Mary over today. I want you to meet her and see if you like and trust her. I think you need someone to talk to besides me."

Your child may feel awkward at first, but later will probably welcome the chance to ventilate his feelings to someone who'll understand.

If your child is really hostile to the idea, it won't work. But if he's not, it can work beautifully—this friend can provide the function that an elder sister or brother would provide in a large family.

Once a week, my daughter, Chrissy, goes to talk to an older friend who works with troubled teen-agers. Chrissy didn't need therapy, but she did need someone, besides Mommy, to talk to about adolescent growing-up problems.

You can also enlist the aid of friends and/or relatives by saying, "Can you help me out? Can Jane eat with you once a week? Can you take Danny to the zoo when you take your kids there?" That way, if you're hurting, your child won't be inundated with morbidity. You have helped provide some fun times for him.

YOUR HEALTH

The stress you experience during Active Bleeding can cause your health to suffer greatly. As many as 50 percent of women in the Active Bleeding Stage end up going, or nearly going, to the hospital. In the first year of separation and/or divorce, the number of operations that take place are also much higher than usual. Women suffer from colitis, asthma, ulcers—all stress-related illnesses. In one group of forty women, four were having mastectomies during the time they were getting their divorces.

To try to prevent this from happening to you, take care of your health. Eat properly and make sure you get enough protein. Take vitamins. Get enough rest. Try to get some exercise every day if you possibly can. One member told me, "I made it my business to bicycle twice a week even though I didn't feel like it. That was a big help for me. I had to force myself, but once I was out, I felt so much better."

Don't expect as much of yourself as you did before. Too many women take on much more than they are able to handle—starting a job and a social life as well as taking on the full responsibilities for the house and children. If any of these things can wait, let them. Often, you won't realize what a terrific strain you are under until you become so run-down that you become sick. And, the minute you find something wrong, go to the doctor.

I repeat: you don't have to do everything at once. I've heard some women say, "I'm going to sell my house, get a new job, get the kids off the school and lose twenty pounds so I can find a new man." If you suggest that they may be taking on too much, the reply usually is, "Well, it has to be done!" But these are the women who, two months later, say, "I don't know why I got so sick," or "I don't know why I'm screaming at the kids all the time." The moral: Try to go easy on yourself.

COPING WITH DIVORCE INSOMNIA

You may have trouble sleeping during this time—for obvious reasons.

Try to prepare yourself mentally for this, and don't get too panicked. Many women do operate on less sleep than usual during this time. Moreover, the insomnia usually subsides after the worst of this period is over.

Perhaps your doctor can provide a mild tranquilizer to help you sleep. I'm not suggesting you rely on pills as a way of life, but I don't think they're a bad idea for some women during an acute Active Bleeding Stage. Or try a glass of wine before bedtime—think of it as an extra treat for yourself. Warm milk can also work.

When you can't sleep, have a plan of action. Don't spend time going over and over what is bothering you, if you can help it. A friend of mine once told me, "When you can't do any more, give your problems to God for the night. You'll get them back the next morning."

Have "toys" in your bedroom, too. I always have a pile of books I want to read close by my bed, notebooks to write in, a tape recorder, a TV set, and a radio. When I can't sleep, I have plenty to do.

You can:

—watch TV

—do needlepoint

—read, if you can concentrate

—have a jigsaw puzzle set up on a card table near your bed. Jigsaw puzzles are great for insomniacs!

—Have some pads and pencils nearby. Write out your feelings and thoughts. Many women never wrote anything before they were divorced—now they spend hours scribbling away! Writing down your feelings can be a catharsis, and then you can look back at a later time and see how you've progressed.

—Do yoga. It's relaxing and calming—and healthy too.

Stage 2
Euphoria

"I'm free at last."

I had gone through such a miserable two years before our separation that I felt happy when Andy finally packed his suitcase and left our house. I felt free. I was blindly optimistic about the future. I was sure life was going to be just great—that I'd meet many Prince Charmings, lead a gay, trouble-free life, and surely end up marrying someone fantastic who would love, cherish, and appreciate me.

I remember Andy saying to me as he left our house for the final time, "You know, you're going to be lonely here, don't you?" I looked at him and thought he had rocks in his head. Me, lonely? I was too optimistic then to think that loneliness was going to strike me.

This blind, optimistic period is what I call the Euphoria Stage. About 40 percent of women who separate from their husbands go into this Euphoria Stage right away, before Active Bleeding. (Remember, more and more women are initiating divorce today.) Other women may experience this stage only after Active Bleeding has taken place.

QUIZ: ARE YOU IN THE EUPHORIA STAGE?

1. Do you feel like everything is rosy?
2. Do you feel that things that used to bother you don't?
3. Do you walk around with a perpetual smile on your face?
4. Are you experiencing a feeling similar to the one experienced when you were first in love?
5. No matter what season it is, do you feel like it's the best season of the year?
6. Do you feel that you don't have any problems?
7. Do you have the feeling that things will work out—someday, somehow?
8. Do you feel you don't want to discuss your problems?
9. Do you feel like you're on a high—perhaps walking a few inches off the ground?
10. When advisors, such as your lawyer, talk to you, do you often feel they are being overly concerned, overly cautious, overly pessimistic?

If you've answered "yes" to three or more of these, you may be in the Euphoria Stage.

Although this stage usually doesn't last for more than two months, you can gain lifelong benefits from it.

While you are feeling so good, write down in a notebook or in your diary all the positive feelings you have about yourself. On another page, note any ideas you have for expanding your life—your desire to get a sales job, move to the West Coast, lose ten pounds. Then, during a more contemplative time, you can evaluate your ideas and act on those you chose.

Whenever possible, however, try to postpone making any major decisions until you have your feet on the ground.

During this Euphoria Stage, one is so imbued with life's glorious possibilities that the harsh realities of daily life don't get enough attention. You feel that you can handle anything and that nothing will ever hurt you again. And because this is such a marvelous feeling to have, you don't *want* to look at the other side of the coin—the fact that there are real problems you may have to face up to in the coming months.

I felt so good after my husband moved out—I wasn't imprisoned in a bad marriage anymore—that I didn't pay enough attention to the legal problems confronting me.

As a result, my legal agreement does not specify that my husband has to pay for the children's orthodontia or college bills. And I regret this very much now. At the time, I felt that the future (the time when the children would be old enough for college) was far, far away. I was sure that by the time the future arrived, those problems would take care of themselves! Surely, I'd be married again. Surely, my children would somehow be taken care of.

I haven't married again. And the problems of these costs face me now.

I've learned since then that many other women also act foolishly during this Euphoria Stage. Many otherwise shrewd women regret the legal and financial mistakes they made during this period—mistakes they may be paying for for years to come.

Betty, a librarian in her twenties, felt "free and marvelous" after she left her husband. She wanted to have as many sexual experiences with other men as she could—a not uncommon fantasy of the newly single woman.

Delirious about the new, liberated life she was about to lead, she rented an expensive, large apartment on the beach (where she'd always wanted to live), bought some new, fashionable clothes, and took a trip to the Caribbean where she met other singles.

Three months later, however, she wasn't sure she wanted to be single any more. She thought she might want to go back to her husband. And on top of that, she was in financial hot water. At the time she'd taken the apartment, she hadn't considered how expensive it was. She wanted it, she'd taken it. She felt that she'd "somehow" be able to manage the rental payments. (This is a common denominator of this stage—a blind optimism, not based on hard facts and figures, that somehow things will work out.) Now, she found that she wasn't able to pay for it (in addition to the bills for clothing and the trips), and that, if she didn't reconcile with her husband, she'd have to consider getting a roommate to share the rent.

Often, too, this stage is so colored by fantasy that you may be colder than necessary to your ex-husband (something you may regret later), and/or neglect your children during this time. Because you're happy, you may assume your children are happy too, whereas they may be going through a difficult time (perhaps experiencing their own Active Bleeding Stage). If you can, try to talk with them to see what they're feeling and what their needs are.

Usually, there is a precipitating factor that causes you to "come down" from your high. Your ex-husband may bring his new girlfriend around; you haven't yet found the job you wanted; you have a problem with your child or a disappointment in love. Soon, you are plunged into the real world again.

When Terry, a lovely woman with a master's degree in special education, and her husband decided to separate, she said, "All I felt was relief. But then, almost immediately, I began to fantasize about a man I'd always been attracted to. I was convinced he was mad about me because we had flirted and chatted from time to time.

"I fantasized calling him and telling him that I was free

and that now we could have an affair. I thought it would all be so easy.

"Well, I went and got my hair done and bought some clothes and went and presented myself to him. He kept putting me off, but he would call me and we would have sex on the phone. That's the first time I'd ever done that and I loved it.

"But this went on for two months, and I wasn't smart enough to question why he wasn't taking me out. I still kept to my fantasy—that he must be wildly in love with me.

"Finally, we did go out, and it was an awful experience. He got very drunk and was very loud. I realized he wasn't the gay, gallant, nice person I had fantasized him to be. He had rented a motel room that night and after all I had done to get him to bed, I couldn't say no. But he was impotent and pretty abusive. He said things to me like, 'All you women want is to get laid'—things like that.

"I never saw him again. But I was certainly jolted by the experience. I was upset about it for a while after."

For the time of its duration, the Euphoria Stage can be a positive experience for you, *as long as you don't make any major decisions* (*legal, personal, or financial*) *during this time*. Let this period expand your mind and work for you. This is a time when you can create new ideas about how you'd like to broaden your horizons at a later date.

Stage 3
Running

"I feel like I should have a
Scarlet Letter on my chest."

It is seven o'clock on Tuesday night. Joan has just taken her children to McDonald's for dinner. The two girls tumble out of the station wagon; Joan's son, Bobby, gets out last. The children go into the den to do their homework and watch TV, and Joan goes upstairs to take a bath. At eight, she puts on a blue pants outfit, a pair of gold earrings, false lashes, plum lipstick.

At eight-thirty, she is with her friends, Nancy and Sue, at Val Anthony's. There are about five men and twenty women in the bar. "It's dead in here," says Nancy. Joan and Sue agree. So they have one quick drink and head for the Hidden Barn. They have two drinks, but it's "dead" too, so they head for The Apartment, another singles bar. By this time, it's eleven-thirty and The Apartment isn't any more lively than the Hidden Barn. "Let's go back to Val Anthony's," Joan suggests. "Maybe it's picked up." So that's what they do.

This scene—the running from bar to bar—is repeated Wednesday evening, Thursday evening, Friday evening.

Joan, along with her friends Nancy and Sue, is in the Running Stage. She can't sit home alone. She can't stop. "After all, I'm not going to meet anybody sitting alone in my kitchen," she says.

In between these nights, she will fill in her other evenings with visits to friends, social clubs, and adult education classes. There may be some nights that she decides to stay home but becomes panicked as it gets later and the children go to bed, perhaps so panicked that she decides to go out after all.

The Running Stage is one approximately 75 percent of separated and divorced women go through. It may occur right after Active Bleeding or the Euphoria Stage or go along with either of them.

Joan says, "I've been running every night for three months. I feel like I'm going crazy because I can't stop." She was in the hospital for a week with a severe infection, came out, and began going out every night again. "I've slept with so many men, I've lost count," she says.

Joan is like someone free-falling in space. She has set no limits for herself. She feels she belongs nowhere.

Although she has a nice apartment, she can't bear to spend any time alone in it. She can't stop to look at it and see how it's being neglected. She can't do anything but prepare to go out. It is as if she has caught a going-out disease. One hears many women in this stage say, "I have to get out of the house."

Many women, I might add, do have children to keep them at home some evenings, yet most find ways to get out as much as they need to.

A woman in this stage will go out whether or not she feels good—it doesn't matter that she has a cold, is exhausted, hasn't had time to clean her house for months. She is egged on by panic, need, and loneliness, and an unwillingness to confront these demons.

In "Running," there's a feeling that no matter where you are there has to be a lot of activity going on—loud activity. There has to be music, the clinking of glasses, raucous laughter. There's the feeling that in order to have something "happen," the climate must be right.

Running is a frenzied time. It's almost as if the lid blew off the pressure cooker, and until the steam is out, you are spinning around and around like a top.

I went through a Running Stage too, but it was different for me, in that I didn't hit the singles bar scene. I did my running by being just about the busiest person in town. I would find errands galore and I was actually never, never in the house. It is almost impossible to stay home during this Running Stage.

During my Running Stage, I experimented with several jobs. I sold linens as an outside saleswoman. I sold encyclopedias. I taught art to senior citizens. A friend and I ran around checking businesses we could start. We pursued every crazy and not so crazy idea—selling printing, sculpture, wigs, opening an antique store, becoming cabinetmakers. I banked on the fact that if I looked long enough, I would find something that would be right for me.

In this frenzied stage, you really aren't looking for an intimate relationship, but for action . . . excitement . . . a Band-Aid to cover the wound of being alone. Running serves as an intoxication to help you avoid feeling pain.

Since Running clearly serves a need, it's important to empathize with that need. And Running can be positive for some women—a woman who needs some confidence-building can find that it's good for her ego to have men find her attractive, interesting, desirable. For a woman whose husband had continually put her down (calling her frigid, stupid, or ugly), the stroking that she gets during Running can do her battered ego much good.

Lenore, a dark-haired woman of forty-two with a lovely

house and two children, tells this story. "For the first two or three months, I had a case of crying bouts. I had to call my sister, and she came to get me out of the house. After the worst of that was over, I said to myself, 'Let's see what I'm worth on the open market.'

"One weekend I picked myself up and went to the Concord, a hotel in the Catskills. I had made up my mind that even if no one spoke to me the whole weekend, I would be okay, and I planned to take tennis lessons and take in the shows. Well, I had a fantastic time; it was just great. At dinner the hostess walked me to a table for eight and it was empty! I said to myself, 'I'm not going to care if no one is here,' and I sat down. There was a piece of melon on the plate. I took the piece of melon in my mouth, but it wouldn't go down. I thought everybody in the place was looking at me by myself. But then two women came in and sat down and then a man came in and sat two seats away, so I introduced myself and I said to him, 'I felt so hungry when I walked in, but I started to eat the melon and it wouldn't go down' . . . They all laughed, and the man said, 'Well, I came in before and there was nobody at the table and I wouldn't sit down.' This was a fifty-year-old man, so I said, 'If you're so afraid, why are you sitting so far away?' He moved over immediately. So the table filled up and we had a wonderful time.

"After dinner, I said, 'Who's going to dance with me tonight?' This man's name was Herb, and I needed somebody at this point. Later, we went up to his room and he was very, very sweet, I was crying and sitting on his lap, he was holding me. I was afraid, lonely, upset. But it was a delightful experience. The next day he wanted me to go to his room again and I just couldn't. He was very nice about it.

"About six weeks later I went back on a singles weekend, and the maître d'hôtel said, 'Oh, you're back,' and he sees three thousand people a week! He remembered me. I felt so flattered.

"Last summer, I don't remember where I got all the strength to run as much as I did. Monday and Tuesday night, I would see friends. Wednesday, go to singles bars in the city. Thursday, Friday, and Saturday nights, go to singles dances.

"I went to Florida last May and a man sat next to me and we made a date for eleven at night. We had one drink, three dances, and I took him to bed, and that's the truth. I was all over him, I was ready. He was a nice guy, but dull as dishwater. Now I probably wouldn't spend more than an hour with him, but then I thought he was the living end.

"On one trip, I met a man named John—he was just separated from his wife. He told me that first night, 'There will be no love, no ties, no marriage, it will only be sex.' We had an absolutely magnificent week. He called me one month later and said he'd be at the Waldorf, would I like to meet him there? How did I feel? Did you ever win the Irish Sweepstakes? That's how I felt. Another time we spent the whole weekend in a motel. We laughed so because we spent the whole time in bed. Twenty-four or forty-eight hours is just not enough time!

"You ask, what is the biggest lesson I've learned about the Running Stage? I really never knew that I was a 'special' kind of person, in terms of being sexual. Now I feel special.

"It has proven something to me. I am not afraid of people, I'm not afraid of the future either. Fear makes us run. I used to think, 'How can I exist alone?' I was looking to see if anyone would want me, or find me attractive. Some people I went out with then I wouldn't go out with today at all. But I always thought men were completely different from women. Men's needs are the same. Running restored my femininity, my sense of feeling like a person. I am more realistic, I think the hysteria is about over."

For Lenore, Running helped her build up her feelings of self-esteem.

On the other hand, a significant number of women have mental or physical breakdowns during this stage because of the *overload* they put on themselves. One woman I know who is now in the Running Stage has a young daughter and a full-time job as a teacher. She goes out every night until three in the morning, then goes to work during the day. On the weekends, she dates or goes to singles dances.

Jane has already been hospitalized two times for mental depression—times when she felt she couldn't cope anymore. And while the reasons that this happened are complex, certainly one would be making an educated guess to say that lack of sufficient rest could be a contributing factor.

In Running, too, there is a continual buildup of excitement usually followed by a letdown. You go out anticipating that something marvelous will happen—you put on your best clothes, spend time on your makeup, have your hair done. Nothing too great happens. The next night, your hopes are built up again, then destroyed. How can this emotional seesawing fail to have a debilitating effect on you? Especially if you've also had a few disillusioning experiences in bars—which happens to most women.

If you feel terribly desperate during this Running Stage, moreover, many of your experiences are likely to be both sad and a little sordid.

Marie, twenty-seven, is a widow: her husband died suddenly at the age of thirty-three. She went through a desperate Running Stage. (There are widows as well in Nexus, and they experience most of the same feelings divorced women do.)

"I tried in the beginning to compensate. I was buying,

buying, buying clothes, doing my hair differently. Then I felt I just needed to be held by somebody, to be cared for, but there was nobody. There aren't any good people in the bars.

"I am an entirely different person than I was when I was married. My husband treated me like a little flower in a glass cage. I dressed to please him. When I started to go out, I would sit there and shake. I had to please the 'average man,' and I was lost, I didn't know what to do. I was a little cutesey, domestic mother at home, and now I had to look sexy. Finally, a girlfriend took me under her wing.

"I started having a love affair. He was married. He was such a gentleman, he lit my cigarette, he sent me a dozen roses. I was too attracted to him to stop, and there was no one else. It was a way for me not to have to go out to the bars anymore. I said okay, this is good, for the first time someone cares about me. I loved that. But he felt he was holding me back from meeting another man and he left at Christmas time.

"After we broke up, I started running. I was out four or five nights a week. Don't forget I am at home every day, with two little kids in a small apartment. I was very unhappy. I would spent all day on the couch in a nightgown. What did I have to do? I would go out every night running away from the house.

"I would feed the children about five o'clock, they would get washed up and put to bed at six o'clock, I would vacuum all the cookie crumbs—I could never leave a dirty apartment. I would start the ritual—bathing, getting dressed, makeup, I had to get out of that house as soon as possible.

"Many men said to me, 'You are so good, you are the woman I always wanted, where were you ten years ago?' Then I would never see them again. I went out Tuesday,

Wednesday, Thursday, Friday, and Saturday. I was out sometimes the whole week. Oh yes, I got sick. I have to have a gallbladder operation, but I don't have time right now."

"I met this huge, big man, very nice, very cool. He said, 'Well, my name is Bill Demery, doesn't it ring a bell?' I said, 'No, should it?' . . . 'I used to play for the Jets.' So I say to myself, 'Oh, Jackpot, whoopee . . .' He did advertising for ski equipment and promotional work for sports stuff. He would call me all the time and bring dinner in. He was getting crazy about me. He said he made about $90,000 per year. I didn't know that men lied.

"One day, he said he wanted me to go to his ranch in Colorado. He said he couldn't go, but he would pay for me and my children to have a great vacation!

"One night I went into a new singles bar and he was there drunk, with a friend who called him John. I said, 'What did you call him?' Finally, his friend told me that this man's name was John, that he was married, had four kids, and was a motorcycle cop. When I confronted him, he said he was an undercover agent. I was so naive I still wasn't sure who was lying. He kept me going for another two weeks.

"Finally I told him one night that he was a liar and a creep. I told him never to come back here again."

Marie then decided to put an end to some of her Running and to spend her time going back to school so she could eventually get a job.

Whether your Running is as desperate as Marie's, or an ego-boosting time, will depend on many factors. However, the Running Stage doesn't last forever. Usually it lasts from six to eighteen months, and some women go through only an abbreviated version of it. Most eventually stop, because it begins to seem empty and futile, or because, as time goes on, your restlessness and anxiety leave you, and you feel more capable of being alone, and of building a more satisfying life for yourself.

QUIZ: ARE YOU IN THE RUNNING STAGE?

1. Do you feel compelled to get out of the house several nights a week?
2. Do you start to grow panicky when you're home alone and the hour gets later and later?
3. Do you find that, in the middle of going out again and again, you ask yourself, "Why am I doing all this?"
4. Do you pick up on the smallest suggestion for a way to get out of your home or apartment?
5. Do you find yourself exhausted much of the time?
6. Do you try to fill up every hour of your day, every day?
7. Do you find yourself unable to concentrate, or read as you used to?
8. Is your health run-down?
9. Do you prefer a "brass band and a three-ring circus" to quiet evenings with friends?
10. Do you feel that the more people around, the merrier?

If you've answered "yes" to three or more, you may be in the Running Stage.

Once a woman's self-esteem is restored and she is less panicked about spending time alone, she will probably be ready to spend her energies in a more creative way. Or, if she does continue to go out frequently to singles bars and parties, she'll do it with less desperation and with more a feeling of "I want to go out and have a good time—to laugh, dance, to be with friends."

Many women, I might add, who feel compelled to have a number of varied sexual experiences, later begin to worry about "being so promiscuous." (Like the Nexus member who said, "I feel like I should have a Scarlet Letter on my chest.") Or a woman may catch a venereal disease (that's not atypical) and find that all the sex is becoming less fun and more sordid.

This feeling of "regret over my mistakes" echoed by so many women is understandable, especially since one has come from a monogamous marriage and value system. However, it's wise to remember that most women do not regret the Running Stage when they are in it, for indeed they seem to have little choice. It is *need* that pushes them, and this need is a very common, normal response to the severe blow of a divorce.

Moreover, I don't see the Running Stage as merely a self-destructive one, although I think some women in it unfortunately buy the stereotype of the loose divorcée. It needn't be; in fact, in many ways, it serves as a great learning experience.

A woman can learn:
—about her sexuality
—that men are very different in bed
—that perhaps her husband wasn't as marvelous in bed as she thought

Used as a learning experience, this stage can help a woman put men in a better perspective and help her evaluate her own needs, values, and goals.

Stage 4
All Work, No Play

All work and no play,
Won't drive the demons away

Jenny is a divorced mother of two. Before she and her husband, Tom, broke up, she had been active in her community, involved in her home and children. After her separation, she told herself, "The kids need me more than ever." She continued all of her activities, didn't date, and didn't make any new single friends. Now, it has been a year since she and Tom have been apart.

Jenny is typical of a certain kind of woman who has not yet come to terms with being single; indeed, she seems frozen in her past. Women who remain in this stage quite possibly are depriving themselves of a personal life and some of the nice things the single life has to offer.

Women in this stage (and only a minority of women go through this one—for example, I didn't) allow themselves little pleasure, fun, or excitement. They don't experience the Running or Euphoria Stages; instead, they concentrate on either a job, finishing school, or motherhood. Life can take on a certain grim quality, e.g., "This is what I have to do, and if I have to, I'll kill myself doing it." You may feel compulsive about "doing things right" or "doing what's best," and you may feel overburdened with no time for yourself and your personal needs.

Choosing to spend time on a goal—working or school—may, however, be the best choice for you at this time. Sometimes, a retrenchment *is* necessary in order to accomplish goals and build strength. As one member said, "There are only so many hours in a day and I have to forego certain needs in order to get the important things done."

Lydia, a woman I admire very much, completed her degree after her divorce at age forty. "I was a failure at marriage," she said, "so I wanted to see if I could be successful at something else. The only men I saw were in between classes. We discussed grades and professors, that's all. I did well at school and proved I could do something right! I got a lot of satisfaction from that."

Six years later, she joined our group. Having achieved her goal, she now wanted to make new friends and expand her social life. "I wanted to bury myself and keep safe while I was in school," she says today. "Now I want to put out feelers to other people."

Carol, another member of our organization, is thirty-three and has two young children. She lives on a suburban street one block from a large shopping center. She was so ashamed of being divorced that she didn't let her neighbors or relatives know she had been separated for nearly two years. She convinced her husband to move back into the house on holidays so that her mother and father would not have to know the real truth—that he had left her and was seeing other women.

During this two-year period, they reconciled for a six-month period of time on the advice of her psychologist. He had advised Carol to put her life in order. She used this time to get her home repaired and to think about what she would do when they were divorced (for she knew by then that the reconciliation wouldn't last).

She happened to read a book about an occupational therapist who was in an unhappy marriage and who finally had the courage to get out. Carol so identified with this woman that when she asked for a divorce, she went back to school to become an occupational therapist. "I had never heard of an occupational therapist before I read the book," she said, "but I thought if she had the courage, I could too. She was my guiding light."

As she set out on her school career, she decided that she would have no sex until she obtained her degree and a job. She said she saw too many women "all mixed up" because of love affairs, and she felt, "I must do what needs to be done." She knew, she says, that her husband would sooner or later stop supporting her.

Carol's decision was a good and wise one—getting a job that would support her (as well as one she could take pride in) was her first priority. So she put her nose to the grindstone and forgot about having a social life during this time.

Few women take this kind of action—yet it would be a good idea for many to do exactly this—to take a cool look at one's situation and to begin to structure a life plan. Carol instinctively knew that her husband wouldn't continue to support her, so she set out determined to be economically independent one day.

This kind of mobilization of one's resources can go a long way toward making a woman become strong and independent. Each woman has to develop at her own rate and make the moves that are best for her when she is ready.

The All-Work, No-Play Stage can last for a short period of weeks or many years.

QUIZ: ARE YOU IN THE ALL WORK, NO PLAY STAGE?
1. Do you feel life is grim?
2. Do you feel your guidelines for living are set around work, school, or motherhood alone?
3. Do you have trouble telling people you're divorced?
4. Do you look down on the single life-style?
5. Do you find you don't leave yourself time for play?
6. Do you look forward to entertainment time?
7. Do you have any leisure time?
8. Do you look forward to dating?
9. Do you look in the papers for plays to see, museums to visit?

If you answered "yes" to several of the first five questions, or "no" to two or more of the last four, you may be in the All Work, No Play Stage.

Whether this stage is of positive or negative value to you will depend on your feelings. Do you feel good about what you're doing, or do you feel as if your life is in a rut? Do you feel you've outgrown this stage? Do you find yourself feeling deprived? Put upon? If you've answered "yes" to any of these questions, you may be ready to put a little more pleasure, social activity, and excitement into your life.

What is it that's keeping you from expanding your social life? If you feel ashamed of your status, you may shrink from confronting anything that draws attention to the fact that you're divorced. You may feel that if you remain "good" and don't think about men or sex, you can still hold your head up high in the neighborhood. You may rightly feel that if the neighbors see a strange man's car pull into your driveway, you'll be the source of gossip and jealousy.

However, if you are uncomfortable, arrange to meet friends at parties and meetings. Moreover, at some point, you are going to have to make a choice between living your own life and living according to the way your old married friends would like you to. It's sad but true that most divorced women do not keep their married friends, except perhaps in the most casual way. For one thing, as a divorced woman you hold up a mirror to the cracks in others' marriages. Your married friends may also be uncomfortable with tales of the fun you're having as a single. They may be jealous, shocked, or threatened. The happiest divorced women are those who make a new network of friends with other singles.

Or ask yourself if you are afraid to get out into the single world? Are you into the All Work, No Play Stage because it is safe and familiar?

Most of us are terrified at venturing out into the single world. We may be frightened by what we've heard about the loose, liberated life-style. We may be bitter about men. We may be frightened of being rejected. We may still be in a mourning period. As one woman said, "After all I've been through with my ex-husband, I want to stay home and bake bread the rest of my life." All of these feelings are perfectly normal.

If you feel this way, it may be a better idea for you to make some single women friends before you begin dating.

Beware, however, of the trap of being taken over by your fear or bitterness. Theresa, a teacher, who had just joined our organization, had been newly single for two years but had not developed any kind of satisfactory social life. When she came to her first meetings, she bitterly complained about all the opportunities her ex-husband had to date, have fun, and meet other women. Yet, while she envied and resented his freedom, she had done little to get out in the world herself. "I don't know if I can make it out there," she said at one point, and then went back to complaining about her husband's gay and carefree life.

While I sympathized with Theresa, and while I agree

that men do usually have an easier time building a social life because they have more time (they don't live with the children) and more money, I also think that Theresa's bitterness at her husband kept her from fully facing her own fears. And I think that one of the things that Nexus did most for Theresa was to help her confront her fears and take one step at a time toward building a personal life for herself.

Marie is another woman who comes to my mind. When I first met her, she was twice-divorced and had a pinched look to her—as if she was drying upon the vine. Her second marriage ended after sixteen years, when her husband left her to "be free." She was understandably bitter that she had been abandoned and had never prepared herself to earn money. Yet her bitterness and her obsession with money had made her a pretty grim person. She was pushing herself too hard, holding two jobs—a full-time beginning office job and a part-time catering position. When I first met her, this drive to make money carried her forward, as any kind of hyperactivity can. But later, I saw her deteriorate—she was still grim, but she was also depressed.

Marie had to save herself by recognizing that even she had a need for a personal life. Work wasn't enough for her, as it isn't for most people. Once she could recognize this and begin to talk about her personal feelings, she was able to search for a way to put her life in better balance.

Retreat from a social life may be necessary in order to accomplish a goal and get your work and financial life straightened out. But be careful that this temporary retreat doesn't last too long. Try not to take a grim "This is my lousy life and I'm resigned to it" approach. Life is harder at some times, easier at others. While you may feel you have to put your mind to the nitty-gritty of survival right now, you should also try to be nice to yourself when you can.

The single life has exciting things to offer you—new experiences, new friends, new areas for self-development. You aren't being fair to yourself if you avoid them all.

If you have been single for over a year and you haven't given a party or had some sexual experiences, perhaps now's the time to get moving.

Stage 5
Post-Love Blues

> She was weeping over the end
> of a cycle. How one must be
> thrust out of a finished cycle
> in life, and that leap the most
> difficult to make—to part with
> one's faith, one's love . . .
> ANAIS NIN

When my first love affair with Jay ended, I was hurt, but I wasn't devastated. However, when my relationship with Al ended, I took to my bed. I was among the walking wounded for the next ten months.

Al, Mr. Man of My Dreams, turned out not to be so perfect. In fact, he was quite sadistic.

He began to let me know in subtle and not so subtle ways that he was seeing other women. He'd deliberately show up in clothes he'd worn the day before so that I'd know he hadn't been in his own bed the night before. He'd drop hints about other women. He even began to suggest that we try swinging with other couples.

I didn't understand anything that was going on. All I

knew was that I wanted him. I was like a baby being ripped apart.

I began to try to find out who he was seeing. I knew that every afternoon at three he visited his stockbroker. So one day, I combed my hair, put on my makeup, and went to spy on him.

I sat in the parking lot, adjacent to his broker's, and waited. Sure enough, Al soon drove up with a blonde at his side. I wanted to get out of the car and kill them both. Instead, I just glared at them, hit the gas pedal, and went home to cry. Having had such a great love, I couldn't believe I'd lost it.

Al didn't call me for a week. When he did, and I told him how horrible and cruel he was, he told me his blonde was "just a friend," but by then, I had had enough fairy tales, and I knew that this year-and-a-half-long relationship was destroying me.

Sitting in that parking lot . . . spying on a man . . . I felt I'd been reduced to lower than an ant.

Even during the worst days of my marriage, I had never felt so low. It became crystal-clear to me that I'd lost all my dignity, that I'd given him the message that I would do anything and take anything. I remember thinking, "I have no dignity, he doesn't give me any, and I want some." I wanted to hold him in my arms again, but I yearned more for a lost pride in myself.

I told Al I would not see him again. I had tried doing this before, but I'd always given in. But this time I meant it.

After it was over, I remember lying in bed, holding my stomach, the pain was so great. I could barely walk, barely talk to other people, barely get dinner for my children. I couldn't get out of bed.

For the next ten months, I tried to heal. I didn't have anything to do with any men. I began to force myself to go out of the house, to face the world even though I was dying inside. I found a friend, Dolores, and I talked out all my pain to her. Without her I don't know how I would have got through this time.

The end of this love affair brought on a crisis I was little prepared for. I began to want my husband back, too; I wanted security, warmth, and comfort rather than the pain and loneliness I felt.

However, what I've learned through working with other divorced women is that the end of the first important love affair often has such devastating effects. In fact, some women feel that they bleed more, suffer more, hurt more over the death of this first relationship than they do over the death of their marriages. It may be that no man will hurt you more deeply than the first man you fall in love with after your divorce.

The main reason for this is that most women who've been in an unhappy marriage dream of falling in love with a man who will love them back. After a divorce, you hope and pray that life will be better. When the first affair ends, it's as if an enormous romantic dream has been dashed. The disappointment is profound—the pain almost overwhelming. Moreover, you have probably given this man all the stored-up, pent-up love you had pushed aside during a bad marriage. As one woman said, "During my affair, I was allowed to be sexy—something my husband disapproved of. I became generous and loving—not the angry person I'd been in my marriage." When the first relationship ended, she felt as if she'd never feel sexy or happy again. Because she hadn't been single long enough to learn that other people would value these qualities, because she hadn't had enough experience to build up self-esteem in these areas, her confidence, for the time being, was destroyed and she was in great pain.

Yet I can tell you this: once having suffered so much in this stage, you'll never suffer so much again. Moreover, the end of the affair can be a new beginning for you—a chance to evaluate yourself and where you're going. It can also be a lesson in dealing with some of the realities of men and the single world.

For one thing, the choice of a partner for this first affair is usually a pretty poor one. You are too vulnerable and too needy to make a wise choice. Later on, after one has dated more, and gotten on more solid ground, women are quick to see how poor a choice that first man often was. As one woman said, "Thank God I didn't marry him as I wanted to. It would have been a complete disaster."

One of the ways to overcome your pain is to sort out your emotions. I've found doing this to be extremely helpful.

Here are some questions you can begin to ask yourself. If you like, write down your answers or talk them into a tape recorder. Both methods will help you concentrate.

1. *What was the "reality quotient" of the affair?*

Many times, the first love affair (and even the second or third) incorporates fantasies left over from adolescence. In adolescence, we had a dream of what romantic love and sex were supposed to be. Most of the time, our marriages didn't live up to those expectations, and that's one of the reasons why the marriage seemed so disappointing. When you fall in love again, it seems as if the fantasy *can* come true. At the end of the affair, therefore, we are often mourning not only the loss of the man but also the loss of our romantic dream of love. Our fantasy is dashed, our expectations of love bloodlessly crushed. It will help you to ask yourself if the dream of your lover was better than the real him. In its totality, was it a good relationship? Or did you keep hoping he would change into what you wanted?

Bertha had been involved with a man for two years. She initially fell in love with him when they were out on his boat together. "It was romantic, fun, wonderful," she says.

"Everything one would want." However, the only times he was so nice were when he was on his boat. The rest of the time he was moody, difficult, unpredictable. Finally Bertha realized that she was hoping he would eventually act in real life the way he acted on the boat.

When she thought about him, she pictured him as he was on the boat—delightful and loving. She was finally forced to confront the real-life man—who was not giving very much satisfaction on a daily basis. When she was able to see how her dream of him was not the real him, she decided to end the affair.

2. *Why did the relationship end?*

Lorraine, thirty-six, had been married to a doctor and had her first important affair, after her divorce, with another doctor. Both men left her. At a meeting, she discussed what had gone wrong. Both men, she said, had complained she was too compliant and submissive. "They said they were bored with me," she admitted, sitting stooped over and looking totally miserable.

"Can you learn something from the two experiences?" I asked her. Lorraine said she would try.

Six months later, Lorraine came to a meeting looking like another person. She held her back up a little straighter and her face had lost that long, sad look. She told the group, "I did some thinking about myself and I learned that there were some things *I* wanted to do in this life. I had never thought about what I wanted to do before. I had always been concerned with pleasing a man. Now I want to please myself."

For a first step, she began to decorate her house. "Before," she said, "I always called in decorators and hated what they did. But I like doing it myself and I'm good at it." At the meeting, she seemed much more like her own person, her own woman.

Lorraine had found that the two men in her life had

criticized what she considered her virtues—her compliancy and desire to please. She then had to ask herself: "If both these men have said the same things about me, that I'm too submissive, are they right? If they are, do I want to change? And if I do, how can I begin?"

Lorraine decided she did want to change, that she didn't want to be so submissive and compliant, that she wanted to be more independent. So she took a small step in the direction of independence by asking herself, "What do I want right now?" (And not, "What does Jim want me to do or what can I do to please Bill?") After that, she began to feel strong enough to do other things on her own—traveling, making new friends. Moreover, once she began to do more things for herself, she realized she felt much more fulfilled. By questioning why her relationships had ended, she had begun a journey of creative growth.

On the other hand, you may find that the relationship ended because the man was a poor choice to begin with— either a newly separated or married man, or a confirmed bachelor. Or perhaps he was a compulsive womanizer, a man who didn't ever really like women very much. If you can see this, you probably will be wary of making the same mistake twice.

3. *Was he the wrong man for me?*

List his characteristics. Which ones did you like? Which ones bothered you? How did he act toward you? With his family? His friends? Sometimes, because you're so deeply involved in a relationship, you can't see the person objectively. But afterwards, you can, and it's very helpful to do this.

One woman said, "I thought Jerry was the man for me. But when I began listing his traits, I realized there was an awful lot I didn't like about him—he was cheap, and I hate that in a man."

You may find that you didn't like many things about

him—his arrogance, his inertia, his lack of feeling, some of his habits.

Upon closer examination, you may see that there was one area in which you felt denied (e.g., that sex wasn't too good, or he hated parties, whereas you love them) which would have begun to bother you more and more had the relationship continued.

4. *Did you feel good with him?*

Or could you consider your relationship an addiction rather than a give-and-take affair on both sides? Were you comfortable or in pain? Did you feel good with him?

Many times women are so busy idealizing a man that they neglect to look at the relationship as an entity in itself—which it is. A woman involved in a destructive relationship often enumerates to herself and to her friends all the "good" things a man is. She'll say he's young or sexy or makes good money or has a good job or whatever else she feels establishes the fact that he is a good catch.

Diane, a woman I've known for some time, has been involved in a relationship for three years. They very rarely have sex, and he is continually putting her down. Yet she can't see her way to ending the affair because, she says, "Where else would I find a man like this? He's good-looking and he's financially stable. Other women envy me. I'm proud of Jim when we go out to parties."

She neglects to see that, aside from the qualities she's listed, their relationship is not a satisfying one. And it seems to me that, in light of this, all his "good" qualities aren't so important. What's important is that a man relates to you with kindness and consideration.

5. *Did I grow at all during the relationship?*

Once you are over the worst of your mourning, perhaps you can look on your affair with less bitterness. What did you learn about yourself? What positive aspects of yourself were developed?

I had idealized Jay, for example, as the perfect person for me—after all, a charming bachelor is hard to find. I'd enumerated to myself all the good things about him—he had no ex-wife, no alimony to pay, no children. He was witty and he had a good job.

However, he was also a man who had a hard time sharing. One day my car had broken down and I asked to borrow one of his (he had two)—the old one. He refused. He was just incapable of giving, beyond a kind of superficial cocktail chatter. In retrospect, I see that I would have been very hurt and frustrated living with that kind of man.

From my experience with Al, I learned two things about myself—that I needed a man who was loyal to me, and a man who would be involved with my children. I want a man to be a whole person, whereas in the beginning of my life as a divorced woman, I had been looking only for romance and excitement. I had been so starved for sex and talk that I'd neglected to consider those less flashy qualities in a man which are much more important to me now.

For all the pain of my relationship with Al, I don't regret the experience. In my own way, I still love the man—that is, I have loving thoughts toward him. But this is a spiritual feeling, not a romantic one.

When I first decided I couldn't see Al anymore, when I knew I had to get over my addiction to him, I'd go over and over in my mind how mean he was. But I kept coming up against the fact that, mean as he was, I still couldn't hate him. I didn't understand this, but eventually I decided to accept it. And from doing so, I learned that I could love someone who wasn't perfect, which made me feel that I'd grown as a person. I finally accepted the fact that this was a man who would always be in my loving thoughts, even though I wanted nothing to do with him. I still find it mysterious to this day, but I accept it.

I also learned two other things. First, that whatever pain I suffered was worth it because I know now that I will never ever again allow myself to be that put down by a man, or by life. Secondly, that out of pain and suffering can come great strength, courage, and even creativity. For it was during my darkest hours alone that I began to fantasize about forming an organization for divorced women. And when I was stronger (into the Yahoo Stage), I acted upon that desire.

WHAT YOU CAN DO TO HELP YOURSELF

Talk over your feelings with friends. When a relationship ends, there's an enormous need to relive it. This is the same need that a widow has when she talks about her deceased husband. As Lynn Caine writes in her book, *Widow*, "So from within and without, there are pressures on the widow not to talk—It takes strength to disregard them . . . There came a day when I knew if I didn't have someone to talk to, I could not go on."

Just because you are not in the same position as the widow doesn't mean you don't feel as bad. You might. Like the widow, you have had a loss, the loss of a man and the loss of a dream. Like her, you *need* to grieve—not in isolation, but with a friend or friends.

You may find friends saying to you, "Don't be sad—he wasn't worth it," or "Stop crying and get yourself somebody else." They may mean to be helpful by saying this, but that's not too helpful. If you can, try to explain to them that you want to talk, and you need someone who'll listen.

I've also found that there's a lot of shame among us for being so shaken by the end of an affair. Women will apologize for crying, for not being able to function too well. As one woman said, "We're supposed to be independent and not need a man. That's the message of the '70s. I feel silly and foolish for not being able to snap out of my depression." However, there shouldn't be any shame attached to grieving over a loss. We're all human!

If you are terribly devastated by the end of an affair, you might consider seeing a therapist. Many women do during this time, and many times it helps.

While you won't feel like going out in the beginning, after a while, force yourself. I found that I had to fight to overcome my immobilization at first. I began by reading— *The Art of Loving* by Erich Fromm about ten times. I went to some Parents Without Partners meetings. I enrolled in an art class, but I couldn't handle painting then and I dropped out.

I was floundering, but I didn't want to give up. Some days were so bad I just gritted my teeth and tried to get through them. Other days I felt a little better and would go out. I was trying to build my self-esteem, even though I felt fragile, like a baby bird trying its wings. I found life was better when I planned my time, and my friend Dolores and I did lots of things together.

I think it's important when getting over the end of an affair to try to find something to do that you can succeed at, and that will give you pleasure. This can be taking a trip you've been wanting to take, learning a new language, starting to play tennis again. *In order to begin to feel like your old self, you have to begin to do things that your old self would do.*

I think, too, that when you begin dating again, you should consider dating a few men at one time. This will be good for your ego.

It's impossible to tell you how soon it will be before you're feeling better. People feel better in different degrees and heal at different rates. One woman may take a long time to get over a relationship, another may find herself in love again after only six weeks. (She's a rarity, but it happens.) If an affair lasted two or three years, be patient with yourself, especially if you find you can't relate to other men right away. It may take as long as a year to get over it.

People may tell you that finding another man will help you, but sometimes that's the last thing that will help. You will heal when you're ready to heal. You may find other men disgusting or repulsive—that's *normal* at this time. When you're ready, you'll feel the way you used to feel about men and about yourself.

Stage 6
Yahoo!

"I feel like I'm a kid again."

After I had healed and was no longer mourning over my lost relationship with Al, I began to have a ball. I began to feel I could do anything and everything. I felt I'd paid my dues, suffered enough. Now it was time to feel and sow my oats.

Later, I came to see that this was a stage 90 percent of all divorced women go through. I call it Yahoo, because that's what you feel like yelling a lot of the time! This is really one of the happiest times in your life.

Yahoo is not as extreme a stage as Active Bleeding, Running, or Euphoria. You won't enter into a Yahoo Stage at the beginning of a divorce or separation; it seems you have to emerge from some of the more extreme stages first. The Yahoo Stage may come after your first big love affair or one or two years after your divorce. For some women, it may come as long as five years after a divorce, but if you have continued to fight for your own growth and have continued to see options in your life, you will experience the Yahoo Stage.

The Yahoo Stage is primarily a good, constructive time and a more natural one. It usually lasts about one to three years. For the first time since your separation, you feel like you're living a regular life—that frenzied quality has left you. You aren't as angry with your ex-husband, and you're not pining away to be married again either. In the Yahoo Stage, your head is on a little straighter and you have some experience with being a single women under your belt. You know the score a little better now.

This period is, for many women, the most solidly adult they have ever felt. For the first time in their lives, they aren't the little girl asking parents (or husband) for permission to live. They are firmly planted on their own two feet, growing and achieving and just really discovering their true strengths. *This period is about achievement, strength, self-worth, and goals all rolled into one.*

Yahoo is an important stage to go through—one of newness, risk, and experimentation. One woman said, "I did so many things that were out of character for me. I really would do almost anything once—that was my attitude. I felt I had to break out of the housewife role and actually see who *I* was." Another said she'd been in a "marriage rut" and now had her eyes and ears open to the world. Women who don't go through this experimental stage often withdraw from the world or become resigned to their fates as mothers or workers.

During this period, you have tremendous energy—almost as if someone were standing behind you pushing you forward, forward, forward. If you have spent the previous years looking for a partner, you may now begin to concentrate on other areas of your life. You may find you are much less dependent on men. It was during my Yahoo Stage that I worked at organizing Nexus and building it into a successful, viable organization.

What kinds of things do women get excited about during this stage? Here are some of the most common examples:

1. *Other people*

Finally, you are getting your head out of the house. You're meeting new people and are involved in new situations.

Often, during this stage, women really begin to relate to other women for the first time. This is especially true of women who have been involved in a group like mine.

When I was married, I knew no one but the women in my neighborhood, and my husband's business associates and their wives. These were the people with whom we socialized. And most of them were the "same" as we were—the same ages, in the same salary bracket, with similar values, attitudes, and goals.

When I was first separated from Andy, there was nobody in my neighborhood who was divorced but me. I intermittently tried to meet other divorced women but had great difficulty finding them. But once I began Nexus and made a concerted effort to reach other divorcées by running an advertisement in the local paper and getting word-of-mouth going, I met many, many women—rich women and poor women, working women as well as women on welfare, younger women and older women, women of different races and religions, women with ideas different from my own. And I began to feel I had been cheated living in my own little ghetto during the time I was married.

I had never had close women friends before. I had never ever discussed my sex life with any of my friends. When I made friends in my group, we discussed our sex lives, including our most far-out fantasies. I can say that those one-to-one conversations helped me grow as much as anything in my life.

2. *Attention from men*

In the Running Stage, numbers count. A woman may date five men a week, or be boosted by the thought that she's been to bed with more men than she can remember. But in the Yahoo Stage, things have settled down, and women are more interested in building more significant relationships. Women also feel freer during this period to date older and younger men, men from different backgrounds, and this can be very exciting, especially for those women who married young, or who married someone mainly because their parents approved of him.

Women often find, too, that they are much more comfortable with men during this stage. They are more self-confident.

The sexual experimentation during this stage can provide a woman with a better understanding and appreciation of her sexual capacity. Often, women who have had sexual problems in their marriages find that they begin to experience orgasm for the first time during the Yahoo Stage.

At the same time, there is not the frantic attention to, and dependence upon, men that there is in the Running Stage. A woman may only be seeing one man during this time, or none at all. But the emphasis is not as much on *finding* a man as it is on *achieving things on one's own and building a more balanced, well-rounded life*. Rather than working on getting married again, women are usually working on other areas of their lives. In fact, many women find their freedom and independence so exciting that the last thing they want to do is get married again.

3. *Freedom*

Many divorced women find their independence absolutely delightful. "You don't have to 'ask permission' to go out," said one woman. "You can choose your own friends, make your own hours, do anything that you want to do." Many women find this freedom utterly delicious.

Naomi said, "I had a husband who ruled the house with an iron hand. He was an autocrat. I wasn't allowed to go out at night unless I had told him before, weeks in advance. And then I had to have his meal cooked before I left. And I'd have to do the dishes when I got back! Now I find that not having to check in with anybody—not having to be afraid that I am going to make another person angry—is a big relief."

I'll never forget one incident during my Yahoo period: I wanted to have my rooms painted, but I couldn't afford to pay professional painters. So I hired some high school kids who painted every day after they got home from their classes. The ladder they used stayed up three weeks. Now if I'd been married, Andy would have nagged and complained about the ladder being in the house, and I would have had to move it every day down into the basement. But because I was living alone, I was able to leave the ladder in the house without anyone griping at me. The ladder became a symbol of my freedom and independence; I draped my clothes over it and I used to pat it when I walked by. I felt liberated and exhilarated by the freedom to do what I wanted to do in my own home—a feeling I'd never had before, a beautiful feeling.

I remember something else, too. One evening a group of women decided to drive to the beach for the weekend. We couldn't find a motel that had rooms to let, so we had to spend one night sleeping in the car. I was uncomfortable and not too happy with the situation, but another woman, Marge, was thrilled by the experience. She loved seeing the sun rise on the beach, having such an unusual adventure, "I feel like a teen-ager," I remember her saying. She was delighted to be able to escape her responsible adult role (the role she'd assumed throughout her married life) and do crazy, silly, fun things.

Overall, most divorced women talk about joy in their

autonomy, in not having to meet someone else's expectations, in being allowed to make decisions and run their own lives. As another woman said, "I don't have to worry about being on schedule. I can cook and do my housework when I want to. And I don't have a man standing over me saying, 'Why isn't the floor clean?' or 'Why aren't the dishes done?' I can be more relaxed—I'm my own boss.

"I also like being able to make decisions about my children without having their father around to put me down or disagree with me. It's more work for me, but he never helped that much with the children anyway. I feel I have a better relationship with them now."

Along with this exhilaration over freedom and independence comes a feeling of pride in one's self-sufficiency. You are beginning to feel that you *can* make it on our own.

4. *Having your own money*

Many married women have had little experience enjoying money that only they are accountable for. Jean says, "I was given a weekly allowance for food, and if I wanted any money I'd have to scrimp and try to scrape money out of that. But it wasn't easy, for my family would always notice if I served cheese casseroles too often and ask where the meat was.

"Even though I didn't have much money after my divorce, I still felt that at least what I had was mine. If I wanted to have something cheap for dinner and buy myself a lipstick with the leftover money, that was okay."

During this Yahoo Stage, women may buy their first cars, balance their own checkbooks for the first time, start their own savings accounts. Deborah used to have a car of her own when she was married, but her husband always picked it out. "He always bought a blue car for me, even though blue wasn't one of my favorite colors," she said. "Now that I bought my own car, I bought bright red! Boy, was I happy about that."

Many women who return to work also love making their own money for the first time. "Every time I get that paycheck, I feel terrific," said one Nexus member. Many women find that knowing that they *can* support themselves makes them more independent in every area of their lives.

5. *Driving or flying for the first time*

Sandra was afraid to drive after dark; when she and her husband went out in the evening, he always drove, and when she had evening PTA meetings, he drove her there and picked her up. After her divorce, however, Sandra had to take the risk and drive alone at night, or otherwise remain stuck in her home. She did take the risk—and found she *liked* driving at night.

Another Nexus member, Joan, drove a car around her neighborhood, but she'd never driven on a long trip by herself. One day, when her daughter, Jill, was getting ready to return to college in California, she said to her, "What if I drive you and we make a nice cross-country trip together?" Jill was delighted with the idea. Joan says, "I had never done anything like this in my life. But I suddenly felt very adventurous. Since my divorce, I've felt more capable. And so the trip together was a real big step for me—a turning point in my own development."

6. *Vacationing alone or with a friend*

Many divorced women are surprised by how well they can manage vacations on their own—that they can rent cars on their own, follow maps, decide on restaurants and hotels.

7. *Going back to school*

Some of the happiest women, those who get the most satisfaction from this Yahoo period, are those who return to school to get a degree or to finish a course or two in preparation for a career.

School also provides a wonderful structure, and for

many women replaces the marital structure. Said Julia, a woman in her thirties who planned to enter the health field, "Sam used to come home on the 6:07 each evening, then we'd have dinner, help the kids with homework, watch some television, and go to bed. I didn't realize it at the time, but his coming home provided a structure for my evenings. I was so lost when he moved out, I didn't know what to do with my time. I felt this great emptiness. When I finally went back to school, I was so busy all the time and I really loved being that busy."

Another Nexus member said, "Boy, it was so great getting A's and B's in school, I really obtained a lot of confidence. I certainly wasn't getting A's and B's in my marriage —there I was failing with a capital F."

Along with increased self-confidence can come tremendous excitement over intellectual stimulation, which many women formerly weren't attuned to or didn't allow themselves in their marriages. Even women who thought they were "too old" for school find, once divorced, that they feel younger, entitled to another chance at life. School isn't out of the question anymore.

Another bonus is the people one meets in an academic environment—professors and young people. Many women talk about feeling "rejuvenated" as they attend classes with men and women younger than themselves.

8. *Accomplishing goals*

Perhaps the main characteristic of this period is that you have many goals. And for some women, this is a pretty new experience.

Once I was divorced and single for a while, I began to see that I should take myself more seriously, that I should settle on some things. I began to concentrate *much* more seriously on what my life was about and what areas in myself I'd like to develop. I also realized that my child-support payments would eventually stop, that my children would get older, and that I had to think about my own future.

Here are some goals organization members have set:

• Jean wanted her bedroom wallpapered but didn't have the money to pay a paperhanger. So she papered the room herself. "I'd take friends to see what I'd done," she said, "and I'd stand back and beam."

• Terry set a goal of losing a hundred pounds and did, with medical help.

• Alma set a goal of organizing a day-care center in her neighborhood so she and other mothers could return to work. "I wanted to feel I'd done something all on my own," she said. "Now I want to get out there and try to make it in the man's world."

All three women felt increased self-esteem and optimism about life once they'd done what they'd set out to do.

Over all, during Yahoo, there is a sense of moving ahead. You are accumulating a lot of "first time" experiences and you feel: "I can't wait for my next adventure!" This can be a rich, creative, and rewarding time in your life, for you are relishing and relaxing in your singleness and growing in many, many different areas.

QUIZ: ARE YOU IN THE YAHOO STAGE?
1. Do you feel in balance?
2. Do you have one or more goals to accomplish?
3. When you close your eyes, can you imagine there are a couple of little people behind you pushing you ever so lightly?
4. Do you feel life is worth living again?
5. Do you feel like a real grown-up person now?
6. Do you feel you can handle things pretty well?
7. Are your feet mostly planted on the ground?

8. Are you excited about things?
9. Are you enjoying a lot of new experiences?

"Yes" to three or more questions indicates you're in the Yahoo Stage.

To help you grow as much as you can during this time, take the following *goal quiz* to find out what goals you'd like to set for yourself. Then, *take action!*

GOAL QUIZ

1. *Would I like to change the way I look?*   Yes   No
   Would I like a new hairdo?
   A new hair color?
   A facelift?
   Would I like to buy some different clothes?
   Take some exercise classes to shape up?
   Go on a diet?
   Buy some new accessories?
   Try out a new makeup?
2. *Do I want to change my surroundings?*
   Do I want to move to a new community?
   Move to another home or apartment?
   Remodel my home?
   Redecorate a room or several rooms?
   Go on a trip?
3. *Do I need more intellectual stimulation?*
   Do I want to get a paid job?
   Go to school and take some courses?
   Read more?
   Join a great books discussion club?

Study art?
Study literature?
Study a language?
Study _____?
      (Fill in the blank)

4. *Do I want more physical activity?*
Do I want to take dance lessons?
Modern?
Ballet?
Tap?
Do I want to join a sports team?
Play tennis?
Jog?
Join a hiking club?
Initiate more sexual activity with
   my partner?
Do yoga?
Swim?
Learn belly dancing?
Ski?
Ice skating?
Any other sport? _____
      (Fill in the blank)

5. *Would I like to give some time to*
   helping others?
Do I want to volunteer at a
   hospital?
Read to the blind?
Work with children?
Work with old people?
Work with animals?
Join an ecology organization?
Work on a political campaign?
Fund-raising for my favorite charity?

Other? _____
> (Fill in the blank)

6. *Do I want an outlet for my creative talents?*
   Do I want to learn a craft?
   Pottery?
   Weaving?
   Other? _____
   > (Fill in the blank)
   Would I like to do some creative writing?
   Would I like to cook more?
   Take a cooking course?
   Garden?
   Sew?
   Take dramatics lessons?
   Join a theater group?
   Join the church choir?
   Learn to play a musical instrument?
   Other? _____
   > (Fill in the blank)

Once you get moving, you'll be amazed at how good you'll feel and how much energy you'll have. For the more you involve yourself in things you like to do, the more interesting your life will be. There's no doubt that new goals, new activities, and new friends can make you feel like a new person—a person with an exciting, stimulating, and challenging life.

Stage 7
Post-Yahoo Blues

"I've accomplished a lot, but so what."

The most difficult times for many divorced women seem to come after a goal has been reached, something major has been accomplished. I tell women in this Post-Yahoo Stage that what they are experiencing is postpartum-accomplishment depression. You'll know you are in this stage if you are feeling bored, listless, or empty and don't know why since you have a lot to be pleased about. Usually this stage only lasts from three to four weeks to two or three months, but it recurs from time to time.

During this stage, many women experience a resurging need to marry. As one woman said, "I feel like I've done it all and seen it all. But it's still empty—there's no love in my life."

Women are often bewildered by the Post-Yahoo Stage because they can spell out their successes and accomplishments: e.g., "I graduated from school, got a job, my kids are functioning well, I'm more at home in the singles world." Here you are listing all the wonderful things you've done, and you don't feel wonderful at all.

Women who aren't used to setting new goals may not be as accustomed to handling these letdowns as men are. But these letdowns are natural and can be overcome.

When I had been involved with my group for over three years, I began to feel slightly depressed. I wondered, "Is this all?" I was bored, vaguely unhappy, and tired of doing the same thing over and over. Then one night we had a rap on what I've come to call the Post-Yahoo Blues. I heard other women describe their symptoms, and most of them were still wishing for a nice man and love and affection in their lives. This seemed to be the biggest lack. And most of the women participating were perplexed at feeling down when other parts of their lives were going all right for a change!

I think that we, as women, usually blame any unidentified problem in our lives on a man (if we have one) or on the lack of one when we don't. However, I think this lack we complain of often has less to do with a man than we think, and more to do with a lack of enough other meaningful goals in our lives. That insight came to me suddenly at that rap session.

When I left there, I knew that I couldn't go out and find the great love of my life, but I could do something for myself. So I became involved in starting a gallery with some other women, and Vicki and I began this book. The Post-Yahoos vanished!

QUIZ: ARE YOU IN THE POST-YAHOO STAGE?
1. Do you feel restless?
2. Do you have a vague "down" feeling?
3. Are you listless?
4. Do you find yourself wondering what's wrong with you since things aren't too bad?
5. Do you feel vague disappointment or unhappiness?
6. Have you just finished accomplishing a major goal?

7. Do you find yourself enumerating your accomplishments over and over?

Three "yes" answers mean that you are probably experiencing the Post-Yahoo Blues.

The best thing you can do for yourself during this stage is to use this period as a time for reflection and reevaluation of your life. Write down in a notebook what you've accomplished. Focusing on the positive is a big help.

Go back to the goal chart in the Yahoo Stage and think about what new goals you'd like to set for yourself.

Since you're in a low period, be aware that your negativism may be stopping you from clearly evaluating your position. You may hear yourself saying: "I can't do ─────" (you fill in the blank) because of your age, your children, your inexperience. However, try not to close off your options and try to be as positive as you can.

Beware of getting in a rut. As one friend told me, "I always thought serious drama wasn't for me. I was a person who liked musicals and that was that. But a date took me to a serious play one evening, and I found myself involved and loving it. I made a point to go back and see another serious play I'd heard about several weeks later. I enjoyed that, too, and feel as if I've really expanded my world."

Don't immediately close off your options for a more rewarding life by saying, "I'm not intellectual" or "I'm not athletic." Learn to take a chance on yourself.

If you *have* accomplished something, give yourself a pat on the back. Georgia had taken many loans to get through college; she'd also held a part-time job. Finally, she graduated, but decided not to go to the graduation exercises because, she said, "I just wanted the degree so I could get a job. Who needs all the pomp and ceremony? I got what I wanted." Yet the day after the ceremony she attended a cousin's birthday party and felt let down that people weren't making a big fuss over her success. When she arrived home and thought about it, she realized that she had cheated herself by not attending her graduation exercises. She needed to feel special—to put an exclamation point to her accomplishment. She knew then she would have enjoyed the graduation exercises if she'd allowed herself that treat.

The moral of this: Don't act in your adult role all the time. Let people make a fuss over you occasionally. After you've accomplished something, celebrate it or let someone else throw a celebration for you.

Here's what some women have done to get out of their Post-Yahoo Blues:

• Marie had wanted to take tap dancing lessons for a long time but felt she couldn't afford them while she was saving for her daughter's schooling. But when her daughter graduated and received a scholarship to a local college, Marie decided it was time for her to take the lessons she'd put off for so long. When she arrived home from her first lesson, feeling excited and exhilarated, she was welcomed by a sign her daughter had put on the front door: "Welcome home, Twinkle-Toes."

• Lisa had a number of jobs, none of which she liked. She also resented having to work since her divorce and wanted her old married life and housewife role back. One day, she answered an ad for a job as a real estate agent. To her surprise, she fell in love with the job; it absolutely fascinated her. "Finding a job I liked got me out of my slump," she said.

What you especially have to guard against during this stage is letting yourself become immobilized or withdrawn. This will only aggravate your depression. You have to try to keep busy, and to include some amount of pleasure in your life *every day*.

Stage 8
The Search for the Real Me

Life has to be faced: to be rejected;
then accepted on new terms with rapture.
VIRGINIA WOOLF

Who am I? Who am I becoming?

Those two questions epitomize the quest for meaning during the Search-for-Me Stage. The stage usually comes only four to seven years after a separation or divorce.

Search for Me is a quieter time—the chaos of Running, the excitement of Yahoo, the pain during Active Bleeding are behind you. While this stage is not a secure one—there is an inherent searching and restlessness to it—it lacks that quality of desperation all too common to many of the other stages.

The Search for Me is motivated by a desire for self-improvement. You're asking, "What can I do to grow as a person?" Some singles become involved in EST, eastern philosophy, and meditation during this stage, trying to find a place where life and answers will be spelled out.

At the same time, a woman in this stage feels "It's okay

to be me." She may have had some psychotherapy, and she's usually pretty insightful as to where she's going. She may even wear her singleness like an old shoe—accepting both herself and her status. By this time, a woman realizes that she doesn't have to run or be perfect or be so dependent upon men. She may look back on some of her past experiences (like Running) with humor, although she in no way wants to be back there. She is more knowledgeable about who she is and more desirous of nourishing her inner person.

There is (finally!) a settled-in feeling of day-in, day-out living. While one isn't bored, one isn't euphoric either—there is a sense of routine, of getting back to regular living with its ups and downs.

A lot of women who have been single this long get past the point of wanting to marry again. Others, who still see marriage as an option, have given up the fantasy of the perfect man who will find them and rescue them from their lot. While they seek and relish companionship, they are sure of the rewards living alone brings too. They don't feel it's painful not to be married. They have worked out a way to get their social and sexual needs met. They are much happier than they would have thought could be possible, living as single women. Women often also feel that, having gotten to this stage, they are in a much better position to choose a mate—that they weren't ready before this time to make a wise choice and weren't able to handle the kind of commitment a good marriage requires.

A woman in this stage is simply more of her own woman. It's a quieter time than before, and you are more comfortable with yourself. Interestingly enough, women in this stage often pick up on old values and interests they had rejected during their earlier single period. Some women return to church or temple. Some renew old friendships that may have been neglected during a more hectic time.

Others pick up their interests in needlepoint, rug hooking, antiquing—"housewifely" arts they often scorned in the first stages of divorce.

I believe I am now in the Search-for-Me Stage. While I am still looking for new things and people to excite me, this has become a quieter pursuit, not such a frantic one.

My painting, for instance, has become more important to me. When I was first separated from my husband, I stopped painting. And I couldn't paint for two years. I wasn't ready; I couldn't concentrate. Finally, an old art teacher forced me to take a painting class and gradually my confidence in myself grew, and I found I loved painting again.

Later, three other women in the art class and myself started a women's art gallery. We worked an entire summer getting our gallery in the works, looking for space, finding four other women to join us. Finally, we were nine women. We each put in five hundred dollars, found a lovely place near the water to house our paintings, and put down two hundred dollars for the first month's rent. We had our first group show seven months later in November.

While I had thought that having a gallery to share would be a great adventure, it turned out to be an even more satisfying experience than I had anticipated. We decided to become a nonprofit organization, and we had to learn how to go about doing that.

I also had a fascinating experience working with my artist colleagues—all of whom are married. I realized, once I began to become involved with these women, how much I had insulated myself from married people. And for the first few meetings, I often found I had knots in my stomach from my jealousy that they were all so happily married. I felt very sorry for myself.

Part of this arose from my fantasy that each and every one of them had terrific married lives. Yet, as we all later became friends, I realized that some of them have happy marriages and some do not. And that helped me put my own complex feelings (loving my independence, but still looking for a loving male companion) into perspective.

Having my own show (each of us has her own show once a year) also gave me more insight into myself, and more courage to continue. Much of my painting during this period has been described as sensual, graphic, tough, but when I got all my chosen paintings on the wall, I had another feeling about them too. They had a light, airy quality, which is a side of my personality, too.

Some of my paintings are very sensual, some have phallic symbols in them. I felt I was exposing the very private part of me, and I was frightened to do that. At the same time, that is what I felt compelled to paint. Having my paintings hang on the gallery's walls for all the world to see strengthened me.

For the divorced woman can't hide if she is to have a fulfilling life. She has to let it all hang out! This is true in terms of her entire life—in her job, in her relationships. You can't hide behind a facade and hope to attain growth or success. You have to be willing to risk exposing yourself, to say, "This is who I am; this is what I need; this is what I want; this is what I have to give."

In a sense, just being a divorced woman exposes you and puts you on the line. A married woman may have a terrible marriage, but no one is going to walk up to her and say, "Gee, I hear you have a terrible marriage." Yet the minute a woman is separated or divorced, the world feels it has a right to probe into her life. People think nothing of walking up to you and saying, "Gee, I hear you are getting a divorce," and then fish for all the gory details. Then they go on from there to make their own judgments about your life after they've inspected it! You're more "on the carpet" than you ever were as a married woman.

The happiest divorced women who reach the Search-for-Me Stage are those who don't mind saying, "This is who I am—a divorced woman." They don't hide, apologize, or try to justify. They have grown into that marvelous stage—self-acceptance.

With this self-acceptance comes tremendous growth. I can't tell you how many women have said to me, "I've grown so much since my divorce. I'm such a different person now." And there isn't one woman I've met who isn't thrilled by her development. I know I've become less of a perfectionist, and less critical and judgmental of others. I feel I understand the human tragedy and comedy a little better now.

Many times, when one is married, growth isn't seen as such an important commodity. The emphasis on preserving the marital unit, particularly in a closed marriage, may cause one or both parties' needs to be stifled. A woman who married young may feel "this is my role and this is his role," and unwittingly seek to preserve the status quo, rather than risking any role change. Individual growth is not brought up, not sought. Many times, it is only out of a crisis (such as a divorce) that growth occurs.

In what areas do most divorced women talk of growth? I'd say primarily two. First, a divorced woman is more likly to recognize her needs as a person and to take them seriously. She is not as into sacrificing herself for her family. She's learned that there is such a thing as *healthy selfishness*.

Secondly, a divorced woman may be more comfortable asserting her own needs. Because she has accepted herself, she is not as compelled to hide who she really is.

I feel that I'm more solidly me now than I've ever been in my life. I have had over seven years of living single, and I have found I can stand pretty well on my own two feet.

I don't think I would have been able to have a good relationship with a man before now—I was too involved with testing myself and finding my independence. But now I think I could make an adjustment to living with someone else, and I think I've learned a lot about men. I'm not intimidated by them any more and I accept them more, too.

I don't know if I ever will find someone and remarry. If I don't, I know, however, that I can still be happy because I have built a satisfying life-style for myself. And I know that every divorced woman can reach this stage—if you keep working at your own growth.

In order to know where you're going, it's helpful to know where you've been. I suggest you chart your own growth experience in the following areas by answering the following questions in your notebook:

AREAS OF GROWTH
My mental health:
How do you function today compared with the way you functioned when you first separated from your husband? Write down what a typical day is like for you. How do you feel about it? Are you pleased with the way you're coping? The way you spend your time?
My relationships with men:
Ask yourself how they differ from those you experienced in the beginning of your divorce and separation? Write a profile of a man you first dated and compare it with a profile of a man you've dated recently whom you liked. Are you choosing more wisely now?
My career:
Do you know the direction in which you're going? Are you making progress? Are you finding satisfaction in your work? Are you going to continue to set goals in this area?

My children:

How did you feel about your children in the beginning of your separation? Did you feel resentful of them? Guilty about them? Did you feel they were a burden? How do you feel now? Do you feel you have more rapport with them? Are you enjoying them more? Are you taking pride in how they are developing?

My spiritual growth:

You can ask yourself if you are more empathetic? More understanding? Do you have better relationships with your friends? Are you more at peace with yourself? Is there harmony in your life?

My creativity:

Have you explored new areas? Reading? Sports? Crafts? Art? Intellectual pursuits? Are you excited about them? Do you feel that you're developing your potential?

Once you answer these questions, don't put them aside. Look over your answers every so often. Go back and answer the questions anew every time you feel the need to. This is a good way of keeping in touch with yourself. Remember, in order to fulfill your potential, you will have to keep expressing the creativity inside you.

It takes time to relax in your singleness. Have patience with yourself. As you progress from stage to stage, you will feel yourself becoming stronger and more resourceful. You will find strengths you didn't know you had. I know I did, and I know many women who have.

I believe that the purpose of life is to grow as a result of our experiences, and I know I have grown immeasurably as a result of my divorce. Some of my experiences have been painful and disappointing, but other parts have been rich and exciting. Today, as I look at my life, I don't regret anything, for even the painful experiences have taught me something about myself and other people.

I have found that the only way to enjoy life as a single woman is to *accept* the fact that you are single—to live your life as it is now, and not to see your single state as just a negative waiting period until you meet the man of your dreams. Maybe your singleness will evolve into something else, but for the moment, live in the present.

One of the hardest things for formerly married women to accomplish is to overcome guilt because the marriage didn't last forever. Divorce has been looked on as a failure—something to be ashamed of. But I think this is changing today, as more and more people realize that it takes courage and strength to divorce. I don't look at divorce as a failure but as a courageous step in the struggle to become a whole person. Sometimes we have to graduate from a marriage just as we graduated from school.

I think, too, to be successfully single you have to overcome the couple mentality, which says that you're not complete unless you have a partner. That simply isn't true. I don't feel anyone needs to be coupled up in order to feel fulfilled. We do live in a two-by-two world and it's sometimes hard to avoid feeling sorry for ourselves. But there are so many people who are divorced today—we are in crowded company.

I have finally accepted my life now, and I pity some of the married people I see who live in a narrow, stunted world and are often out of touch with their own feelings and the needs of others. I would never wish to be back where I was in my cozy, married cocoon. What I've learned has become part of me—something nobody can take away.

Every formerly married woman can build a satisfactory life-style for herself, with time and effort. In order to do this, you have to welcome a challenge and be open to new experiences. And this is true no matter how old you are. *For living a satisfying single life has little to do with age, and much to do with your state of mind.* A divorce gives you the chance for a new life, a different life, a better life. But *you* have to be the one to make it happen. And you can do this by adopting a positive attitude and cultivating an independent spirit.

In order to live successfully as a single woman, you have to create a life that fits your needs. You have to enrich your world with friendships and to develop yourself so that, more and more, you become the person you want to be. The good life is a process, not a state of being. As a single woman, you are going against everything the culture taught you in terms of finding fulfillment through a marriage. If you can rise above the "poor me, I'm not married" syndrome, you will know that you are growing.

There are a lot of advantages to being single. You have options to get your social and sexual needs met. There's the freedom . . . the independence . . . the liberation. There is the joy of handling your own money, learning to cope as a single mother, and the freedom to manage your time as you see fit. How I love spending a Sunday morning in bed without having to feel guilty or justify myself.

The satisfaction of being single may not happen the first year, or even the second. But it can happen. I wouldn't trade where I am today for anything in the world.

Right now, you may be in the process of shifting gears. You may not quite know where you're at because you're allowing new ideas to come into your consciousness. It's often easier, at this stage, to tie up with what is familiar—to go home again. But don't retreat yet. Soon you'll know in what direction you're heading.

If I never remarry, I now know I can live quite nicely by myself. I know what I need to make me happy—to keep busy, to exercise my creativity, and to have people around whom I care about and who care about me. This is my recipe for living. What I've learned most is that I can accept myself for who I am today . . . and that the search for the real me will probably continue for the rest of my life. The single life has much to offer women—it has certainly given a lot to me.

Groups to Help You

Nexus is an organization for separated, divorced, or widowed women. Its purpose is to provide mutual support, to offer a haven or halfway house to a woman after a breakup and help her in her new life-style. Usually, groups have twenty-five to thirty members each. For more information on starting or joing a Nexus group, write to: Nexus, P.O. Box 176, Garden City, New York 11530.

Focus means FOR OUR CHILDREN AND US. Fran Mattera is the President and founder. Write to her at P.O. Box 325, Levittown, New York 11756. The purpose of the organization is to a) consult with legislators, b) work to promote changes in the court system, and c) educate women. They try to share what they have learned about the law, Family Court, and lawyers, and actually accompany women to the courtroom. Women in other states can start a similar organization, and Focus will help you.

National Organization for Women, is the first and oldest organization fighting for women's rights. There are chapters across the country. They will provide you with information on divorce laws in your state. Services for divorced women vary from chapter to chapter, but this is an excellent organization to contact, and they have a national task force fighting to help divorced women get a fairer shake.

Women's Action Alliance, 370 Lexington Avenue, New York, New York 10017. A resource center for women. Carries booklets, including one on starting a daycare center, which costs $1.50.

Parents Without Partners. There are chapters across the country. This is an excellent organization. It has many activities for parents and children, and is also a good place for men and women to meet.

Reading List

Carmel Berman, *Woman's Guide to the Care and Feeding of an Automobile*, Stein and Day, $6.95

Helen De Rosis, M.D. and Victoria Pellegrino, *The Book of Hope: How Women Can Overcome Depression*, Mac-Millan, $9.95

Ira J. Tanner, *Loneliness, the Fear of Love*, Perennial Library, $1.50.

Raoul Lionel Felder, *Divorce, the Way Things are, Not the Way Things Should Be*, World, $7.95

Richard Gardner, M.D., *The Boys and Girls Book about Divorce*, Bantam, $1.25

Margaret Higgins and Thomas Quick, *The Ambitious Woman's Guide to a Successful Career*, American Management Association, $9.95

Michael Korda, *Male Chauvinism*, Random House, $6.95

Mildred Newman and Bernard Berkowitz, *How to Be Your Own Best Friend*, Random House, $4.95

Cathryn Paulsen and Ryan A. Kuhni, *Woman's Almanac*, Lippincott, $6.95

Tom Philben, *Home Repairs Any Woman Can Do*, Prentice Hall, $5.95

Letty Cottin Pogrebin, *How to Make It in a Man's World*, Doubleday, $5.95

Sylvia Porter, *Sylvia Porter's Money Book*, Doubleday, $14.95

Ruth Roosevelt and Janette Lofas, *Living in Step*, Stein and Day, $7.95

Lila Swell, *Success: You Can Make It Happen*, Simon & Schuster, $7.95

Warren Farrell, *The Liberated Man*, Random House, $10.00

Borrowing Basics for Women, Public Affairs Dept., First Natl. City Bank, 399 Park Avenue, New York 10022, free

Women in Transition, A Feminist Handbook in Separation and Divorce. Charles Scribner's Sons, $6.95